LETTERS AND SERMONS,

WITH

A REVIEW OF

ECCLESIASTICAL HISTORY,

AND

HYMNS.

By JOHN NEWTON,

RECTOR OF ST MARY, WOOLNOTH, LONDON.

IN SIX VOLUMES.

VOL. II.

WILDSIDE PRESS

CARDIPHONIA:

OR, THE

UTTERANCE

OF THE

HEART;

IN THE COURSE OF

A REAL CORRESPONDENCE.

Hæc res et jungit, junctos et servat amicos.
HOR. Lib. i. Sat. 3.

As in water face answereth to face, so the heart of man to man.
PROV. xxvii. 19.

ADVERTISEMENT.

THE deference due to the Public feems to require an apology for committing letters of private correfpondence to the Prefs, while the Writer is yet living. He is fenfible that fending them abroad without his name prefixed, will not of itfelf be fufficient to obviate the charge of egotifm. The manner of expreffion and thinking, where an author has been repeatedly in print, will mark him out to good judges when they fee him again, fo as to render any farther defcription unneceffary.

The folicitation of friends, though a trite, is not always an improper plea, and would probably in the prefent cafe be admitted, if he had not determined to conceal the names of his correfpondents likewife, and to fupprefs, as far as poffible, every circumftance which might lead to difcover them. For *they* certainly did recommend the publication, and return him their letters purpofely that a felection might be made. But as he does not think himfelf at liberty to declare them, he muft forego the advantage of fcreening himfelf under the fanction of their judgement.

Pofthumous Letters are ufually publifhed to a difadvantage. If it be fuppofed that the Author
thor

thor has friends whofe regard to his memory will make them willing to purchafe what appears under his name, that circumftance has fometimes given occafion to an indifcriminate and injudicious publication of Letters collected from all quarters, in which more attention is paid to the bulk than the value. For amongft a number of letters written to intimate friends, fome will be too trivial to deferve notice, and others may be fo intermingled with details of private or domeftic concerns, as perhaps to give pain to thofe who are interefted in them, when they fee them in print. The writer of the following Letters thought himfelf more competent to decide at prefent, which and how much of the papers before him might be not utterly unworthy of being preferved, than a ftranger could be after his deceafe.

Farther, he finds that between an increafe of engagements on the one hand, and the unavoidable effects of advancing years on the other, he can expect but little leifure or ability for writing letters in future, except upon necef-fary bufinefs. By this method of fending to each of his correfpondents many letters at once, he takes leave of them with the lefs regret, perfuaded that he thus communicates the fubftance of all he could offer, if he was able to write to them feverally as often and as much at large as in times paft.

Though

Though fome attention has been paid to variety, it was not practicable wholly to avoid what may be thought repetition, without deftroying the texture and connection of many Letters; particularly in thofe which treat of affliction. But where the fame fubject recurs, it is ufually placed in fomething of a different point of view, or illuftrated in a different manner.

Thus much to befpeak the Reader's favourable and candid perufal of what is now put into his hands. But the Writer ftands before a higher tribunal; and would be much to be pitied if he were not confcious, that in this publication he has no allowed aims, but to be fubfervient to the gracious defigns of God by the Gofpel, and to promote the good of his fellow-creatures.

November 29. 1780.

CON-

CONTENTS.

TWEN-

TWENTY-SIX

LETTERS

TO A

NOBLEMAN.

LETTER I.

My Lord,   *March* — 1765.

I Remember, when I once had the pleasure of waiting on you, you were pleased to begin an interesting conversation, which, to my concern, was soon interrupted. The subject was concerning the causes, nature, and marks of a decline in grace; how it happens that we lose that warm impression of divine things, which in some favoured moments we think it almost impossible to forget; how far this change of frame is consistent with a spiritual growth in other respects; how to form a comparative judgement of our proficiency upon the whole; and by what steps the losses we sustain from our necessary connection with a sinful nature and a sinful world may be retrieved from time to time. I beg your Lordship's permission to fil up the paper with a view to these inquiries. I do not mean to offer a laboured essay on them, but such thoughts as shall occur while the pen is in my hand.

The awakened soul (especially when after a season of distress and terror it begins to taste that the Lord is gracious) finds itself as in a new world. No change in outward life can be so sensible, so affecting. No wonder, then, that at such a time little else can be thought of;—the transition from darkness to light, from a sense of wrath to a hope of glory, is the greatest that can be imagined, and is oftentimes as sudden as wonderful. Hence the general characteristics of young converts are zeal and love. Like Israel at the Red Sea they have

A 2   just

juſt ſeen the wonderful works of the Lord, and
they cannot but ſing his praiſe ; they are deeply affected with the danger they have lately eſcaped,
and with the caſe of multitudes around them, who
are ſecure and careleſs in the ſame alarming ſituation ; and a ſenſe of their own mercies, and a compaſſion for the ſouls of others, is ſo tranſporting,
that they can hardly forbear preaching to every one
they meet.

This emotion is highly juſt and reaſonable, with
reſpect to the cauſes from whence it ſprings ; and it
is doubtleſs a proof, not only of the imperfection,
but the depravity of our nature, that we are not always thus affected ; — yet it is not entirely genuine.
If we examine this character cloſely, which ſeems
at firſt ſight a pattern and a reproof to Chriſtians
of longer ſtanding, we ſhall for the moſt part find it
attended with conſiderable defects.

1. Such perſons are very weak in faith. Their
confidence ariſes rather from the lively impreſſions
of joy within, than from a diſtinct and clear appre-
henſion of the work of God in Chriſt. The comforts which are intended as *cordials* to animate them
againſt the oppoſition of an unbelieving world, they
miſtake and reſt in as the *proper evidences* of their
hope. And hence it comes to paſs, that when the
Lord varies his diſpenſations, and hides his face,
they are ſoon troubled and at their wits end.

2. They who are in this ſtate of their firſt love
are ſeldom free from ſomething of a cenſorious ſpirit. They have not yet felt all the deceitfulneſs of
their own hearts ; they are not well acquainted with
the devices or temptations of Satan ; and therefore
know not how to ſympathize or make allowances,
where allowances are neceſſary and due, and can
hardly bear with any who do not diſcover the ſame
earneſtneſs as themſelves.

3. They are likewiſe more or leſs under the influence

fluence of felf-righteoufnefs and felf-will. They mean well; but not being as yet well acquainted with the fpiritual meaning and proper ufe of the law, nor eftablifhed in the life of faith, a part (often-times a very confiderable part) of their zeal fpends itfelf in externals and non-effentials, prompts them to practice what is not commanded, to refrain from what is lawful, and to obferve various and needlefs aufterities and fingularities, as their tempers and circumftances differ.

However, with all their faults, methinks there is fomething very beautiful and engaging in the honeft vehemence of a young convert. Some cold and ri-gid judges are ready to reject thefe promifing ap-pearances on account of incidental blemifhes. But would a gardener throw away a fine nectarine, be-caufe it is *green,* and has not yet attained all that beauty and flavour which a few more fhowers and funs will impart ? Perhaps it will hold for the moft part in grace as in nature, (fome exceptions there are), if there is not fome *fire* in youth, we can hardly expect a proper warmth in *old* age.

But the great and good Hufbandman watches over what his own hand has planted, and carries on his work by a variety of different and even con-trary difpenfations. While their mountain ftands thus ftrong, they think they fhall never be moved; but at length they find a change. Sometimes it comes on by infenfible degrees. That part of their affection which was purely natural will abate of courfe when the power of novelty ceafes : they will begin, in fome inftances, to perceive their own in-difcretions; and an endeavour to correct the ex-ceffes of imprudent zeal will often draw them to-wards the contrary extreme of remiffnefs : the evils of their hearts, which, though overpowered, were not eradicated, will revive again : the enemy will watch his occafions to meet them with fuitable

A 3   temptations;

temptations; and as it is the Lord's design that they
should experimentally learn and feel their own
weakness, he will in some instances be permitted to
succeed. When guilt is thus brought upon the conscience, the heart grows hard, the hands feeble,
and the knees weak; then confidence is shaken, the
spirit of prayer interrupted, the armour gone, and
thus things grow worse and worse, till the Lord is
pleased to interpose: for though we can fall of ourselves, we cannot rise without his help. Indeed
every sin, in its own nature, has a tendency towards
a final apostacy: but there is a provision in the
covenant of grace, and the Lord, in his own time,
returns to convince, humble, pardon, comfort, and
renew the soul. He touches the rock, and the waters flow. By repeated experiments and exercises
of this sort, (for this wisdom is seldom acquired by
one or a few lessons), we begin at length to learn,
that we are nothing, have nothing, can do nothing
but sin. And thus we are gradually prepared to
live more out of ourselves, and to derive all our
sufficiency of every kind from Jesus, the fountain
of grace. We learn to tread more warily, to trust
less to our own strength, to have lower thoughts of
ourselves, and higher thoughts of *him*; in which
two last particulars, I apprehend, what the scripture means by a growth of grace does properly con-
sist. Both are increasing in the lively Christian; —
every day shews him more of his own heart, and
more of the power, sufficiency, compassion, and
grace of his adorable Redeemer; but neither will
be complete till we get to heaven.

I apprehend, therefore, that though we find an
abatement of that sensible warmth of affection which
we felt at first setting out; — yet if our views are
more evangelical, our judgement more ripened, our
hearts more habitually humbled under a sense of inward depravity, our tempers more softened into
　　　　　　　　　　　　　　　　　　sympathy

sympathy and tenderness; if our prevailing desires are spiritual, and we practically esteem the precepts, ordinances, and people of God; we may warrantably conclude, that his good work of grace in us is, upon the whole, on an increase.

But still it is to be lamented, that an increase of knowledge and experience should be so generally attended with a decline of fervour. If it was not for what has passed in my own heart, I should be ready to think it impossible. But this very circum- stance gives me a still more emphatical conviction of my own vileness and depravity. The want of humiliation humbles me, and my very indifference rouses and awakens me to earnestness. There are, however, seasons of refreshment, ineffable glances of light and power upon the soul, which, as they are derived from clearer displays of divine grace, if not so tumultuous as the first joys, are more pe- netrating, transforming, and animating. A glance of these, when compared with our sluggish stupidi- ty when they are with-held, weans the heart from this wretched state of sin and temptation, and makes the thoughts of death and eternity desirable. Then this conflict shall cease;—I shall sin and wander no more, see him as he is, and be like him for ever.

If the question is, How are these bright moments to be prolonged, renewed, or retrieved? We are directed to faith and diligence. A careful use of the appointed means of grace, a watchful endeavour to avoid the occasions and appearances of evil, and especially assiduity in secret prayer, will bring us as much of them as the Lord sees good for us. He knows best why we are not to be trusted with them continually. Here we are to walk by faith, to be exercised and tried; by and by we shall be crown- ed, and the desires he has given shall be abundantly satisfied.

I am, &c.

A 4

L E T T E R   II.

My Lord,   *April* — 1766.

I Shall embrace your permiſſion to fill my paper.
—As to ſubjeƈt, that which has been a frequent
theme of my heart of late, I ſhall venture to lay
before your Lordſhip,—I mean the remarkable and
humbling difference which I ſuppoſe all who know
themſelves may obſerve, between their acquired and
their experimental knowledge, or, in other words,
between their judgement and their praƈtice.   To
hear a believer ſpeak his apprehenſions of the evil
of ſin, the vanity of the world, the love of Chriſt,
the beauty of holineſs, or the importance of eternity, who would not ſuppoſe him proof againſt
temptation ?   To hear with what ſtrong arguments
he can recommend watchfulneſs, prayer, forbear-
ance, and ſubmiſſion, when he is teaching or advi-
ſing others, who would not ſuppoſe but he could
alſo teach himſelf, and influence his own conduƈt ?
Yet, alas !   *Quam diſpar ſibi !*   The perſon who roſe
from his knees before he left his chamber a poor
indigent, fallible, dependent creature, who ſaw and
acknowledged that he was unworthy to breathe
the air or to ſee the light, may meet with many occaſions before the day is cloſed, to diſcover the corruptions of his heart, and to ſhew how weak and
faint his beſt principles and cleareſt convictions
are in their actual exerciſe.   And in this view,
how vain is man ! what a contradiƈtion is a believer to himſelf ! He is called a *Believer* empha-
tically, becauſe he cordially aſſents to the word
of God ; but, alas ! how often unworthy of the
name !   If I was to deſcribe him from the ſcrip-
                                                        ture.

ture-character, I fhould fay, he is one whofe heart
is athirft for God, for his glory, his image, his
prefence : his affections are fixed upon an unfeen Saviour ; his treafures, and confequently his
thoughts are on high, beyond the bounds of fenfe.
Having experienced much forgivenefs, he is full of
bowels of mercy to all around ; and having been
often deceived by his own heart, he dares truft it
no more, but lives by faith in the Son of God, for
wifdom, righteoufnefs, and fanctification, and derives from him grace for grace ; fenfible that without him he has not fufficiency even to think a good
thought. In fhort — He is dead to the world, to
fin, to felf, but alive to God, and lively in his
fervice. Prayer is his breath, the word of God his
food, and the ordinances more precious to him
than the light of the fun. Such is a believer — in
his judgement and prevailing defires.

But was I to defcribe him from experience, efpecially at fome times, how different would the
picture be ? Though he knows that communion
with God is his higheft privilege, he too feldom
finds it fo ; on the contrary, if duty, confcience,
and neceffity did not compel, he would leave the
throne of grace unvifited from day to day. He
takes up the Bible, confcious that it is the fountain
of life and true comfort ; yet perhaps while he is
making the reflection, he feels a fecret diftafte,
which prompts him to lay it down, and give his
preference to a newfpaper. He needs not to be
told of the vanity and uncertainty of all beneath
the fun ; and yet is almoft as much elated or caft
down by a trifle, as thofe who have their portion
in this world. He believes that all things fhall
work together for his good, and that the moft
high God appoints, adjufts, and over-rules all his
concerns ; yet he feels the rifings of fear, anxiety,
and difpleafure, as though the contrary was true.

A 5   He

He owns himfelf ignorant, and liable to be de-ceived by a thoufand fallacies; yet is eafily betrayed into pofitivenefs and felf-conceit. He feels himfelf an unprofitable, unfaithful, unthankful fervant, and therefore blufhes to harbour a thought of de-firing the efteem and commendation of men, yet he cannot fupprefs it. Finally, (for I muft obferve fome bounds), on account of thefe and many other inconfiftencies, he is ftruck dumb before the Lord, ftripped of every hope and plea, but what is pro-vided in the free grace of God, and yet his heart is continually leaning and returning to a covenant of works.

Two queftions naturally arife from fuch a view of ourfelves. Firft,—How can thefe things be, or why are they permitted? Since the Lord hates fin, teaches his people to hate it and cry againft it, and has promifed to hear their prayers, how is it that they go thus burdened? Surely if he could not or would not over-rule evil for good, he would not permit it to continue. By thefe exercifes he teaches us more truly to know and feel the utter depravity and corruption of our whole nature, that we are indeed defiled in every part. His method of falva-tion is likewife hereby exceedingly endeared to us; we fee that it is and muft be of grace, wholly of grace; and that the Lord Jefus Chrift, and his per-fect righteoufnefs, is and muft be our all in all. His power likewife in maintaining his own work, notwithftanding our infirmities, temptations, and enemies, is hereby difplayed in the cleareft light, his ftrength is manifefted in our weaknefs. Satan likewife is more remarkably difappointed and put to fhame, when he finds bounds fet to his rage and policy, beyond which he cannot pafs; and that thofe in whom he finds fo much to work upon, and over whom he fo often prevails for a feafon, efcape at laft out of his hands. He cafts them
down,

down, but they are raifed again; he wounds them,
but they are healed; he obtains his defire to fift
them as wheat, but the prayer of their great Advocate prevails for the maintenance of their faith.
Farther, by what believers feel in themfelves they
learn by degrees how to warn, pity, and bear with
others. A foft, patient, and compaffionate fpirit,
and a readinefs and fkill in comforting thofe who
are caft down, is not perhaps attainable in any
other way. And laftly, I believe nothing more habitually reconciles a child of God to the thought
of death, than the wearifomnefs of this warfare.
Death is unwelcome to nature;—but then, and
not till then, the conflict will ceafe. Then we fhall
fin no more. The flefh, with all its attendant evils,
will be laid in the grave;—then the foul, which
has been partaker of a new and heavenly birth,
fhall be freed from every incumbrance, and ftand
perfect in the Redeemer's righteoufnefs before God
in glory.

But though thefe evils cannot be wholly removed,
it is worth while to enquire, Secondly, How they
may be mitigated? This we are encouraged to hope
for. The word of God directs and animates to a
growth in grace. And though we can do nothing
fpiritually of ourfelves, yet there is a part affigned
us. We cannot conquer the obftacles in our way
by our own ftrength; yet we *can* give way to them;
and if we do, it is our fin, and will be our forrow.
The difputes concerning inherent power in the
creature, have been carried to inconvenient lengths;
for my own part, I think it fafe to ufe fcriptural
language.—The apoftles exhort us, to give all diligence, to refift the devil, to purge ourfelves from
all filthinefs of flefh and fpirit, to give ourfelves to
reading, meditation, and prayer, to watch, to put
on the whole armour of God, and to abftain from
all appearance of evil. Faithfulnefs to light re i-

A 6. ved.

ved, and a fincere endeavour to conform to the
means prefcribed in the word of God, with an
humble application to the blood of fprinkling, and
the promifed Spirit, will undoubtedly be anfwered
by increafing meafures of light, faith, ftrength, and
comfort; and we fhall know, if we follow on to
know the Lord.

I need not tell your Lordfhip that I am an ex-
tempore writer. I dropt the confideration of whom
I was addreffing from the firft paragraph; but I
now return and fubfcribe myfelf, with the greateft
deference, &c.

L E T T E R   III.

My Lord,   *April —* 1770.

I Have a defire to fill the paper, and muft therefore betake myfelf to the expedient I lately
mentioned. Glorious things are fpoken of the city
of God, or (as I fuppofe) the ftate of glory, in
Rev. xxi. from verfe 10. *ad finem.* The defcription
is doubtlefs myftical, and perhaps nothing fhort of
a happy experience and participation will furnifh an
adequate expofition. One expreffion, in particular,
has I believe puzzled wifer heads than mine to explain. *The ftreet of the city was pure gold, as it
were tranfparent glafs.* The conftruction likewife
in the Greek is difficult. Some render it *pure gold
tranfparent as glafs;* this is the fenfe, but then it
fhould be neuter διαφανες to agree with χρυσιον.
If our reading is right, we muft underftand it either
of *gold pure,* bright and perfpicuous as the fineft
tranfparent glafs, (for all glafs is not tranfparent),
or elfe, as two diftinct comparifons, fplendid and
durable

durable as the pureſt gold, clear and tranſparent as
the fineſt glaſs. In that happy world the beauties
and advantages, which here are divided and incompatible, will unite and agree. Our glaſs is clear,
but brittle ; our gold is ſhining and ſolid, but it is
opaque, and diſcovers only a ſurface. And thus it
is with our minds. The powers of the imagination
are lively and extenſive, but tranſient and uncertain. The powers of the underſtanding are more
ſolid and regular, but at the ſame time more ſlow
and limited, and confined to the outſide properties
of the few objects around us. But when we arrive
within the vail, the perfections of the glaſs and the
gold will be combined, and the imperfections of
each will entirely ceaſe. Then we ſhall *know* more
than we can now imagine. *The glaſs will be all
gold.* And then we ſhall apprehend Truth in its
relations and conſequences ; not (as at preſent) by
that tedious and fallible proceſs which we call,
Reaſoning, but by a ſingle glance of thought, as
the ſight pierces in an inſtant through the largeſt
tranſparent body. *The gold will be all glaſs.*

I do not offer this as the ſenſe of the paſſage, but
as a thought which once occurred to me while
reading it. I daily groan under a deſultory un-
governable imagination, and a palpable darkneſs of
underſtanding, which greatly impede me in my attempts to contemplate the truths of God. Perhaps
theſe complaints, in a greater or leſs degree, are
common to all our fallen race, and exhibit mournful proofs that our nature is eſſentially depraved.
The grace of God affords ſome aſſiſtance for cor-
recting the wildneſs of the fancy, and enlarging
the capacity of the mind: yet the cure at preſent is
but palliative ; but ere long it ſhall be perfect, and
our complaints ſhall ceaſe for ever. Now it coſts
us much pains to acquire a *pittance* of ſolid and
uſeful knowledge ; and the ideas we have collected
are

are far from being at the difpofal of judgement,
and, like men in a crowd, are perpetually clafhing
and interfering with each other. But it will not be
fo, when we are completely freed from the effects
of fin. Confufion and darknefs will not follow us
into the world where light and order reign. Then,
and not till then, our knowledge will be perfect,
and our poffeffion of it uninterrupted and fecure.

Since the radical powers of the foul are thus en-
feebled and difordered, it is not to be wondered at
that the beft of men, and under their higheft attainments, have found caufe to make the acknowledgement of the apoftle, " When I would do good,
" evil is prefent with me." But, bleffed be God,
though we muft feel hourly caufe for fhame and
humiliation for what we are in ourfelves, we have
caufe to rejoice continually in Chrift Jefus, who,
as he is revealed unto us under the various names,
characters, relations, and offices, which he bears
in the fcripture, holds out to our faith a balm for
every wound, a cordial for every difcouragement,
and a fufficient anfwer to every objection which fin
or Satan can fuggeft againft our peace. If we are
guilty, he is our righteoufnefs ; if we are fick, he
is our infallible phyfician ; if we are weak, helplefs, and defencelefs, he is the compaffionate and
faithful Shepherd who has taken charge of us, and
will not fuffer any thing to difappoint our hopes,
or to feparate us from his love. He knows our
frame, he remembers that we are but duft, and
has engaged to guide us by his counfel, fupport
us by his power, and at length to receive us to his
glory, that we may be with him for ever.

I am, with the greateft deference, &c.

LETTER IV.

My Lord,   *February,* — 1772.

I Have been fitting perhaps a quarter of an
 hour with my pen in my hand, and my finger
upon my upper lip, contriving how I fhould begin
my letter. — A detail of the confufed incoherent
thoughts which have fucceffively paffed through
my mind, would have more than filled the fheet ;
but your Lordfhip's patience, and even your charity for the writer, would have been tried to the uttermoft, if I could have penned them all down. At
length my fufpence reminded me of the Apoftle's
words, Gal. v. 17. " Ye cannot do the things that
" ye would." This is an humbling but a juft account
of a Chriftian's attainments in the prefent life, and is
equally applicable to the ftrongeft and to the weakeft. The weakeft need not fay *lefs*, the ftrongeft will
hardly venture to fay *more*. The Lord has given
his people a defire and will aiming at great things,
without this they would be unworthy the name of
Chriftians ; but they cannot do as they would : their
beft defires are weak and ineffectual, not abfolutely
fo, (for he who works in them to will, enables them
in a meafure to do likewife), but in comparifon with
the mark at which they aim. So that while they
have great caufe to be thankful for the defire he
has given them, and for the degree in which it is anfwered, they have equal reafon to be afhamed and
abafed under a fenfe of their continual defects, and
the evil mixtures which taint and debafe their beft
endeavours. It would be eafy to make out a long
lift of particulars which a believer would do if he
could, but in which, from firft to laft, he finds a
mortifying inability. Permit me to mention a few,
which

which I need not tranfcribe from books, for they
are always prefent to my mind.

He would willingly enjoy God in prayer:—he
knows that prayer is his duty; but, in his judgement, he confiders it likewife as his greateft honour
and privilege. In this light he can recommend it
to others, and can tell them of the wonderful con-
defcenfion of the great God, who humbles himfelf
to behold the things that are in heaven, that he
fhould ftoop fo much lower, to afford his gracious
ear to the fupplications of finful worms upon earth.
He can bid them expect a pleafure in waiting upon
the Lord, different in kind and greater in degree
than all that the world can afford. By prayer he
can fay, You have liberty to caft all your cares upon him that careth for you. By one hour's intimate accefs to the throne of grace, where the Lord
caufes his glory to pafs before the foul that feeks
him, you may acquire more true fpiritual knowledge and comfort, than by a day or a week's converfe with the beft of men, or the moft ftudious
perufal of many folios : And in this light he would
confider it and improve it for himfelf. But, alas!
how feldom can he do as he would ? How often
does he find this privilege a mere tafk, which he
would be glad of a juft excufe to omit? and the
chief pleafure he derives from the performance, is
to think that his tafk is finifhed:— he has been
drawing near to God with his lips, while his heart
was far from him. Surely this is not doing as he
would, when (to borrow the expreffion of an old
woman here) he is dragged before God like a flave,
and comes away like a thief.

The like may be faid of reading the fcripture.
He believes it to be the word of God : he admires
the wifdom and grace of the doctrines, the beauty
of the precepts, the richnefs and fuitablenefs of the
promifes ; and therefore, with David, he accounts

it

it preferable to thoufands of gold and filver, and fweeter than honey or the honeycomb. Yet while he thus thinks of it, and defires that it may dwell in him richly, and be his meditation night and day, he cannot do as he would. It will require fome refolution to perfift in reading a portion of it every day; and even then his heart is often lefs engaged than when reading a pamphlet. Here again his privilege frequently dwindles into a tafk. His ap- petite is vitiated, fo that he has but little relifh for the food of his foul.

He would willingly have abiding, admiring thoughts of the perfon and love of the Lord Jefus Chrift. Glad he is, indeed, of thofe occafions which recal the Saviour to his mind; and with this view, notwithftanding all difcouragements, he per- ferveres in attempting to pray and read, and waits upon the ordinances. Yet he cannot do as he would. Whatever claims he may have to the exercife of gratitude and fenfibility towards his fellow-creatures, he muft confefs himfelf mourn- fully ungrateful and infenfible towards his beft Friend and Benefactor. Ah! what trifles are capable of fhutting *him* out of our thoughts, of whom we fay, He is the Beloved of our fouls, who loved us, and gave himfelf for us, and whom we have deliberately chofen as our chief good and portion. What can make us amends for the lofs we fuffer here? Yet furely if we *could*, we *would* fet him always before us; his love fhould be the delightful theme of our hearts

> *From morn to noon, from noon to dewy eve.*

But though we aim at this good, evil is prefent with us; we find we are renewed but in part, and have ftill caufe to plead the Lord's promife, To take away the heart of ftone, and give us a heart of flefh.

He

He would willingly acquiefce in all the difpenfations of Divine Providence. He believes that all
events are under the direction of infinite wifdom
and goodnefs, and fhall furely iffue in the glory of
God, and the good of thofe who fear him. He
doubts not but the hairs of his head are all numbered, that the bleffings of every kind which he
poffeffes, were beftowed upon him, and are preferved
to him, by the bounty and fpecial favour of the
Lord whom he ferves ;—that afflictions fpring not
out of the ground, but are fruits and tokens of
Divine love, no lefs than his comforts ;—that there
is a need-be, whenever for a feafon he is in heavinefs. Of thefe principles he can no more doubt,
than of what he fees with his eyes ; and there are
feafons when he thinks they will prove fufficient to
reconcile him to the fharpeft trials. But often
when he aims to apply them in an hour of *prefent*
diftrefs, he cannot do what he would. He feels a law
in his members warring againft the law in his mind ;
fo that, in defiance of the cleareft convictions, feeing
as though he perceived not, he is ready to complain, murmur, and defpond. Alas ! how vain is
man in his beft eftate ! How much weaknefs and
inconfiftency, even in thofe whofe hearts are right
with the Lord ! and what reafon have we to confefs that we are unworthy, unprofitable fervants !

It were eafy to enlarge in this way, would paper
and time permit. But, bleffed be God, we are not
under the law, but under grace. And even thefe
diftreffing effects of the remnants of indwelling fin
are over-ruled for good. By thefe experiences the
believer is weaned more from felf, and taught more
highly to prize and more abfolutely to rely on him,
who is appointed unto us of God, Wifdom, Righteoufnefs, Sanctification, and Redemption. The
more vile we are in our own eyes, the more precious he will be to us ; and a deep repeated fenfe of
the

the evil of our hearts is neceffary to preclude all
boafting, and to make us willing to give the whole
glory of our falvation where it is due. Again, a
fenfe of thefe evils will (when hardly any thing elfe
can do it) reconcile us to the thoughts of death ;
yea make us defirous to depart that we may fin no
more, fince we find depravity fo deep rooted in our
nature, that (like the leprous houfe) the whole
fabric muft be taken down, before we can be freed
from its defilement. Then, and not till then, we
fhall be able to do the thing that we would : when
we fee Jefus, we fhall be transformed into his image,
and have done with fin and forrow for ever.

I am, with great deference, &c.

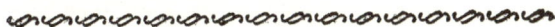

∞∞∞∞∞∞∞∞∞∞∞∞∞∞∞∞

L E T T E R   V.

My Lord,   *March* — 1772.

I Think my laft letter turned upon the Apoftle's
thought, Gal. v. 17. " Ye cannot do the things
that ye would." In the parallel place, Rom. vii. 19.
there is another claufe fubjoined, " The evil which
" I would not, that I do." This, added to the former, would complete the dark fide of my experience. Permit me to tell your Lordfhip a little
part (for fome things muft not, cannot be told),
not of what I have read, but of what I have felt,
in illuftration of this paffage.

I *would not* be the fport and prey of wild, vain,
foolifh and worfe imaginations ; but this evil is
prefent with me : my heart is like a highway, like
a city without walls or gates. Nothing fo falfe, fo
frivolous, fo abfurd, fo impoffible, or fo horrid, but
it

it can obtain accefs, and that at any time, or in any
place : neither the ftudy, the pulpit, or even the
Lord's table, exempt me from their intrufion. I
fometimes compare my *words* to the treble of an
inftrument, which my *thoughts* accompany with a
kind of bafe, or rather anti-bafe, in which every
rule of harmony is broken, every poffible combination of difcord and confufion is introduced, utterly inconfiftent with, and contradictory to the intended melody.   Ah! what mufic would my praying and preaching often make in the ears of the
Lord of Hofts, if he liftened to them as they are
mine only ! By men, the upper part only (if I may
fo fpeak) is heard ; and fmall caufe there is for felf-
gratulation, if *they* fhould happen to commend,
when confcience tells me, they would be ftruck
with aftonifhment and abhorrence could they hear
the whole.

But if this awful effect of heart-depravity cannot
be wholly avoided in the prefent ftate of human
nature, yet at leaft I would not allow and indulge
it ; yet this I find I do.   In defiance of my beft
judgement, and beft wifhes, I find fomething within me which cherifhes and cleaves to thofe evils,
from which I ought to ftart and flee, as I fhould
if a toad or a ferpent was put in my food or in my
bed.   Ah! how vile muft the heart (at leaft my
heart) be, that can hold a parley with fuch abominations, when I fo well know their nature and their
tendency.   Surely he who finds himfelf capable of
this, may, without the leaft affectation of humility,
(however fair his outward conduct appears), fubfcribe himfelf lefs than the leaft of all faints, and
of finners the very chief.

I would not be influenced by a principle of felf
on any occafion ; yet this evil I often do.   I fee
the bafenefs and abfurdity of fuch a conduct as
clearly as I fee the light of the day.   I do not affect
                                                    to

to be thought ten feet high; and I know that a
defire of being thought wife or good, is equally
contrary to reafon and truth.   I fhould be grieved
or angry if my fellow-creatures fuppofed I had
fuch a defire; and therefore I fear the very principle of felf, of which I complain, has a confiderable fhare in prompting my defires to conceal it.
The pride of others often offends me, and makes
me ftudious to hide my own; becaufe their good
opinion of me depends much upon their not perceiving it.   But the Lord knows how this dead fly
taints and fpoils my beft fervices, and makes them
no better than fpecious fins.

I would not indulge vain reafonings concerning
the counfels, ways, and providences of God; yet
I am prone to do it.   That the judge of all the
earth will do right, is to me as evident and neceffary as that two and two make four.   I believe that
he has a fovereign right to do what he will with
his own, and that this fovereignty is but another
name for the unlimited exercife of wifdom and
goodnefs.   But my reafonings are often fuch, as if
I had never heard of thefe principles, or had for-
mally renounced them.   I feel the workings of a
prefumptuous fpirit that would account for every
thing, and venture to difpute whatever it cannot
comprehend.   What an evil is this, for a potfherd
of the earth to contend with its Maker!   I do not
act thus towards my fellow-creatures; I do not
find fault with the decifions of a judge, or the difpofitions of a general, becaufe, though I know they
are fallible, yet I fuppofe they are wifer in their re-
fpective departments than myfelf.   But I am often
ready to take this liberty when it is moft unreafonable and inexcufable.

I would not cleave to a covenant of works: it
fhould feem from the foregoing particulars, and
many others which I could mention, that I have
reafons

reasons enough to deter me from this. Yet even this I do. Not but that I say, and I hope from my heart, Enter not into judgement with thy servant, O Lord; I embrace it as a faithful saying, and worthy of all acceptation, that Jesus Christ came into the world to save sinners; and it is the main pleasure and business of my life, to set forth the necessity and all-sufficiency of the Mediator between God and man, and to make mention of his righteousness, even of his only. But here, as in every thing else, I find a vast difference between my judgement and my experience. I am invited to take the water of life *freely*, yet often discouraged, because I have nothing wherewith to pay for it. If I am at times favoured with some liberty from the above-mentioned evils, it rather gives me a more favourable opinion of myself, than increases my admiration of the Lord's goodness to so unworthy a creature; and when the returning tide of my corruptions convinces me that *I am still the same*, an unbelieving legal spirit would urge me to conclude that the Lord is changed: at least, I feel a weariness of being beholden to him for such continued multiplied forgiveness; and I fear that some part of my striving against sin, and my desires after an increase of sanctification, arises from a secret wish that I might not be so absolutely and entirely indebted to him.

This, my Lord, is only a faint sketch of my heart; but it is taken from the life: it would require a volume rather than a letter to fill up the outlines. But I believe you will not regret that I chuse to say no more upon such a subject. But though my disease is grievous, it is not desperate; I have a gracious and infallible physician. I shall not die, but live, and declare the works of the Lord.

I remain, my Lord, &c.

LET-

L E T T E R   VI.

My Lord,   *April—* 1772.

MY two laſt letters turned upon a mournful ſubject, the depravity of the heart, which im-
pedes us when we would do good, and pollutes our
beſt intended ſervices with evil. We have cauſe,
upon this account, to go ſoftly all our days ; yet
we need not ſorrow as they who have no hope.
The Lord has provided his people relief under thoſe
complaints, and teaches us to draw improvement
from them. If the evils we feel were not capable
of being over-ruled for good, he would not permit
them to remain in us. This we may infer from
his hatred to ſin, and the love which he bears to
his people.

As to the remedy, neither our ſtate nor his honour are affected by the workings of indwelling ſin,
in the hearts of thoſe whom he has taught to wreſtle,
ſtrive, and mourn, on account of what they feel.
Though ſin wars, it ſhall not reign ; and though
it breaks our peace, it cannot ſeparate from his
love. Nor is it inconſiſtent with his holineſs and
perfection, to manifeſt his favour to ſuch poor defiled creatures, or to admit them to communion
with himſelf ; for they are not conſidered as in
themſelves, but as one with Jeſus, to whom they
have fled for refuge, and by whom they live a life
of faith. They are accepted in the Beloved, they
have an advocate with the Father, who once made
an atonement for their ſins, and ever lives to make
interceſſion for their perſons. Though they cannot
fulfil the law, he has fulfilled it for them ; though
the obedience of the members is defiled and imperfect, the obedience of the head is ſpotleſs and
                                        complete ;

complete; and though there is much evil in them,
there is something good, the fruit of his own gracious Spirit. They act from a principle of love,
they aim at no less than his glory, and their habitual desires are supremely fixed upon himself.
There is a difference in kind between the feeblest
efforts of faith in a real believer, while he is covered with shame at the thoughts of his miscarriages,
and the highest and most specious attainments of
those who are wise in their own eyes, and prudent
in their own sight. Nor shall this conflict remain
long, or the enemy finally prevail over them. They
are supported by almighty power, and led on to
certain victory. They shall not always be as they
are now; yet a little while, and they shall be freed
from this vile body, which, like the leprous house,
is incurably contaminated, and must be entirely taken down. Then they shall see Jesus as he is, and
be like him and with him for ever.

The gracious purposes to which the Lord makes
the sense and feeling of our depravity subservient,
are manifold. Hereby his own power, wisdom,
faithfulness, and love, are more signally displayed.
His power, in maintaining his own work in the
midst of so much opposition, like a spark burning
in the water, or a bush unconsumed in the flames.
His wisdom, in defeating and controuling all the
devices which Satan, from his knowledge of the
evil of our nature, is encouraged to practise against
us. He has overthrown many a fair professor,
and, like Goliath, he challenges the whole army of
Israel: yet he finds there are some against whom,
though he thrusts sorely, he cannot prevail; not-
withstanding any seeming advantage he gains at
some seasons, they are still delivered, for the Lord
is on their side. The unchangeableness of the
Lord's love, and the riches of his mercy, are likewise more illustrated by the multiplied pardons he
bestows

beftows upon his people, than if they needed no forgivenefs at all.

Hereby the Lord Jefus Chrift is more 'endeared to the foul; all boafting is effectually excluded, and the glory of a full and free falvation is afcribed to him alone. If a mariner is furprifed by a ftorm, and after one night fpent in jeopardy is prefently brought fafe into port; though he may rejoice in his deliverance, it will not affect him fo fenfibly, as if, after being tempeft-toffed for a long feafon, and experiencing a great number and variety of hair-breadth efcapes, he at laft gains the defired haven. The righteous are faid to be fcarcely faved, not with refpect to the certainty of the event, for the purpofe of God in their favour cannot be difappointed, but in refpect to their own apprehenfions, and the great difficulties they are brought through. But when, after a long experience of their own deceitful hearts, after repeated proofs of their weaknefs, wilfulnefs, ingratitude, and infenfibility, they find that none of thefe things can feparate them from the love of God in Chrift, Jefus becomes more and more precious to their fouls. They love much, becaufe much has been forgiven them. They dare not, they will not afcribe any thing to themfelves, but are glad to acknowledge, that they muft have perifhed (if poffible) a thoufand times over, if Jefus had not been their Saviour, their fhepherd, and their fhield. When they were wandering he brought them back, when fallen he raifed them, when wounded he healed them, when fainting he revived them. By him out of weaknefs they have been made ftrong; he has taught their hands to war, and covered their heads in the day of battle. In a word, fome of the cleareft proofs they have had of his excellence, have been occafioned by the mortifying proofs they have had of their own vilenefs. They would not have known fo much of

him, if they had not known fo much of themfelves.

Farther, a fpirit of humiliation, which is both
the *Decus et Tutamen,* the ftrength and beauty of
our profeffion, is greatly promoted by our feeling,
as well as reading, that when we would do good
evil is prefent with us. A broken and contrite fpirit is pleafing to the Lord, he has promifed to dwell
with thofe who have it; and experience fhews, that
the exercife of all our graces is in proportion to the
humbling fenfe we have of the depravity of our
nature. But that we are fo totally depraved, is a
truth which no one ever truly learned by being only told it. Indeed if we could receive, and habitually maintain a right judgement of ourfelves, by
what is plainly declared in fcripture, it would probably fave us many a mournful hour; but experience is the Lord's fchool, and they who are taught
by him ufually learn, that they have no wifdom by
the miftakes they make, and that they have no
ftrength by the flips and falls they meet with. Every day draws forth fome new corruption which before was little obferved, or at leaft difcovers it in a
ftronger light than before. Thus by degrees they
are weaned from leaning to any fuppofed wifdom,
power, or goodnefs in themfelves; they feel the
truth of our Lord's words, " without me ye can do
" nothing;" and the neceffity of crying with David,
" O lead me and guide me for thy name's fake." It
is chiefly by this frame of mind that one Chriftian
is differenced from another; for though it is an
inward feeling, it has very obfervable outward effects, which are expreffively intimated, Ezek. xvi. 63.
Thou fhalt be dumb and not open thy mouth, in
the day when I am pacified towards thee, faith the
Lord God. The knowledge of my full and free
forgivenefs, of thy innumerable backflidings and
tranfgreffions, fhall make thee afhamed, and filence
the

the unruly workings of thine heart. Thou fhalt open thy mouth in praife; but thou fhalt no more boaft in thyfelf, or cenfure others, or repine at my difpenfations. In thefe refpects we are exceedingly prone to fpeak unadvifedly with our lips. But a fenfe of great unworthinefs and much forgivenefs checks thefe evils. Whoever is truly humbled will not be eafily angry, will not be pofitive and rafh, will be compaffionate and tender to the infirmities of his fellow-finners, knowing, that if there be a difference, it is grace that has made it, and that he has the feeds of every evil in his own heart; and under all trials and afflictions, he will look to the hand of the Lord, and lay his mouth in the duft, acknowledging, that he fuffers much lefs than his iniquities have deferved. Thefe are fome of the advantages and good fruits which the Lord enables us to obtain from that bitter root, indwelling fin.

I am, with great deference, &c.

ഗ‍ഗ‍ഗ‍ഗ‍ ‍ഗ‍ ‍ഗ‍ഗ‍ഗ‍ഗ‍ഗ‍ഗ‍ഗ‍ഗ‍ഗ‍ഗ‍ഗ‍ഗ‍ഗ

LETTER   VII.

My Lord,   *September —* 1772.

WEak, unfkilful, and unfaithful, as I am in practice, the Lord has been pleafed to give me fome idea of what a Chriftian ought to be, and of what is actually attainable in the prefent life, by thofe whom he enables earneftly to afpire towards the prize of their high calling. They who are verfed in mechanics can, from a knowledge of the combined powers of a complicated machine, make an exact calculation of what it is able to perform, and what refiftance it can counteract; but who can

compute

compute the poffible effects of that combination of
principles and motives revealed in the gofpel, upon a heart duly impreffed with a fenfe of their importance and glory ?   When I was lately at Mr
Cox's Mufeum, while I was fixing my attention upon fome curious movements, imagining that I faw
the whole of the artift's defign, the perfon who
fhewed it touched a little fpring, and fuddenly a
thoufand new and unexpected motions took place,
and the whole piece feemed animated from the top
to the bottom.   I fhould have formed but a very
imperfect judgement of it, had I feen no more than
what I faw at firft.   I thought it might in fome meafure illuftrate the vaft difference that is obfervable
amongft profeffors, even amongft thofe who are, it
is to be hoped, fincere.   There are perfons who
appear to have a true knowledge (in part) of the
nature of the gofpel-religion, but feem not to be
apprifed of its properties, in their comprehenfion
and extent.   If they have attained to fome hope of
their acceptance, if they find at feafons fome communion with God in the means of grace, if they
are in meafure delivered from the prevailing and
corrupt cuftoms of the world, they feem to be fatisfied, as if they were poffeffed of all.   Thefe are
indeed great things; *Sed meliora latent.* The profeffion of too many, whofe fincerity charity would
be unwilling to impeach, is greatly blemifhed, notwithftanding their hopes and their occafional comforts, by the breakings forth of unfanctified tempers, and the indulgence of vain hopes, anxious
cares, and felfifh purfuits.   Far, very far, am I
from that unfcriptural fentiment of finlefs perfection in fallen man.   To thofe who have a due fenfe
of the fpirituality and ground of the divine precepts,
and of what paffes in their own hearts, there will
never be wanting caufes of humiliation and felf-
abafement on the account of fin; yet ftill there is a
                                        liberty

liberty and privilege attainable by the gofpel, beyond
what is ordinarily thought of. Permit me to mention two or three particulars, in which thofe who
have a holy ambition of afpiring to them fhall not
be altogether difappointed.

A delight in the Lord's all-fufficiency, to be fatisfied in him as our prefent and eternal portion.
This, in the fenfe in which I underftand it, is not
the effect of a prefent warm frame, but of a deeply
rooted and abiding principle; the habitual exercife of which is to be eftimated by the comparative
indifference with which other things are regarded.
The foul thus principled is not at leifure to take or
to feek fatisfaction in any thing but what has a
known fubferviency to this leading tafte. Either
the Lord is prefent, and then he is to be rejoiced
in; or elfe he is abfent, and then he is to be fought
and waited for. They are to be pitied, who, if
they are at fome times happy in the Lord, can at
other times be happy without him, and rejoice in
broken cifterns, when their fpirits are at a diftance
from the fountain of living waters. I do not plead
for an abfolute indifference to temporal bleffings;
he gives us all things richly to *enjoy*; and a capacity of relifhing them is his gift likewife; but then
the confideration of his love in beftowing fhould
exceedingly enhance the value, and a regard to
his will fhould regulate their ufe. Nor can they
all fupply the want of *that* which we can only receive immediately from himfelf. This principle
likewife moderates that inordinate fear and forrow
to which we are liable upon the profpect or the occurrence of great trials, for which there is a fure
fupport and refource provided in the all-fufficiency
of infinite goodnefs and grace. What a privilege
is this, to poffefs God *in all things* while we have
them, and all things in God when they are taken
from us.

B 3   An

An acquiescence in the Lord's will, founded in a persuasion of his wisdom, holiness, sovereignty, and goodness. This is one of the greatest privileges and brightest ornaments of our profession. So far as we attain to this, we are secure from disappointment. Our own limited views and short-sighted purposes and desires, may be, and will be, often over-ruled; but then our main and leading desire, that the will of the Lord may be done, must be accomplished. How highly does it become us, both as creatures and as sinners, to submit to the appointments of our Maker! and how necessary is it to our peace! This great attainment is too often unthought of, and overlooked; we are prone to fix our attention upon the second causes and immediate instruments of events; forgetting that whatever befalls us is according to his purpose, and therefore must be right and seasonable in itself, and shall in the issue be productive of good. From hence arise impatience, resentment, and secret repinings, which are not only sinful, but tormenting: Whereas, if all things are in his hand, if the very hairs of our head are numbered; if every event, great and small, is under the direction of his providence and purpose; and if he has a wise, holy, and gracious end in view, to which every thing that happens is subordinate and subservient;—then we have nothing to do, but with patience and humility to follow as he leads, and chearfully to expect a happy issue. The path of present duty is marked out; and the concerns of the next and every succeeding hour are in his hands. How happy are they who can resign all to him, see his hand in every dispensation, and believe that he chuses better for them than they possibly could for themselves!

A single eye to his glory, as the ultimate scope of all our undertakings. The Lord can design nothing

thing fhort of his own glory; nor fhould we. The conftraining love of Chrift has a direct and marvellous tendency, in proportion to the meafure of faith, to mortify the corrupt principle, *Self*, which for a feafon is the grand fpring of our conduct, and by which we are too much biaffed after we know the Lord. But as grace prevails, felf is renounced. We feel that we are not our own, that we are bought with a price; and that it is our duty, our honour, and our happinefs, to be the fervants of God and of the Lord Jefus Chrift. To devote foul and body, every talent, power, and faculty, to the fervice of his caufe and will; to let our light fhine (in our feveral fituations) to the praife of his grace; to place our higheft joy in the contemplation of his adorable perfections; to rejoice even in tribulations and diftreffes, in reproaches and infirmities, if thereby the power of Chrift may reft upon us, and be magnified in us; to be content, yea glad to be nothing, that he may be all in all; — to obey *him*, in oppofition to the threats or folicitations of men; to truft *him*, tho' all outward appearances feem againft us; to rejoice in *him*, though we fhould (as will fooner or later be the cafe) have nothing elfe to rejoice in; — to live above the world, and to have our converfation in heaven, to be like the angels, finding our own pleafure in performing his : — This, my Lord, is the prize, the mark of our high calling, to which we are encouraged with a holy ambition continually to afpire. It is true, we fhall ftill fall fhort; we fhall find, that when we would do good, evil will be prefent with us. But the attempt is glorious, and fhall not be wholly in vain. He that gives us thus *to will*, will enable us to perform with growing fuccefs, and teach us to profit even by our miftakes and imperfections.

O bleffed man ! that thus fears the Lord, that

delights

delights in his word, and derives his principles, motives, maxims, and confolations, from that unfailing fource of light and ftrength. He fhall be like a tree planted by the rivers of water, whofe leaf is always green, and fruit abundant. The wifdom that is above fhall direct his plans, infpire his counfels; and the power of God fhall guard him on every fide, and prepare his way through every difficulty : he fhall fee mountains fink into plains, and ftreams fpring up in the dry wildernefs. The Lord's enemies will be his; and they may be permitted to fight againft him, but they fhall not prevail, for the Lord is with him to deliver him. The conduct of fuch a one, though in a narrow and retired fphere of life, is of more real excellence and importance, than the moft fplendid actions of kings and conquerors, which fill the annals of hiftory, Prov. xvi. 32. And if the God whom he ferves is pleafed to place him in a more public light, his labours and cares will be amply compenfated, by the fuperior opportunities afforded him, of manifefting the power and reality of true religion, and promoting the good of mankind.

I hope I *may* fay, that I *defire* to be thus entirely given up to the Lord; I am fure I *muft* fay, that what I have written is far from being my actual experience. Alas! I might be condemned out of my own mouth, were the Lord ftrict to mark what is amifs. But, O the comfort! we are not under the law, but under grace. The gofpel is a difpenfation for finners, and we have an Advocate with the Father. *There* is the unfhaken ground of hope. A reconciled Father, a prevailing Advocate, a powerful Shepherd, a compaffionate Friend, a Saviour, who is able and willing to fave to the uttermoft. He knows our frame; he remembers that we are but duft; and has opened for us a new and blood-befprinkled way of accefs to the throne of
grace,

grace, that we may obtain mercy, and find grace to help in every time of need.

I am, &c.

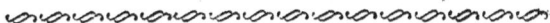

L E T T E R   VIII.

My Lord,   *April* 1773.

FOR five or fix weeks paft I have been a good deal indifpofed.   The ground of my complaint was a cold, attended with a flight fever, and for fome time with a cough, which made me feel fome inconvenience in preaching; to this fucceeded a deafnefs, fo great as to cut me off from converfation; for I could not hear the found of a voice, unlefs it was fpoken loud in my ear.   But the Lord has mercifully removed the fever and cough, opened my ears, and I am now nearly as well as ufual. I had caufe to be thankful, efpecially for two things, under this difpenfation : Firft, that I was enabled, though fometimes with a little difficulty, to go on with my public work.   It is a fingular favour I have to acknowledge, that for the fpace of almoft nine years, fince I have been in the miniftry, our fabbath and weeekly opportunities have not been once fufpended : whereas I have feen many of the Lord's fervants laid by for a confiderable fpace, within that time.   My other great mercy was, that the Lord was pleafed to preferve me in a peaceful refigned frame ; fo that when I was deaf, and could not be certain that I fhould recover my hearing any more, I was in general as chearful and eafy as at other times.   This was the effect of his goodnefs :—for though I know enough of his fovereignty, wifdom, and faithfulnefs, of his right to do

B 5   what

what he pleafes, and the certainty that he does all
things well, to furnifh me with arguments enough
to prove that fubmiffion to his will is our abfolute
duty; yet I am fenfible, that when the trial actually comes, notwithftanding all the advice I may
have offered to others, I fhould myfelf tofs like a
wild bull in a net; rebel and repine; forget that I
am a finner, and that he is fovereign: this I fay
would always and invariably be the cafe, unlefs he
was gracioufly pleafed to fulfil his word, that
ftrength fhall be according to the day. I hope my
deafnefs has been inftructive to me. The exercife
of our fenfes is fo eafily and conftantly performed,
that it feems a thing of courfe; but I was then
reminded how precarious the tenure is by which
we hold thofe bleffings which feem moft our own,
and which are moft immediately neceffary to the
comfortable enjoyment of life. Outward fenfes,
mental faculties, health of body, and peace of mind,
are extremely valuable; but the continuance of
them for a fingle moment depends upon him who
if he opens none can fhut, and when he fhuts none
can open. A minute is more than fufficient to
deprive us of what we hold moft dear, or to prevent us from deriving the leaft comfort from it
if it is not taken away. I am not prefuming to
give your Lordfhip information; but only mention-
ing the thoughts that were much upon my mind
while I was incapable of converfation. Thefe are
indeed plain and obvious truths, which I have long
acknowledged as indifputable; but I have reafon
to be thankful when the Lord impreffes them with
frefh power upon my heart, even though he fees
fit to do it by the medium of afflictions. I have
feen of late fomething of the weight and importance of that admonition, Jer. ix. 23. 24. A paffage which, though addreffed to the wife, the
mighty, and the rich, is of univerfal application;—
for

for felf, unlefs corrected and mortified by grace, will find fomething whereof to glory, in the meaneft characters and the loweft fituation.   And indeed, when things come to be weighed in the balance of the fanctuary, the lunatics in Bedlam, fome of whom glory in their ftraw or their chains, as marks of fplendor, or enfigns of royalty, have as much reafon on their fide, as any perfons upon earth who glory in themfelves.   This alone is the proper ground of glory and joy, if we know the Lord.—Then all is fafe at prefent, and all will be happy for ever.   Then, whatever changes may affect our temporal concernments, our beft interefts and hopes are fecured beyond the reach of change; and whatever we may lofe or fuffer during this little fpan of time, will be abundantly compenfated in that glorious ftate of eternity, which is juft at hand.

I am, &c.

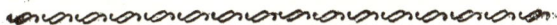

L E T T E R   IX.

My Lord,   *December* — 1772.

I Lately employed fome of my leifure hours (which when I am not indolent are but few) in reading the Memoirs of the Duke of Sully, which occafionally came in my way.   It afforded me matter for variety of reflections.   I pity the Duke of Sully, whofe attachment to the name of a Proteftant feems to have been little more than a point of honour, who drew all his refources from himfelf, and whofe chief aim feems to have been to approve himfelf faithful to an earthly mafter. He acted as well as could be expected from natural
B 6.   principles;

principles; and the Lord, who employed him as an
inſtrument of his providence, rewarded his fidelity
with ſucceſs, honour, and riches: A reward which,
though in itſelf a poor one, is ſuited to the deſires of men who place their happineſs in worldly
things, and is ſo far a compenſation of their ſervices. It is given to your Lordſhip to act from nobler principles, and with more enlarged views. You
ſerve a Maſter, of whoſe favour, protection, and
aſſiſtance you cannot be deprived, who will not o-
verlook or miſconſtrue the ſmalleſt ſervice you attempt for him, who will liſten to no inſinuations
againſt you, who is always near to comfort, direct,
and ſtrengthen you, and who is preparing for you
ſuch honours and bleſſings as he only can give, an
inheritance (the reverſe of all earthly good) αφθαρ-
τον και αμιαντον και αμαραντον *. Thus animated
and thus ſupported, aſſiſted likewiſe by the prayers
of thouſands, may we not warrantably hope that
your Lordſhip will be an inſtrument of great good,
and that both church and ſtate will be benefited by
your example, counſels, and care.

In another view the Duke of Sully's Hiſtory
exhibits a comment upon the Pſalmiſt's words,
" Surely man in his beſt eſtate is altogether vanity."
View him in one light, he ſeems to have poſſeſſed
all that the moſt aſpiring mind could aim at—the
favour and confidence of his prince, accumulated
wealth, great honours, and ſuch power by his offices and influence with the king, that he could almoſt do what he pleaſed. Yet he had ſo much to
ſuffer from the fatigues and difficulties of his ſta-
tion, and the cabals and malice of his enemies,
that in the midſt of all his grandeur a diſpaſſionate
mind would rather pity than envy him. And how
ſuddenly were his ſchemes broken by the death of

* Incorruptible, undefiled, unfading.

the

the king. Then he loft his friend, his protector, his influence. The remainder of his days were imbittered by many inquietudes; he lived indeed (if that could afford any confolation) in much ftate and pageantry afterwards; but after having toiled through more than fourfcore years, died at laft almoft of a broken heart from domeftic uneafi-neffes. And is this all that the world can do for thofe who are accounted moft fuccefsful! Alas!

Too low they build who build below the fkies.

And what a picture of the inftability of human things have we in his Mafter, Henry! Admired, beloved, dreaded. Full of vaft defigns, fondly fuppofing himfelf born to be the arbiter of Europe, in an awful moment, and in the midft of his friends, fuddenly ftruck from the height of his grandeur, and fnatched into the invifible, unchangeable world. In that moment all his thoughts perifhed. How unfpeakably awful fuch a tranfition! How remarkable were his own forebodings of the approaching hour! O Lord, how doft thou pour contempt upon princes, and teach us that the great and the mean are equally in thy hands, and at thy difpofal, as clay in the hands of the potter! Poor king! while he expected obedience to his own commands, he lived in habitual defiance of the commands of God. Men may refpect his memory, for his fincerity, benevolence, and other amiable qualities; but befides that, he was engroffed by a round of fenfual pleafure, (when bufinefs of ftate did not interfere), his life was ftained with adultery. Happy, if in the hours he fpent in retirement, when the pre-intimation of his death hung heavy upon his mind, the Lord humbled and foftened his heart, and gave him repentance unto life! I wifh the hiftory afforded a proof of this. However, in

his

his death, we fee an affecting proof, that no human dignity or power can ward off the ftroke of the Almighty, who by fuch fudden and unexpected difpenfations often fhews himfelf terrible to the princes and great men of the earth. O! that they could fee his hand, and wifely confider his doing, in them.

But happy is the man who fears the Lord, and delights in his commandments; who fets God always before him, and acts under the conftraining influence of redeeming love. *He* is the real friend and the beft champion of his country, who makes, not the vague notions of human wifdom and honour, but the precepts and example of the bleffed Jefus, the model and the motive of his conduct. He inculcates (as occafion offers) the great truths of religion in his converfation, and demonftrates them by his practice; yet the beft part of his life is known only to God and himfelf. His time is divided between ferving his country in public, and wreftling for it in private. Nor fhall his labours or his prayers be loft. Either he fhall have the defire of his heart, and fhall fee the religion and the liberty he fo highly values tranfmitted to pofterity; or, if he fhould live when wrath is decreed, and there is no remedy, the promife and the providence of God fhall feal him as the peculiar charge of angels, in the midft of public calamity. And when all things are involved in confufion, when the hearts of the wicked fhall fhake like the leaves of the foreft, he fhall be kept in perfect peace, trufting in the Lord.

I am, with the greateft deference, &c.

LETTER X.

My Lord,   *March* — 1773.

USually for some days before I purpose writing
to your Lordship my thoughts are upon the
stretch for a subject; I do not mean all day long,
but it is so more or less: but I might as well spare
my inquiries, I can come to no determination, and
for the most part begin to write at an absolute uncertainty how I am to proceed. Since I cannot pre-
meditate, my heart prays that it may be given me
in the same hour what I shall offer. A simple dependence upon the teaching and influence of the
good Spirit of God, so as not to superfede the use
of appointed means, would, if it could be uni-
formly maintained, make every part of duty easy
and successful. It would free us from much solici-
tude, and prevent many mistakes.—Methinks I
have a subject in view already, a subject of great
importance to myself, and which perhaps will not
be displeasing to your Lordship: How to walk
with God in the daily occurrences of life, so as to
do every thing for his sake, and by his strength.

When we are justified by faith, and accepted in
the Beloved, we become heirs of everlasting life ;
but we cannot know the full value of our privileges
till we enter upon the state of glory. For this,
most who are converted have to wait some time
after they are partakers of grace. Though the
Lord loves them, hates sin, and teaches them to
hate it, he appoints them to remain a while in a
sinful world, and to groan under the burden of a
depraved nature. He could put them in immediate
possession of the heaven for which he has given
them a meetness, but he does not. He has a service
for

for them here, an honour which is worth all they
can fuffer, and for which eternity will not afford
an opportunity, namely, to be inftruments of promoting his defigns, and manifefting his grace in
the world. Strictly fpeaking, this is the whole of
our bufinefs here, the only reafon why life is prolonged, or for which it is truly defirable, that we
may fill up our connections and fituations, improve
our comforts and our croffes, in fuch a manner
as that God may be glorified in us and by us.   As
he is a bountiful Mafter and a kind Father, he is
pleafed to afford a variety of temporal bleffings,
which fweeten our fervice, and as coming from his
hand are very valuable, but are by no means worth
living for, confidered in themfelves, as they can
neither fatisfy our defires, preferve us from trouble,
or fupport us under it.   That light of God's countenance, which can pervade the walls and diffipate
the gloom of a dungeon, is unfpeakably preferable
to all that can be enjoyed in a palace without it.
The true end of life is, to live not to ourfelves, but
to him who died for us ; and while we devote ourfelves to his fervice upon earth, to rejoice in the
profpect of being happy with him for ever in heaven.   Thefe things are generally known and acknowledged by profeffors; but they are a *favoured
few* who act confiftently with their avowed principles; who honeftly, diligently, and without referve, endeavour to make the moft of their talents
and ftrength in promoting the Lord's fervice, and
allow themfelves in no views or defigns but what
are plainly fubordinate and fubfervient to it.   Yea,
I believe the beft of the Lord's fervants fee caufe
enough to confefs, that they are not only unprofitable in comparifon of what they with to be, but
in many inftances unfaithful likewife.   They find
fo many fnares, hinderances, and temptations, arifing from without, and fo much embarraffment
                                                    from

from fin which dwells within, that they have more
caufe for humiliation than felf-complacence, when
they feem moft earneft and moft ufeful.   However, we have no fcriptural evidence that we ferve
the Lord at all, any farther than we find an habitual defire and aim to ferve him wholly.   He is
gracious to our imperfections and weaknefs; yet he
requires all the heart, and will not be ferved by
halves, nor accept what is performed by a divided
fpirit.   I lately met with fome profane fcoffs of
Voltaire upon the fentiment of doing all to the
glory of God; (fuch as might be expected from
fuch a man); however, *this* is the true alchimy
which turns every thing to gold, and ennobles the
common actions of life into acts of religion, 1 Cor.
x. 31.   Nor is there a grain of real goodnefs in
the moft fpecious actions which are performed
without a reference to God's glory.   This the
world cannot underftand; but it will appear highly
reafonable to thofe who take their ideas of God
from the fcripture, and who have felt the neceffity,
and found the benefits of redemption. — We are
debtors many ways.   The Lord has a right to us
by creation, by redemption, by conqueft, when he
freed us from Satan's power, and took poffeffion
of our hearts by his grace; and laftly, by our own
voluntary furrender in the day when he enabled us
to fix our choice on himfelf, as our Lord and our
portion.   Then we felt the force of our obligations,
we faw the beauty and honour of his fervice, and
that nothing was worthy to ftand in the leaft degree of competition with it.   This is always equally
true, though our perceptions of it are not always
equally ftrong.   But where it has been once really
known, it cannot be wholly forgotten, or ceafe to
be the governing principle of life; and the Lord
has promifed to revive the impreffion in thofe who
wait upon him, and thereby to renew their ftrength.

For

For in proportion as we feel by what ties we are his, we shall embrace his service as perfect freedom.

Again, when the eye is thus single, the whole body will be full of light. The principle, of acting simply for God, will in general make the path of duty plain, solve a thousand otherwise dubious questions, lead to the most proper and obvious means, and preclude that painful anxiety about events, which upon no other plan can be avoided. The love of God is the best casuist; especially as it leads us to a careful attendance to his precepts, a reliance on his promises, and a submission to his will. Most of our perplexities arise from an undue, though perhaps unperceived attachment to self. Either we have some scheme of our own too closely connected with our general view of serving the Lord, or lay some stress upon our own management, which, though we suspect it may possibly fail us, we cannot entirely help trusting to. In these respects the Lord permits his servants occasionally to feel their own weakness; but if they are sincerely devoted to him, he will teach them to profit by it, and bring them by degrees to a simplicity of dependence, as well as of intention. Then all things are easy. Acting from love, and walking by faith, they can neither be disappointed or discouraged. Duty is their part, care is his, and they are enabled to cast it upon him. They know that when their expedients seem to fail, he is still all-sufficient. They know that, being engaged in his cause, they cannot miscarry; and that, though in some things they may seem to fall short of success, they are sure of meeting acceptance, and that he will estimate their services not by their actual effects, but according to the gracious principle and desire he has put into their hearts, 2 Chron. vi. 7. 8.

I am, with the greatest respect, &c.

LET-

LETTER XI.

My Lord,   *June,* — 1773.

MY old caft-off acquaintance, Horace, occafionally came in my way this morning.—I opened
it upon lib. 3. od. 29   Did I not know the pro-
pofal to be utterly impracticable, how gladly fhould
I imitate it, and fend your Lordfhip, in honeft profe,
if not in elegant verfe, an invitation.   But I muft
content myfelf with the idea of the pleafure it
would give me to fit with you half a day under my
favourite great tree, and converfe with you, not
concerning the comparatively petty affairs of human governments, but of the things pertaining to
the kingdom of God.   How many delightful fubjects would fuggeft themfelves in a free and retired
converfation.   The excellency of our King, the
permanency and glory of his kingdom, the beauty
of his adminiftration, the privileges of his fubjects,
the review of what he has done for us, and the
profpect of what he has prepared for us in future;
—and if, while we were converfing, he fhould be
pleafed to join us, (as he did the difciples when
walking to Emmaus), how would our hearts burn
within us.   Indeed, whether we are alone or in
company, the moft interefting topics ftrike us but
faintly, unlefs he is pleafed to afford his gracious
influence; but when he is prefent, light, love, liberty, and joy, fpring up in the hearts that know
him.—This reminds me (as I have mentioned
Horace) to reftore fome beautiful lines to their
proper application.   They are impious and idolatrous as he ufes them, but have an expreffive propriety in the mouth of a believer :——

                                             Lucem

Lucem redde tuæ, Dux bone, patriæ,
Inftar veris enim vultus ubi tuus
Affulfit populo, gratior it Dies
Et Soles melius nitent.

But we cannot meet. All that is left for me, is
to ufe the liberty you allow me of offering a few
hints upon thefe fubjects by letter, not becaufe you
know them not, but becaufe you love them. The
hour is coming, when all impediments fhall be removed.—All diftinctions fhall ceafe that are founded upon fublunary things, and the earth and all its
works fhall be burnt up. Glorious day! May our
fouls be filled with the thought, and learn to eftimate all things around us *now*, by the view in
which they will appear to us *then*. Then it will be
of fmall moment who was the prince, and who was
the beggar in this life ;—but who in their feveral
fituations fought, and loved, and feared, and honoured the Lord. Alas! how many of the kings
of the earth, and the rich men, and the chief cap-
tains, and the mighty men, will then fay (in vain)
to the mountains and the rocks, fall on us, and
hide us ! In this world they are for the moft part
too bufy to regard the commands of God, or too
happy to feek his favour ; they have their good
things here ; they pleafe themfelves for a while,
and in a moment they go down to the grave : in
that moment their thoughts perifh, their fchemes
are left unfinifhed, they are torn from their poffeffions, and enter upon a new, an untried, an unchangeable, a never ending ftate of exiftence. Alas,
is this all the world can afford ! I congratulate
you, my Lord, not becaufe God has appointed
you to appear in an elevated rank, (this, abftracted
from the opportunity it affords you of greater ufefulnefs, would perhaps be a more proper fubject
for condolance) ; but that he has admitted you to
                                        thofe

thofe honours and privileges which come *from him only*, and which fo few in the fuperior ranks of life think worthy of their attention. I doubt not but you are often affected with a fenfe of this diftinguifhing mercy. But though we know that we are debtors, great debtors to the grace of God, which alone has made us to differ, we know it but imperfectly at prefent. It doth not yet appear what we fhall be, nor can we form a juft conception of the mifery from which we are redeemed, much lefs of the price paid for our redemption. How little do we know of the Redeemer's dignity, and of the unutterable diftrefs he endured when his foul was made an offering for fin, and it pleafed the Father to bruife him, that by his ftripes we might be healed. Thefe things will ftrike us quite in another manner, when we view them in the light of eternity. Then, to return to the thought from which I have rambled, then and there I truft we fhall meet to the higheft advantage, and fpend an everlafting day together in happinefs and praife. With this thought I endeavour to comfort myfelf, under the regret I fometimes feel that I can have fo little intercourfe with you in this life.

May the chearing contemplation of the hope fet before us, fupport and animate us to improve the interval, and fill us with an holy ambition of fhining as lights in the world, to the praife and glory of his grace, who has called us out of darknefs. Encompaffed as we are with fnares, temptations, and infirmities, it is poffible (by his promifed affiftance) to live in fome good meafure above the world while we are in it; above the influence of its cares, its fmiles, or its frowns. Our converfation, πολιτευμα, our citizenfhip is in heaven. We are not at home, but only refident here for a feafon, to fulfil an appointed fervice; and the Lord, whom we ferve, has encouraged us to hope, that he will

guide

guide us by his wifdom, ftrengthen us by his power, and comfort us with the light of his countenance, which is better than life. Every bleffing we receive from him is a token of his favour, and a pledge of that far more exceeding and eternal weight of glory, which he has referved for us. O! to hear him fay at laft, Well done, good and faithful fervant, enter thou into the joy of thy Lord! will be a rich amends for all that we can lofe, fuffer, or forbear, for his fake.

I fubfcribe myfelf, with great fincerity, &c.

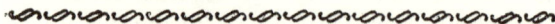

LETTER XII.

My Lord,   *February —* 1774.

THE firft line of Horace's epiftle to Auguftus, when rightly applied, fuggefts a grand and chearing idea. As addreffed by the poet, nothing can be more blafphemous, idolatrous, and abfurd; but with what comfort and propriety may a Chriftian look up to him, to whom all power is committed in heaven and earth, and fay, *Cum tot fuftineas et tanta negotia Solus!* Surely a more weighty and comprehenfive fentence never dropped from an uninfpired pen. And how beautifully and expreffively is it clofed by the word *folus!* The government is upon his fhoulders: and though he is concealed by a veil of fecond caufes from common eyes, fo that they can perceive only the means, inftruments, and contingencies by which he works, and therefore think he does nothing; yet in reality he does *all*, according to his own counfel and pleafure, in the armies of heaven, and among the inhabitants of the earth.

Who

Who can enumerate the *Tot et tanta negotia,* which are inceſſantly before his eye, adjuſted by his wiſdom, dependent on his will, and regulated by his power, in his kingdoms of providence and grace? If we conſider the heavens, the work of his fingers, the moon and the ſtars which he has ordained ; if we call in the aſſiſtance of aſtronomers and glaſſes, to help us in forming a conception of the number, diſtances, magnitudes, and motions of the heavenly bodies ; the more we ſearch, the more we ſhall be confirmed, that theſe are but a portion of his ways.—But he calls them all by their names, upholds them by his power, and without his continual energy they would ruſh into confuſion, or ſink into nothing. If we ſpeak of intelligences, he is the life, the joy, the ſun of all that are capable of happineſs. Whatever may be ſignified by the thrones, principalities, and powers in the world of light, they are all dependant upon his power, and obedient to his command ; it is equally true of angels as of men, that without him they can do nothing. The powers of darkneſs are likewiſe under his ſubjection and controul. Though but little is ſaid of them in ſcripture, we read enough to aſſure us that their number muſt be immenſely great, and that their ſtrength, ſubtlety, and malice, are ſuch, as we may tremble to think of them as our enemies, and probably ſhould, but for our ſtrange inſenſibility to whatever does not fall under the cognizance of our outward ſenſes. But he holds them all in a chain, ſo that they can do or attempt nothing but by his permiſſion ; and whatever he permits them to do (though they mean nothing leſs) has its appointed ſubſerviency in accompliſhing his deſigns.

But to come nearer home, and to ſpeak of what ſeems more ſuited to our ſcanty apprehenſions,— ſtill we may be loſt in wonder.—Before this bleſſed and only potentate, all the nations of the earth are
but

but as the duft upon the balance, and the fmall
drop of a bucket, and might be thought (if compared with the immenfity of his works) fcarcely
worthy of his notice : yet here he prefides, per-
vades, provides, protects, and rules. In him his
creatures live, move, and have their being : from
him is their food and prefervation. The eyes of
all are upon him : what he gives they gather, and
can gather no more ; and at his word they fink into
the duft.—There is not a worm that crawls upon
the ground, or a flower that grows in the pathlefs
wildernefs, or a fhell upon the fea-fhore, but bears
the imprefs of his wifdom, power, and goodnefs.
With refpect to men, he reigns with uncontrouled
dominion over every kingdom, family, and individual. Here we may be aftonifhed at his wifdom,
in employing free agents, the greater part of whom
are his enemies, to accomplifh his purpofes. But,
however reluctant, they all ferve him. His patience likewife is wonderful. Multitudes, yea nearly our whole fpecies, fpend the life and ftrength
which he affords them, and abufe all the bounties
he heaps upon them, in the ways of fin. His commands are difregarded, his name blafphemed, his
mercy difdained, his power defied, yet ftill he
fpares. It is an eminent part of his government, to
reftrain the depravity of human nature, and in various ways to check its effects, which if left to itfelf, without his providential controul, would prefently make earth the very image of hell. For the
vileft men are not fuffered to perpetrate a thoufandth part of the evil which their hearts would
prompt them to. The earth, though lying in the
wicked one, is filled with the goodnefs of the Lord.
He preferveth man and beaft, fuftains the young
lion in the foreft, feeds the birds of the air, which
have neither ftore-houfe or barn, and adorns the
infects and the flowers of the field with a beauty
and

and elegance beyond all that can be found in the
courts of kings.

Still more wonderful is his adminiftration in his
kingdom of grace. He is prefent with all his creatures, but in a peculiar manner with his own people.
Each of thefe are monuments of a more illuftrious
difplay of power, than that which fpread abroad the
heavens like a curtain and laid the foundations of
the earth : for he finds them all in a ftate of rebellion and enmity, and makes them a willing people ;
and from the moment he reveals his love to them,
he efpoufes their caufe, and takes all their concerns into his own hands. He is near and attentive
to every one of them, as if there was only that one.
This high and lofty One, who inhabits eternity,
before whom the angels veil their faces, conde-
fcends to hold communion with thofe whom men
defpife. He fees not as man feeth —— rides on a
cloud difdainful by a Sultan or a Czar, to manifeft himfelf to an humble foul in a mud-walled
cottage. He comforts them when in trouble,
ftrengthens them when weak, makes their beds in
ficknefs, revives them when fainting, upholds them
when falling, and fo feafonably and effectually manages for them, that though they are perfecuted
and tempted, though their enemies are many and
mighty, nothing that they feel or fear is able to feparate them from his love.

And all this He does *folus*. All the abilities,
powers, and inftincts, that are found amongft creatures, are emanations from his fullnefs. All changes, fucceffes, difappointments,—all that is memo-
rable in the annals of hiftory, all the rifings and
falls of empires, all the turns in human life, take
place according to his plan. In vain men contrive
and combine to accomplifh their own counfels, unlefs they are parts of his counfel likewife, the efforts of their utmoft ftrength and wifdom are crofs-

ed and reverfed by the feebleft and moft unthought-
of circumftances. But when he has a work to accomplifh, and his time is come, however inadequate
and weak the means he employs may feem to a carnal eye, the fuccefs is infallibly fecured : for all
things ferve him, and are in his hands as clay in
the hands of the potter. Great and marvellous are
thy works, Lord God Almighty ! juft and true are
thy ways, thou King of faints !

This is the God whom we adore. This is he
who invites us to lean upon his almighty arm, and
promifes to guide us with his unerring eye. He
fays to you, my Lord, and even to me, Fear not,
I am with thee ; be not difmayed, I am thy God ;
I will ftrengthen thee, yea I will help thee, yea I
will uphold thee, with the right hand of my righteoufnefs. Therefore, while in the path of duty,
and following his call, we may chearfully pafs on,
regardlefs of apparent difficulties ; for the Lord,
whofe we are, and who has taught us to make his
glory our higheft end, will go before us, and at his
word crooked things become ftraight, light fhines
out of darknefs, and mountains fink into plains.
Faith may and muft be exercifed, experience muft
and will confirm what his word declares, that the
heart is deceitful, and that man in his beft eftate is
vanity. But his promifes to them that fear him
fhall be confirmed likewife, and they fhall find him,
in all fituations, a fun, a fhield, and an exceeding
great reward.

I have loft another of my people ; a mother in
our Ifrael ; a perfon of much experience, eminent
grace, wifdom, and ufefulnefs. She walked with
God forty years : fhe was one of the Lord's poor ;
but her poverty was decent, fanctified, and honourable : fhe lived refpected, and her death is
confidered as a public lofs, It is a great lofs to me ;
I fhall mifs her advice and example, by which I
have

have been often edified and animated. But Jefus ftill lives. Almoft her laft words were, The Lord is my portion, faith my foul.

I am, &c.

LETTER XIII.

My Lord,   *March* 10. 1774.

FOR about fix weeks paft I have had occafion to fpend feveral hours of almoft every day with the fick and the dying. Thefe fcenes are to a minifter like walking the hofpitals to a young furgeon. The various cafes which occur exemplify, illuftrate, and explain, with a commanding energy, many truths, which may be learned indeed at home, but cannot be fo well underftood, or their force fo fenfibly felt, without the advantage of experience and obfervation. As phyficians, befides that competent general knowledge of their profeffion which fhould be common to them all, have ufually their feveral favourite branches of ftudy, fome applying themfelves more to botany, others to chymiftry, others to anatomy; fo minifters, as their inclinations and gifts differ, are led more clofely to confider fome particular branch of the fyftem of divine truth. Some are directed to ftate and defend the doctrines of the gofpel; fome have a talent for elucidating difficult texts of fcripture; fome have a turn for explaining the prophetical parts, and fo of the reft. For myfelf, if it be lawful to fpeak of myfelf, and fo far as I can judge, anatomy is my favourite branch; I mean the ftudy of the human heart, with its workings and counter-workings, as it is differently affected in a ftate of nature or of

grace,

grace, in the different feafons of profperity, adverfity, conviction, temptation, ficknefs, and the approach of death. The Lord, by fending me hi-
ther, provided me a good fchool for thefe purpofes. I know not where I could have had a better, or affording a greater variety of characters, in
proportion to the number of people ; and as they
are moftly a poor people, and ftrangers to that addrefs which is the refult of education and converfe
with the world, there is a fimplicity in what they fay
or do, which gives me a peculiar advantage in judging of their cafes.

But I was about to fpeak of death. Though the
grand evidence of thofe truths upon which our
hopes are built arifes from the authority of God
fpeaking them in his word, and revealing them by
his Spirit, to the awakened heart, (for till the heart
is awakened it is incapable of receiving this evidence) ; yet fome of thefe truths are fo myfterious,
fo utterly repugnant to the judgement of depraved
nature, that, through the remaining influence of
unbelief and vain reafoning, the temptations of
Satan, and the fubtle arguments with which fome
men reputed wife attack the foundations of our
faith, the minds even of believers are fometimes
capable of being fhaken. I know no better cor-
roborating evidence for the relief of the mind under
fuch affaults than the teftimony of dying perfons,
efpecially of fuch as have lived out of the noife of
controverfy, and who perhaps never heard a fyllable
of what has been ftarted in thefe evil days, againft
the Deity of Chrift, his atonement, and other important articles. Permit me, my Lord, to relate,
upon this occafion, fome things which exceedingly
ftruck me in the converfation I had with a young
woman whom I vifited in her laft illnefs about two
years ago. She was a fober prudent perfon, of
plain fenfe, could read her Bible, but had read
little

little beſide : her knowledge of the world was nearly confined to the pariſh ; for I ſuppoſe ſhe was
ſeldom if ever twelve miles from home in her life.
She had known the goſpel about ſeven years before
the Lord viſited her with a lingering conſumption,
which at length removed her to a better world.   A
few days before her death, I had been praying by
her bed-ſide, and in my prayer I thanked the Lord,
that he gave her now to ſee that ſhe had not followed cunningly-deviſed fables.   When I had fi-
niſhed, ſhe repeated that word, " No, ſhe ſaid,
not cunningly-deviſed fables ; theſe are realities indeed ; I feel their truth, I feel their comfort.   O
tell my friends, tell my acquaintance, tell inquiring
ſouls, tell poor ſinners, tell all the daughters of
Jeruſalem, (alluding to Solomon's Song, v. 16.
from which ſhe had juſt before deſired me to
preach at her funeral), what Jeſus has done for
my ſoul.   Tell them, that now in the time of need
I find him my beloved and my friend, and as ſuch
I commend him to them."   She then fixed her
eyes ſtedfaſtly upon me, and proceeded, as well as
I can recollect, as follows : " Sir, you are highly
favoured in being called to preach the goſpel.   I
have often heard you with pleaſure ; but give me
leave to tell you, that I now ſee all you have ſaid,
or can ſay, is comparatively but little.   Nor till
you come into my ſituation, and have death and
eternity full in your view, will it be poſſible for
you to conceive the vaſt weight and importance of
the truths you declare.   Oh ! Sir, it is a ſerious
thing to die ; no words can expreſs what is needful
to ſupport the ſoul in the ſolemnity of a dying
hour."
    I believe it was the next day when I viſited her
again. After ſome diſcourſe as uſual, ſhe ſaid, with
a remarkable vehemence of ſpeech, Are you ſure I
cannot be miſtaken ? I anſwered without heſitation,

Yes, I am fure; I am not afraid to fay, my foul for
your's that you are right. She paufed a little, and
then replied, " You fay true, I know I am right.
I feel that my hope is fixed upon the rock of ages;
I know in whom I have believed. Yet if you could
fee with my eyes, you would not wonder at my
queftion. But the approach of death prefents a
profpect, which is till then hidden from us, and
which cannot be defcribed." She faid much more
to the fame purpofe, and in all fhe fpoke there was
a dignity, weight, and evidence, which I fuppofe
few profeffors of divinity, when lecturing from the
chair, have at any time equalled. We may well
fay with Elihu, Who teacheth like him? Many
inftances of the like kind I have met with here. I
have a poor girl near me who looks like an idiot,
and her natural capacity is indeed very fmall; but
the Lord has been pleafed to make her acquainted
alternately with great temptations, and proportionably great difcoveries of his love and truth. Sometimes, when her heart is enlarged, I liften to her
with aftonifhment. I think no books or minifters
I ever met with have given me fuch an impreffion and underftanding of what the apoftle ftyles
τα βαθη του Θεου, as I have upon fome occafions
received from her converfation.

But I am rambling again. My attendance upon
the fick is not always equally comfortable, but
could I learn aright, it might be equally inftructive.
Some confirm the precioufnefs of a Saviour to me,
by the chearfulnefs with which, through faith in
his name, they meet the king of terrors. Others
no lefs confirm it, by the terror and reluctance
they difcover when they find they muft die; for
though there are too many who fadly flight the
bleffed gofpel while they are in health, yet in this
place moft are too far enlightened to be quite
thoughtlefs about their fouls, if they retain their
                                        fenfes.

fenfes in their laft illnefs. Then, like the foolifh
virgins, they fay, Give us of your oil: Then they
are willing that minifters and profeffors fhould pray
with them and fpeak to them. Through the Lord's
goodnefs, feveral whom I have vifited in thefe circumftances have afforded me good hope; they
have been favingly changed by his bleffing upon
what has paffed at the eleventh hour. I have feen
a marvellous and bleffed change take place in their
language, views, and tempers, in a few days. I
now vifit a young perfon, who is cut fhort in her
nineteenth year by a confumption, and I think cannot live many days. I found her very ignorant and
infenfible, and fhe remained fo a good while; but
of late I hope her heart is touched.—She feels her
loft ftate, fhe feems to have fome right defires, fhe
begins to pray, and in fuch a manner as I cannot
but hope the Lord is teaching her, and will reveal
himfelf to her before fhe departs. But it is fometimes otherwife. I faw a young woman die laft
week: I had been often with her; but the night fhe
was removed fhe could only fay, O, I cannot live,
I cannot live! She repeated this mournful complaint as long as fhe could fpeak; for as the vital
powers were more oppreffed, her voice was changed into groans; her groans grew fainter and fainter, and in about a quarter of an hour after fhe had
done fpeaking fhe expired. Poor thing, I thought,
as I ftood by her bed-fide, if you were a Duchefs,
in this fituation, what could the world do for you
now! I thought, likewife, how many things are
there that now give us pleafure or pain, and affume
a mighty importance in our view, which, in a dying
hour, will be no more to us than the clouds which
fly unnoticed over our heads. Then the truth of
our Lord's aphorifm will be feen, felt, and acknowledged, "One thing is needful;" and we fhall
be ready to apply Grotius's dying confeffion to

C 4   (alas!)

(alas !) a great part of our lives, *Ah vitam perdidi,
nihil agendo laboriosè.*

Your Lordſhip allows me to ſend unpremeditated
letters. I need not aſſure you this is one.

    I am, &c.

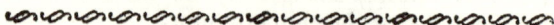

LETTER XIV.

My Lord,   *May* 24. 1774.

WHat a mercy is it to be ſeparated in ſpirit,
conversation, and intereſt, from the world
that knows not God ! where all are alike by nature. Grace makes a happy and unſpeakable difference. Believers were once under the ſame influence of that ſpirit who ſtill worketh in the children of diſobedience, purſuing different paths, but
all equally remote from truth and peace ; ſome
hatching cockatrice eggs, others weaving ſpiders
webs. Theſe two general heads of miſchief and
vanity include all the ſchemes, aims, and atchieve-
ments of which man is capable, till God is pleaſed
to viſit the heart with his grace. The buſy part of
mankind are employed in multiplying evils and mi-
ſeries ; the more retired, ſpeculative, and curious,
are amuſing themſelves with what will hereafter appear as unſubſtantial, unſtable, and uſeleſs as a cobweb. Death will ſoon ſweep away all that the phi-
loſophers, the virtuoſi, the mathematicians, the an-
tiquarians, and other learned triflers, are now weaving with ſo much ſelf-applauded addreſs. Nor will
the fine-ſpun dreſſes, in which the moraliſt and the
ſelf-righteous clothe themſelves, be of more advantage to them, either for ornament or defence, than
the produce of a ſpider. But it is given to a few

                       to

to know their prefent ftate and future deftination.
—Thefe build upon the immovable rock of ages
for eternity: Thefe are trees fpringing from a living
root, and bear the fruits of righteoufnefs, which
are by Jefus Chrift to the glory and praife of God:
Thefe only are awake, while the reft of the world
are in a fleep, indulging in vain dreams, from which
likewife they will fhortly awake; but, O with what
confternation, when they fhall find themfelves irre-
coverably divorced from all their delufive attach-
ments, and compelled to appear before that God to
whom they have lived ftrangers, and to whom they
muft give an account! O for a thoufand tongues
to proclaim in the ears of thoughtlefs mortals
that important aphorifm of our Lord, " One thing
" is needful!" Yet a thoufand tongues would be
and are employed in vain, unlefs fo far as the Lord
is pleafed to fend the watchman's warning, by the
power and agency of his own Spirit. I think the
Poet tells us, that Caffandra had the gift of truly
foretelling future events; but fhe was afterwards
laid under a painful embarraffment, that no body
fhould believe her words. Such, with refpect to
the bulk of their auditories, is the lot of gofpel-
minifters: they are enlightened to fee, and fent
forth to declare, the awful confequences of fin;
but alas, how few believe their report! To illuftrate our grief and difappointment, I fometimes
fuppofe there was a dangerous water in the way of
travellers, over which there is a bridge, which thofe
who can be prevailed upon may pafs with fafety.
By the fide of this bridge watchmen are placed, to
warn paffengers of the danger of the waters; to affure them, that all who attempt to go through them
inevitably perifh; to invite, intreat, and befeech
them, if they value their lives, to crofs the bridge.
Methinks this fhould be an eafy tafk: Yet if we
fhould fee in fact the greater part ftopping their

ears to the friendly importunity; many so much
offended by it, as to account the watchman's care
impertinent, and only deferving of fcorn and ill
treatment; hardly one in fifty betaking themfelves
to the friendly bridge, the reft eagerly plunging into the waters, from which none return, as if they
were determined to try who fhould be drowned firft:
this fpectacle would be no unfit emblem of the reception the gofpel meets with from a blinded world.
The minifters are rejected, oppofed, vilified; they
are accounted troublers of the world, becaufe they
dare not, cannot ftand filent, while finners are pe-
rifhing before their eyes; and if, in the courfe of
many fermons, they can prevail but on one foul to
take timely warning, and to feek to Jefus, who is
the way, the truth, and the life, they may account
it a mercy and an honour, fufficient to overbalance
all the labour and reproaches they are called to endure. From the moft they muft expect no better
reception than the Jews gave to Jeremiah, who told
the prophet to his face, As to the word thou haft
fpoken to us in the name of the Lord, we will not
hearken to thee at all; but we will certainly do
whatfoever thing goeth forth out of our own mouth.
Surely, if the Lord has given us any fenfe of the
worth of our fouls, any compaffion towards them,
this muft be a painful exercife; and experience
muft teach us fomething of the meaning of Jeremiah's pathetic exclamation, O that my head were
waters, and mine eyes fountains of tears, that I
might weep day and night for the flain of the
daughters of my people. It is our *duty* to be thus
affected. Our relief lies in the wifdom and fovereignty of God. He reveals his falvation to whom
he pleafes, for the moft part to babes; from the
bulk of the wife and the prudent it is hidden. Thus
it hath pleafed him, and therefore it muft be right.
Yea, he will one day condefcend to juftify the pro-

priety and equity of his proceedings to his creatures; then every mouth will be ftopped, and none
will be able to reply againft their judge. Light is
come into the world, but men prefer darknefs.
They hate the light, refift it, and rebel againft it.
It is true, all do fo; and therefore, if all were to
perifh under the condemnation, their ruin would
be their own act. It is of grace that any are faved,
and in the diftribution of that grace, he does what
he will with his own : A right which moft are ready enough to claim in their own concerns, though
they are fo unwilling to allow it to the Lord of all.
Many perplexing and acrimonious difputes have
been ftarted upon this fubject; but the redeemed
of the Lord are called, not to difpute, but to admire and rejoice; to love, adore, and obey. To
know that he loved us, and gave himfelf for us, is
the conftraining argument and motive to love him,
and furrender ourfelves to him; to confider ourfelves as no longer our own, but to devote ourfelves,
with every faculty, power, and talent, to his fervice and glory. He deferves our all; for he parted
with all for us. He made himfelf poor,—he endured fhame, torture, death, and the curfe for us,
that we through him might inherit everlafting life.
Ah! the hardnefs of my heart, that I am no
more affected, aftonifhed, overpowered with this
thought !

    I am, &c.

L E T T E R   XV.

My Lord,   *April* 20. 1774.

I Have been pondering a good while for a subject,
and at last I begin without one, hoping that (as
it has often happened) while I am writing one line,
something will occur to fill up another.   Indeed I
have an inexhaustible fund at hand; but it is to me
often like a prize in the hand of a fool, I want
skill to improve it.   O for a warm, a suitable, a
seasonable train of thought, that might enliven my
own heart, and not be unworthy your Lordship's
perusal !   Methinks the poets can have but cold
comfort, when they invocate a fabled muse; but
we have a warrant, a right, to look up for the influence of the Holy Spirit, who ordains strength
for us, and has promised to work in us.   What
a comfort, what an honour is this, that worms
have liberty to look up to God ! and that he, the
high and holy One who inhabiteth eternity, is
pleased to look down upon us, to maintain our
peace, to supply our wants, to guide us with his
eye, and to inspire us with wisdom and grace suitable to our occasions !   They who profess to know
something of this intercourse, and to depend upon
it, are by the world accounted enthusiasts, who
know not what they mean, or perhaps hypocrites,
who pretend to what they have not, in order to
cover some base designs.—But we have reason to
bear their reproaches with patience.   Could the
miser say,

———— *Populus me fibilat, at mihi plaudo*
Ipfe domi, fimul ac nummos contemplor in arca.

Well

Well then may the believer fay, Let them laugh,
let them rage, let them, if they pleafe, point at me
for a fool as I walk the ftreets; if I do but take up
the Bible, or run over in my mind the inventory of
the bleffings with which the Lord has enriched me,
I have fufficient amends. Jefus is mine; in him I
have wifdom, righteoufnefs, fanctification, and redemption, an intereft in all the promifes and in all
the perfections of God; he will guide me by his
counfel, fupport me by his power, comfort me with
his prefence, while I am here, and afterwards,
when flefh and heart fail, he will receive me to
his glory.

Let them fay what they will, they fhall not difpute or laugh us out of our fpiritual fenfes. If all
the blind men in the kingdom fhould endeavour
to bear me down, that the fun is not bright, or
that the rainbow has no colours, I would ftill believe my own eyes. I have feen them both, they
have not. I cannot prove to their fatisfaction what
I affert, becaufe they are deftitute of fight, the neceffary medium; yet their exceptions produce no
uncertainty in my mind: they would not, they
could not hefitate a moment, if they were not blind.
Juft fo, they who have been taught of God, who
have tafted that the Lord is gracious, have an experimental perception of the truth, which renders
them proof againft all the fophiftry of infidels. I
am perfuaded we have many plain people here, who,
if a wife man of the world was to fuggeft that the
Bible is a human invention, would be quite at a lofs
how to anfwer him, by arguments drawn from external evidences; yet they have found fuch effects
from this bleffed book, that they would be no more
moved by the infinuation, than if they were told,
that a cunning man, or fet of men, invented the
fun, and placed it in the firmament. So, if a wife
Socinian was to tell them, that the Saviour was only

a

a man like themfelves, they would conceive juft
fuch an opinion of his fkill in divinity, as a philofo-
pher would do of a clown's fkill in aftronomy, who
fhould affirm that the fun was no bigger than a cart-
wheel.

It remains therefore a truth, in defiance of all
the cavils of the ignorant, that the Holy Spirit does
influence the hearts of all the children of God, or,
in other words, they are infpired, not with new
revelations, but with grace and wifdom to underftand, apply and feed upon the great things already revealed in the fcriptures, without which the
fcriptures are as ufelefs as fpectacles to the blind.
Were it not fo, when we become acquainted with
the poverty, ignorance, and wickednefs of our
hearts, we muft fit down in utter defpair of being
ever able to think a good thought, to offer a fingle
petition aright in prayer, or to take one fafe ftep
in the path of life. But now we may be content
with our proper weaknefs, fince the power and
fpirit of Chrift are engaged to reft upon us ; and
while we are preferved in a fimple dependence upon
this help, though unable of ourfelves to do any
thing, we fhall find an ability to do every thing
that our circumftances and duty call for. What is
weaker than a worm ? Yet the Lord's worms fhall,
in his ftrength, threfh the mountains, and make the
hills as chaff. But this life of faith, this living
and acting by a power above our own, is an inex-
plicable myftery, till experience makes it plain. I
have often wondered that St Paul has obtained fo
much quarter at the hands of fome people, as to
pafs with them for a man of fenfe ; for furely the
greateft part of his writings muft be to the laft degree abfurd and unintelligible upon their principles.
How many contradictions muft they find, for inftance, if they give any attention to what they read
in that one paffage, Gal. ii. 20. " I am crucified with
                                        " Chrift ;

" Chrift: Neverthelefs I live ; yet not **I,** but Chrift
" liveth in me : and the life which I now live in the
" flefh, I live by faith in the Son of God, who loved
" me, and gave himfelf for me."

And as believers are thus infpired by the holy
Spirit, who furnifhes them with defires, motives,
and abilities, to perform what is agreeable to his
will ; fo I apprehend, that they who live without
God in the world, whom the apoftle ftyles *fenfual,
not having the fpirit,* are in a greater or lefs degree
ad captum recipientis, under what I may call a *black
infpiration.* After making the beft allowances I
can, both for the extent of human genius, and the
deplorable evil of the human heart, I cannot fuppofe that one half of the wicked wit, of which
fome perfons are fo proud, is properly their own.
Perhaps fuch a one as Voltaire would neither have
written, or have been read or admired fo much, if
he had not been the amanuenfis of an abler hand
in his own way. Satan is always near when the
heart is difpofed to receive him ; and the Lord
withdraws his reftraints, to heighten the finner's
ability of finning with an *eclat,* and affifting him
with fuch ftrokes of blafphemy, malice, and falfehood, as perhaps he could not otherwife have attained. Therefore, I do not wonder that they are
clever and fmart, that they raife a laugh, and are
received with applaufe among thofe who are like-
minded with themfelves. But unlefs the Lord is
pleafed to grant them repentance, (though it is rather to be feared fome of them are given up to ju-
dicial hardnefs of heart), how much better would
it have been for them had they been born idiots or
lunatics, than to be diftinguifhed as the willing, in-
duftrious, and fuccefsful inftruments of the powers
of darknefs, in beguiling, perverting, and ruining
the fouls of men ! Alas, what are parts and talents,
or any diftinctions which give pre-eminence in life,
unlefs

unlefs they are fanctified by the grace of God, and
directed to the accomplifhment of his will and
glory ! From the expreffion, *Bind them in bundles
and burn them*, I have been led to think, that the
deceivers and the deceived, they who have pro-
ftituted their gifts or influence to encourage others
in fin, and they who have perifhed by their means,
may in another world have fome peculiar and infeparable connection, and fpend an eternity in
fruitlefs lamentations, that ever they were connected here.

Your Lordfhip, I doubt not, feels the force of
that line,

O to grace how great a debtor !——

Had not the Lord feparated you for himfelf,
your rank, your abilities, your influence, which
now you chiefly value as enlarging your opportunities of ufefulnefs, might, nay certainly would,
have been diverted into the oppofite channel.

I am, &c.

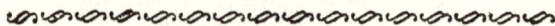

L E T T E R   XVI.

My Lord,   *November 5. 1774.*

I Have not very lately had recourfe to the expedient of defcanting upon a text, but I believe it
the beft method I can take to avoid ringing changes
upon a few obvious topics, which I fuppofe uni-
formly prefent themfelves to my mind when I am
about to write to your Lordfhip. Juft now that
fweet expreffion of David occurred to my thoughts,
The Lord is my Shepherd! Permit me, without plan

or premeditation, to make a few obſervations upon
it; and may your Lordſhip feel the peace, the confidence, the bleſſedneſs, which a believing application of the words is ſuited to inſpire.

The Socinians and others, in their unhappy laboured attempts to darken the principal glory and
foundation-comfort of the goſpel, employ their
critical ſophiſtry againſt thoſe texts which expreſsly
and doctrinally declare the Redeemer's character;
and affect to triumph, if in any manuſcript or an-
cient verſion they can find a variation from the received copies which ſeems to favour their cauſe.
But we may venture to wave the authority of every
diſputed or diſputable text, and maintain the truth
againſt their cavils, from the current language and
tenor of the whole ſcripture.   David's words in
Pſal. xxiii. are alone a deciſive proof that Jeſus is
Jehovah, if they will but allow two things, which
I think they cannot deny :—1. That our Saviour
aſſumes to himſelf the character of the Shepherd of
his people;—and 2. That he did not come into the
world to abridge thoſe advantages which the ſer-
vants of God enjoyed before his incarnation. Upon
theſe premiſſes, which cannot be gainſayed without
ſetting aſide the whole New Teſtament, the concluſion is undeniable : for if Jehovah was David's
Shepherd, unleſs Jeſus be Jehovah, we who live
under the goſpel have an unſpeakable diſadvantage,
in being entruſted to the care of one who, according to the Socinians, is a mere man; and upon the
Arian ſcheme, is at the moſt a creature, and infinitely ſhort of poſſeſſing thoſe perfections which
David contemplated in his Shepherd. He had a
Shepherd whoſe wiſdom and power were infinite,
and might therefore warrantably conclude he ſhould
not want, and need not fear. And we alſo may
conclude the ſame, if our Shepherd be the Lord
or Jehovah, but not otherwiſe. Beſides, the very
                                             nature

nature of the Shepherd's office respecting the state
of such frail creatures as we are, requires those attributes for the due discharge of it, which are in-
communicably divine. He must intimately know
every individual of the flock.—His eye must be
upon them every one, and his ear open to their
prayers, and his arm stretched out for their relief,
in all places and in all ages.—Every thought of
every heart must be open to his view, and his wisdom must penetrate, and his arm controul and
over-rule all the hidden and complicated machina-
tions of the powers of darkness.—He must have
the administration of universal providence over all
the nations, families, and persons upon earth, or
he could not effectually manage for those who put
their trust in him, in that immense variety of cases
and circumstances in which they are found. Reason, as well as scripture, may convince us, that he
who gathereth the outcasts of Israel, who healeth
the broken in heart, who upholdeth all that fall,
raiseth up all that are bowed down, and upon
whom the eyes of all wait for their support, can
be no other than he who telleth the number of the
stars and calleth them all by their names, who is
great in power, and whose understanding is infinite.
To this purpose, likewise, the prophet Isaiah de-
scribes this mighty Shepherd, chap. xl. 9.—17.
both as to his person and office.

But is not this indeed the great mystery of god-
liness! How just is the apostle's observation, that
no man can say Jesus Christ is Lord, but by the
Holy Ghost! How astonishing the thought,—that
the Maker of heaven and earth, the Holy One of
Israel, before whose presence the earth shook, the
heavens dropped, when he displayed a faint emblem of his majesty upon Sinai, should afterwards
appear in the form of a servant, and hang upon a
cross, the sport and scorn of wicked men! I cannot

not wonder that to the wife men of the world this appears abfurd, unreafonable, and impoffible; yet to right reafon, to reafon enlightened and fanctified, however amazing the propofition be, yet it appears true and neceffary, upon a fuppofition, that a holy God is pleafed to pardon finners in a way fuited to difplay the awful glories of his juftice. The fame arguments which prove the blood of bulls and goats infufficient to take away fin, will conclude againft the utmoft doings or fufferings of men or angels. The Redeemer of finners muft be mighty; he muft have a perfonal dignity to ftamp fuch a value upon his undertakings, as that thereby God may appear juft, as well as merciful, in juftifying the ungodly for his fake; and he muft be all-fufficient to blefs, and almighty to protect, thofe who come unto him for fafety and life.

Such a one is our Shepherd. This is he of whom we through grace are enabled to fay we are *his* people, and the fheep of *his* pafture. We are his by every tie and right; he made us, he redeemed us, he reclaimed us from the hand of our enemies, and we are his by our own voluntary furrender of ourfelves; for though we once flighted, defpifed, and oppofed him, he made us willing in the day of his power: he knocked at the door of our hearts; but we (at leaft I) barred and faftened it againft him as much and as long as poffible. But when he revealed his love, we could ftand out no longer. Like fheep, we are weak, deftitute, defencelefs, prone to wander, unable to return, and always furrounded with wolves. But all is made up in the fulnefs, ability, wifdom, compaffion, care, and faithfulnefs of our great Shepherd. He guides, protects, feeds, heals, and reftores, and will be our guide and our God even until death. Then he will meet us, receive us, and prefent us unto himfelf, and we

fhall

fhall be near him, and like him, and with him for
ever.

Ah! my Lord, what a fubject is this? I truft it
is the joy of your heart. Placed as you are by his
hand in a fuperior rank, you fee and feel that the
higheft honours, and the moft important concernments that terminate with the prefent life, are trivial as the fports of children, in comparifon with
the views and the privileges you derive from the
glorious gofpel; and your fituation in life renders
the grace beftowed upon you the more confpicu-
ous and diftinguifhing. I have fomewhere met
with a fimilar reflection of Henry the Fourth of
France, to this purpofe, that though many came into the world the fame day with him, he was probably the only one among them that was born to
be a King. Your Lordfhip is acquainted with many, who if not born on the fame day with you,
were born to titles, eftates, and honours; but how
few of them were born to the honour of making a
public and confiftent profeffion of the glorious gofpel! The hour is coming, when all honours and
poffeffions, but this which cometh of God only,
will be eclipfed and vanifh; and, like the bafelefs
fabric of a vifion, leave not a wreck behind. How
miferable will they then be, who muft leave their
all! What a mortifying thought does Horace put in
the way of thofe who difdain to read the Scripture?

> *Linquenda tellus, et domus, et placens*
> *Uxor: neque harum, quas colis, arborum*
> *Te, præter invifas cupreffos,*
> *Ulla brevem dominum fequetur.*

But grace and faith can make the loweft ftate of
life fupportable, and make a difmiffion from the
higheft defirable. Of the former I have many living

ving proofs and witneſſes around me. Your Lordſhip, I truſt, will have ſweet experience of the latter, when, after having fulfilled the will of God
in your generation, you ſhall be called (I hope in
ſome yet diſtant day) to enter into your Maſter's
joy. In the mean time, how valuable are life, talents, influence, and opportunities of every kind,
if we are enabled to improve and lay out all for him
who has thus loved us, thus provided for us? As
to myſelf, I would hope there are few who have ſo
clear a ſenſe of their obligations to him, who make
ſuch unſuitable and languid returns as I do. I
think I have a deſire to ſerve him better; but,
alas! evil is preſent with me. Surely I ſhall feel
ſomething like ſhame and regret for my coldneſs,
even in heaven;—for I find I am never happier
than when I am moſt aſhamed of myſelf upon this
account here.

    I am, &c.

LETTER XVII.

My Lord,   *December* 8. 1774.

HOW wonderful is the patience of God towards
ſinful men! In him they live, and move, and
have their being; and if he were to withdraw his
ſupport for a ſingle moment, they muſt periſh. He
maintains their lives, guards their perſons, ſup-
plies their wants, while they employ the powers
and faculties they receive from him in a ſettled
courſe of oppoſition to his will. They trample upon his laws, affront his government, and deſpiſe
his grace; yet ſtill he ſpares. To ſilence all his ad-
verſaries in a moment, would require no extraordinary

ordinary exertion of his power; but his forbear-
ance towards them manifests his glory, and gives us
cause to say, Who is a God like unto thee?

Sometimes, however, there are striking instances
of his displeasure against sin. When such events
take place, immediately upon a public and preme-
ditated contempt offered to Him that sitteth in the
heavens; I own they remind me of the danger of
standing, if I may so speak, in the Lord's way:
for though his long-suffering is astonishing, and
many dare him to his face daily, with seeming impunity; yet he sometimes strikes an awful and unexpected blow, and gives an illustration of that so-
lemn word, "Who ever hardened himself against
"the Lord and prospered?" But who am I to make
this observation? I ought to do it with the deepest
humiliation, remembering that I once stood (according to my years and ability) in the foremost
rank of his avowed opposers; and with a determined and unwearied enmity, renounced, defied, and
blasphemed him. "But he will have mercy on
"whom he will have mercy;" and therefore I was
spared, and reserved to speak of his goodness.

Josephus, when speaking of the death of Herod
Agrippa, ascribes it to a natural cause, and says, he
was seized with excruciating pains in his bowels.
But Luke informs us of the *true* cause: an angel of
the Lord smote him. Had we a modern history,
written by an inspired pen, we should probably often be reminded of such an interposition where
we are not ordinarily aware of it. For though the
springs of actions and events are concealed from us
for the most part, and vain men carry on their
schemes with confidence, as though the Lord had
forsaken the earth; yet they are under his eye and
controul; and faith, in some measure, instructed
by the specimens of his government recorded in
the scripture, can trace and admire his hand, and
                                            can

can fee how he takes the wife in their own crafti-
nefs, ftains the pride of human glory; and that
when finners fpeak proudly, he is above them, and
makes every thing bend or break before him.

While we lament the growth and pernicious
effects of infidelity, and fee how wicked men and
feducers wax worfe and worfe, deceiving, and being deceived; what gratitude fhould fill our hearts
to him, who has been pleafed to call us out of the
horrid darknefs in which multitudes are bewildered
and loft, into the glorious light of his gofpel?
Faint are our warmeft conceptions of this mercy.
In order to underftand it fully, we fhould have a
full and adequate fenfe of the evil from which we
are delivered; the glory to which we are called;
and efpecially of the aftonifhing means to which
we owe our life and hope, the humiliation, fufferings, and death of the Son of God. But our views
of thefe points, while in our prefent ftate, are and
muft be exceedingly weak and difproportionate.
We know them but in part, we fee them δι εσοπῖρν,
by *reflection*, rather the images than the things
themfelves; and though they are faithfully reprefented in the mirror of God's word, to us they appear indiftinct, becaufe we fee them through a
grofs medium of ignorance and unbelief. Hereafter every vail fhall be removed; we fhall know,
in another manner than we do now, the unfpeakable evil of fin, and the infupportable dreadfulnefs
of God's difpleafure againft it, when we fee the
world in flames, and hear the final fentence de-
nounced upon the ungodly. We fhall have far
other thoughts of Jefus when we fee him as he is;
and fhall then be able to make a more affecting eftimate of the love which moved him to be made a
fubftitute and a curfe for us; and we fhall then
know what great things God has prepared for them
that love him. Then with tranfport we fhall adopt
the

the Queen of Sheba's language, It was a true report we heard in yonder dark world; but behold
the half, the thoufandth part, was not told us! In
the mean time, may fuch conceptions as we are enabled to form of thefe great truths, fill our hearts,
and be mingled with all our thoughts, and all our
concerns; may the Lord, by faith, give us an
abiding evidence of the reality and importance of the
things which cannot yet be feen : fo fhall we be enabled to live above the world while we are in it,
uninfluenced either by its blandifhments or its
frowns; and, with a noble fimplicity and fingulari-
ty, avow and maintain the caufe of God in truth,
in the midft of a crooked and perverfe generation.
He whom we ferve is able to fupport and protect
us; and he well deferves, at our hands, that we
fhould be willing to endure, for his fake, much
more than he will ever permit us to be exercifed
with. The believer's call, duty, and privilege, is
beautifully and forcibly fet forth in Milton's character of Abdiel, at the end of the Fifth Book :

> ———— *Faithful found*
> *Among the faithlefs, faithful only he :*
> *Among innumerable falfe, unmov'd,*
> *Unfhaken, unfeduc'd, unterrify'd,*
> *His loyalty he kept, his love, his zeal;*
> *Nor number, nor example, with him wrought*
> *To fwerve from truth, or change his conftant mind*
> *Though fingle.* ————————

Methinks your Lordfhip's fituation particularly
refembles that in which the Poet has placed Abdiel.
You are not indeed called to ferve God quite alone;
but amongft thofe of your own rank, and with
whom the ftation in which he has placed you ne-
ceffitates you to converfe, how few are there who
can underftand, fecond, or approve, the principles
upon

upon which you act, or eafily bear a conduct which muft imprefs conviction, or reflect difhonour upon themfelves! But you are not alone; the Lord's people (many of whom you will not know till you meet them in glory) are helping you here with their prayers; his angels are commiffioned to guard and guide your fteps;—yea, the Lord himfelf fixes his eye of mercy upon your private and your public path, and is near you at your right hand, that you may not be moved! That he may com-fort you with the light of his countenance, and up-hold you with the arm of his power, is my frequent prayer.

I am, &c.

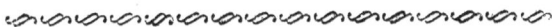

L E T T E R   XVIII.

My Lord,   *January* 20. 1775.

WE have entered upon another year!—So have thoufands, perhaps millions, who will not fee it clofe! An alarming thought to the world-ling! at leaft it fhould be fo. I have an imperfect remembrance of an account I read when I was a boy, of an ice-palace, built one winter at Peterf-burg. The walls, the roof, the floors, the furni-ture, were all of ice, but finifhed with tafte; and every thing that might be expected in a royal pa-lace was to be found there; the ice, while in the ftate of water, being previoufly coloured, fo that to the eye all feemed formed of proper materials; but all was cold, ufelefs, and tranfient. -Had the froft continued till now, the palace might have been ftanding; but with the returning fpring it melted away, like the bafelefs fabric of a vifion. Methinks

there ſhould have been one ſtone in the building, to
have retained the inſcription, *Sic tranſit gloria mundi !* for no contrivance could exhibit a fitter illu-
ſtration of the vanity of human life. Men build
and plan as if their work were to endure for ever;
but the wind paſſes over them, and they are gone.
In the midſt of all their preparations, or at fartheſt
when they think they have juſt compléted their deſigns, their breath goeth forth, they return to their
earth; in that very day their thoughts periſh.

   How many ſleep who kept the world awake !

Yet this ice houſe had ſomething of a leiſurely
diſſolution, though, when it began to decay, all the
art of man was unable to prop it; but often death
comes haſtily, and, like the ſpringing of a mine,
deſtroys to the very foundations without previous
notice. Then all we have been concerned in here
(all but the conſequences of our conduct, which
will abide to eternity) will be no more to us than
the remembrance of a dream. This truth is too
plain to be denied; but the greater part of mankind
act as if they were convinced it was falſe : they
ſpend their days in vanity, and in a moment they
go down to the grave. What cauſe of thankfulneſs
have they who are delivered from this deluſion, and
who, by the knowledge of the glorious goſpel, have
learned their true ſtate and end, are ſaved from the
love of the preſent world, from the heart-diſtreſſ-
ing fear of death; and know, that if their earthly houſe were *diſſolved*, like the ice-palace, they
have a houſe not made with hands, eternal in the
heavens.

   Yet even theſe are much concerned to realize the
brevity and uncertainty of their preſent ſtate, that
they may be ſtimulated to make the moſt and the
beſt of it; to redeem their time, and manage their
precarious

precarious opportunities, fo as may moft tend to
the praife and glory of him who has called them
out of darknefs into marvellous light.   Why fhould
any that have tafted that the Lord is gracious wifh
to live another day, but that they may have the
honour to be fellow-workers with him, inftrumental
in promoting his defigns, and of laying themfelves
out to the utmoft of their abilities and influence in
his fervice !   To enjoy a fenfe of his loving kindnefs, and to have the light of his countenance lifted
up upon our fouls, is indeed, refpecting ourfelves,
the beft part of life, yea better than life itfelf; but
this we fhall have to unfpeakably greater advantage,
when we have finifhed our courfe, and fhall be
wholly freed from the body of fin.   And therefore
the *great defirable* while here feems to be grace,
that we may *ferve* him and *fuffer* for him in the
world.   Though our firft wifh immediately upon
our own accounts might be, to depart and be with
Jefus, which is πολλω μαλλον κρεισσον, yet a lively thought of our immenfe obligations to his redeeming love, may reconcile us to a much longer
continuance here, if we may by any means be fubfervient to diffufe the glory of his name, and the
bleffings of his falvation, which is God's great
and principal end in preferving the world itfelf.
When hiftorians and politicians defcant upon the
rife and fall of empires, with all their profeffed fa-
gacity, in tracing the connection between caufes
and effects, they are totally unacquainted with the
great mafter-wheel which manages the whole movement; that is, the Lord's defign in favour of his
church and kingdom.   To this every event is fubordinate ; to this every interfering intereft muft ftoop.
How eafily might this pofition be proved, by re-
viewing the hiftory of the period about the Reformation.   Whether Dr Robertfon confiders things
in this light, in his hiftory of Charles V. I know

not,

not, as I have not feen his books; but if not, however elaborate his performance may be in other refpects, I muft venture to fay, it is effentially defective, and cannot give that light and pleafure to
a fpiritual reader of which the fubject is capable.
And I doubt not but fome who are yet unborn will
hereafter clearly fee and remark, that the prefent
unhappy difputes between Great Britain and America, with their confequences, whatever they may
be, are part of a feries of events, of which the ex-
tention and interefts of the church of Chrift were
the principal final caufes. In a word, that Jefus
may be known, trufted, and adored, and finners,
by the power of his gofpel, be refcued from fin and
Satan, is comparatively the To εν—the one great
bufinefs, for the fake of which the fucceffion of day
and night, fummer and winter, is ftill maintained;
and when the plan of redemption is confummated,
fin, which now almoft fills the earth, will then fet
it on fire; and the united intereft of all the reft of
mankind, when detached from that of the people
of God, will not plead for its prefervation a fingle
day. In this view, I congratulate your Lordfhip,
that, however your beft endeavours to ferve the
temporal interefts of the nation may fall fhort of
your wifhes; yet, fo far as your fituation gives you
opportunity of fupporting the gofpel-caufe, and fa-
cilitating its progrefs, you have a profpect both of
a more certain and more important fuccefs. For
inftance, it was, under God, your Lordfhip's favour
and influence that brought me into the miniftry.
And though I be nothing, yet he who put it into
your heart to patronife me, has been pleafed not to
fuffer what you then did for his fake to be wholly
in vain. He has been pleafed, in a courfe of years,
by fo unworthy an inftrument as I am, to awaken
a number of perfons, who were at that time dead
in trefpaffes and fins; but now fome of them are
                                              preffing

preffing on to the prize of their high calling in Chrift Jefus; and fome of them are already before the throne. Should I fuggeft in fome companies, that the converfion of a hundred finners (more or lefs) to God is an event of more real importance than the *temporal* profperity of the greateft nation upon earth, I fhould be charged with ignorance and arrogance; but your Lordfhip is fkilled in fcriptural arithmetic, which alone can teach us to eftimate the value of fouls, and will agree with me, that one foul is worth more than the whole world, on account of its redemption-price, its vaft capacities and its duration. Should we fuppofe a nation to confift of forty millions, the whole and each individual to enjoy as much good as this life can afford, without abatement, for a term of fifty years each;—all this good, or an equal quantity, might be exhaufted by a fingle perfon in two thoufand million of years, which would be but a moment, in comparifon of the eternity which would ftill follow.—And if this good were merely temporal good, the whole aggregate of it would be evil and mifery, if compared with that happinefs in God, of which only they who are made partakers of a divine life are capable. On the other hand, were a whole nation to be deftroyed by fuch accumulated miferies as attended the fiege of Jerufalem, the fum-total of thefe calamities would be but trifling, if fet in competition with what every fingle perfon that dies in fin has to expect, when the fentence of everlafting deftruction from the prefence of the Lord, and the glory of his power, fhall be executed.

What an unexpected round have my thoughts taken fince I fet out from the ice-palace? It is time to relieve your Lordfhip, and to fubfcribe myfelf, &c.

L E T T E R   XIX.

My Lord,   *February* 23. 1775.

I Assent to our Lord's declaration, " Without
" me ye can do nothing;" not only upon the
authority of the speaker, but from the same irre-
sistible and experimental evidence, as if he had told
me, that I cannot make the sun to shine, or change
the course of the seasons. Though my pen and my
tongue sometimes move freely, yet the total inca-
pacity and stagnation of thought I labour under at
other times, convinces me, that in myself I have not
sufficiency to think a good thought ; and I believe
the case would be the same, if that little measure of
knowledge and abilities, which I am too prone to
look upon as my own, were a thousand times greater than it is. For every new service I stand in need
of a new supply, and can bring forth nothing of
my supposed store into actual exercise, but by his
immediate assistance. His gracious influence is that
to those who are best furnished with gifts, which
the water is to the mill, or the wind to the ship,
without which the whole apparatus is motionless
and useless. I apprehend that we lose much of the
comfort which might arise from a sense of our continual dependence upon him, and of course fall
short of acknowledging, as we ought, what we receive from him, by mistaking the manner of his
operation. Perhaps we take it too much for granted, that communications from himself must bear
some kind of sensible impression that they are *his,*
and therefore are ready to give our own industry
or ingenuity credit for those performances in which
we can perceive no such impression : yet it is very
possible that we may be under his influence when
we

we are leaft aware : and though what we fay, or
write, or do, may feem no way extraordinary ; yet
that we fhould be led to fuch a particular turn of
thought at one time rather than at another, has, in
my own concerns, often appeared to me remarkable, from the circumftances which have attended,
or the confequences which have followed. How
often, in the choice of a text, or in the courfe of a
fermon, or in a letter to a friend, have I been led
to fpeak a word in feafon ! and what I have expreffed at large, and in general, has been fo exactly
fuited to fome cafe which I was utterly unacquainted with, that I could hardly have hit it fo well, had
I been previoufly informed of it. Some inftances of
this kind have been fo ftriking, as hardly to admit
a doubt of fuperior agency. And indeed, if believers in Jefus, however unworthy in themfelves, are
the temples of the Holy Ghoft ; if the Lord lives,
dwells, and walks in them; if he is their life and
their light; if he has promifed to guide them with
his eye, and to work in them to will and to do of
his own good pleafure ; methinks what I have mentioned, and more, may be reafonably expected. That
line in the hymn,

Help I every moment need,

is not an hyperbolical expreffion, but ftrictly and
literally true, not only in great emergencies, but
in our fmoother hours, and moft familiar paths.
This gracious affiftance is afforded in a way imperceptible to ourfelves, to hide pride from us, and
to prevent us from being indolent and carelefs with
refpect to the ufe of appointed means ; and it would
be likewife more abundantly, and perhaps more
fenfibly afforded, were our fpirits more fimple in
waiting upon the Lord. But, alas ! a divided heart,
an undue attachment to fome temporal object, fad-

ly deadens *our* fpirits, (I fpeak for myfelf), and
grieves the Lord's fpirit; fo that we walk in darknefs and at a diftance, and though called to great
privileges, live far below them. But methinks the
thought of him who is always near, and upon whom
we do and muft inceffantly depend, fhould fuggeft
a powerful motive for the clofeft attention to his
revealed will, and the moft punctual compliance with
it; for fo far as the Lord withdraws we become as
blind men, and with the cleareft light, and upon
the plaineft ground, we are liable, or rather fure,
to ftumble at every ftep.

Though there is a principle of confcioufnefs, and
a determination of the will, fufficient to denomi-
nate our thoughts and performances our own; yet
I believe mankind in general are more under an invifible agency than they apprehend. The Lord,
immediately from himfelf, and perhaps by the miniftry of his holy angels, guides, prompts, reftrains,
or warns his people. So there undoubtedly is what
I may call a *black infpiration,* the influence of the
evil fpirits who work in the hearts of the difobe-
dient, and not only excite their wills, but affift
their faculties, and qualify as well as incline them
to be more affiduoufly wicked, and more extenfive-
ly mifchievous, than they could be of themfelves.
I confider Voltaire, for inftance, and many writers
of the fame ftamp, to be little more than fecreta-
ries and amanuenfes of one who has unfpeakably
more wit and adroitnefs in promoting infidelity and
immorality, than they of themfelves can juftly pretend to. They have, for a while, the credit (if I
may fo call it) of the fund from whence they draw;
but the world little imagines who is the real and
original author of that philofophy and poetry, of
thofe fine turns and fprightly inventions, which are
fo generally admired. Perhaps many, now ap-
plauded for their genius, would have been comparatively

ratively dolts, had they not been engaged in a caufe
which Satan has fo much intereft in fupporting.

But to return to the more pleafing fubject.—How
great and honourable is the privilege of a true believer ! That he has neither wifdom or ftrength
in himfelf is no difadvantage ; for he is connected
with infinite wifdom and almighty power. Though
weak as a worm, his arms are ftrengthened by the
mighty God of Jacob, and all things become poffible, yea eafy to him, that occur within the compafs of his proper duty and calling. The Lord,
whom he ferves, engages to proportion his ftrength
to his day, whether it be a day of fervice or of
fuffering : and though he be fallible and fhort-
fighted, exceeding liable to miftake and impofition ;
yet, while he retains a fenfe that he is fo, and
with the fimplicity of a child afks counfel and direction of the Lord, he feldom takes a wrong ftep,
at leaft not in matters of confequence ; and even
his inadvertencies are over-ruled for good. If he
forgets his true ftate, and thinks himfelf to be fomething, he prefently finds he is indeed nothing ; but
if he is content to be nothing, and to have nothing,
he is fure to find a feafonable and abundant communication of all that he wants. Thus he lives,
like Ifrael in the wildernefs, upon mere bounty ;
but then it is a bounty unchangeable, unwearied,
inexhauftible, and all-fufficient. Mofes, when fpeaking of the methods the Lord took to humble Ifrael,
mentions his feeding them with manna, as one method. I could not underftand this for a time. I
thought they were rather in danger of being proud,
when they faw themfelves provided for in fuch an
extraordinary way.—But the manna would not
keep ; they could not hoard it up ; and were therefore in a ftate of abfolute dependence from day to
day : this appointment was well fuited to humble
them. Thus it is with us in fpirituals. We fhould

be better pleafed, perhaps, to be fet up with a ftock
or fufficiency at once,—fuch an inherent portion
of wifdom and power, as we might depend upon,
at leaft for common occafions, without being con-
ftrained by a fenfe of indigence, to have continual
recourfe to the Lord for every thing we want. But
his way is beft. His own glory is moft difplayed,
and our fafety beft fecured, by keeping us quite
poor and empty in ourfelves, and fupplying us from
one minute to another, according to our need.
This, if any thing, will prevent boafting, and keep
a fenfe of gratitude awake in our hearts. This is
well adapted to quicken us to prayer, and furnifhes
us with a thoufand occafions for praife, which
would otherwife efcape our notice.

But who or what are we, that the Moft High
fhould thus notice us! fhould vifit us every morning, and water us every moment! It is an aftonifhing thought, that God fhould thus dwell with men!
That he, before whom the mightieft earthly poten-
tates are lefs than nothing and vanity, fhould thus
ftoop and accommodate himfelf to the fituation,
wants, and capacities of the weakeft, meaneft, and
pooreft of his children! But fo it hath pleafed
him. He feeth not as man feeth.

  I am, &c.

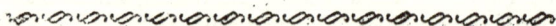

LETTER XX.

My Lord,   *Auguft —* 1775.

I Have no apt preface or introduction at hand,
 and as I have made it almoft a rule not to ftudy
for what I fhould offer your Lordfhip, I therefore
beg leave to begin abruptly. It is the future promifed

mifed privilege of believers in Jefus, that they fhall be as the angels; and there is a fenfe in which we fhould endeavour to be as the angels now. This is intimated to us where we are taught to pray, Thy will be done on earth, as it is in heaven. I have fometimes amufed myfelf with fuppofing an angel fhould be appointed to refide awhile upon earth in a human body; not in finful flefh like ours, but in a body free from infirmity, and ftill preferving an unabated fenfe of his own happinefs in the favour of God, and of his unfpeakable obligation to his goodnefs;—and then I have tried to judge, as well as I could, how fuch an angel would comport himfelf in fuch a fituation. I know not that I ever enlarged upon the thought, either in preaching or writing. Permit me to follow it a little in this paper.

Were I acquainted with this heavenly vifitant, I am willing to hope I fhould greatly reverence him; and, if permitted, be glad, in fome cafes, to confult him. In fome, but not in all; for I think my fear would be equal to my love. Methinks I could never venture to open my heart freely to him, and unfold to him my numberlefs complaints and infirmities; for, as he could have no experience of the like things himfelf, I fhould fuppofe he would not know how fully to pity me, indeed hardly how to bear with me, if I told him all. Alas! what a prepofterous, ftrange, vile creature fhould I appear to an angel, if he knew me as I am! It is well for me that Jefus was made lower than the angels, and that the human nature he affumed was not diftinct from the common nature of mankind, though fecured from the common depravity; and becaufe he fubmitted to be under the law in our name and ftead, though he was free from fin himfelf, yet fin, and its confequences, being (for our fakes) charged upon him, he acquired, in the days of his hu-

miliation,

miliation, an experimental fympathy with his poor
people. He knows the effects of fin and temptation
upon us, by that knowledge whereby he knows all
things; but he knows them likewife in a way more
fuitable for our comfort and relief, by the fufferings and exercifes he paffed through for us. Hence
arifes encouragement. We have not an high prieft
who cannot be touched with a feeling of our infirmities, but was in all points tempted even as we
are. When I add to this, the confideration of his
power, promifes, and grace, and that he is exalted on purpofe to pity, relieve, and fave, I gather
courage. With him I dare be free, and am not
forry, but glad, that he knows me perfectly, that
not a thought of my heart is hidden from him.
For without this infinite and exact knowledge of
my difeafe, how could he effectually adminifter to
my cure? But whither am I rambling? I feem to
have loft fight of the angel already. I am now coming back, that if he cannot effectually pity me, he
may at leaft animate and teach me.

In the firft place, I take it for granted this angel
would think himfelf a ftranger and pilgrim upon
earth. He would not forget that his πολιτευμα
was in heaven. Surely he would look upon all the
buftle of human life (farther than the defign of his
miffion might connect him with it) with more indifference than we look upon the fports of children,
or the amufements of idiots and lunatics, which
give us an uneafinefs, rather than excite a defire of
joining in them. He would judge of every thing
around him, by the reference and tendency it had
to promote the will of him that fent him; and the
moft fpecious or fplendid appearances, confidered
in any other view, would make no impreffion upon
him.

Confequently, as to his own concernment, all
his aim and defire would be to fulfil the will of
                                        God.

God. All fituations would be alike to him; whether he was commanded, as in the cafe of Sennacherib, to deftroy a mighty army with a ftroke; or, as in the cafe of Hagar, to attend upon a woman, a fervant, a flave; both fervices would be to him equally honourable and important, becaufe he was in both equally pleafing his Lord, which would be his element and his joy, whether he was appointed to guide the reins of empire, or to fweep the ftreets.

Again, the angel would doubtlefs exhibit a ftriking example of benevolence; for being free from felfifh bias, filled with a fenfe of the love of God, and a knowledge of his adorable perfections; his whole heart, and foul, and ftrength, would be engaged and exerted, both from duty and inclination, to relieve the miferies, and advance the happinefs of all around him; and in this he would follow the pattern of him who doth good to all, commanding his fun to rife, and his rain to fall, upon the juft and the unjuft;—though, from the fame pattern, he would fhew an efpecial regard to the houfehold of faith. An angel would take but little part in the controverfies, contentions, and broils, which might happen in the time of his fojourning here, but would be a friend to all, fo far as confiftent with the general good.

The will and glory of God being the angel's great view, and having a more lively fenfe of the realities of an unfeen world than we can at prefent conceive, he would certainly, in the firft and chief place, have the fuccefs and fpread of the glorious gofpel at heart. Angels, though not redeemed with blood, yet feel themfelves nearly concerned in the work of redemption. They admire its myfteries. We may fuppofe them well informed in the works of creation and providence. But (unlike too many men,

men, who are fatisfied with the knowledge of a-
ftronomy, mathematics, or hiftory), they fearch and
pry into the counfels of redeeming love, rejoice at
the converfion of a finner, and think themfelves
well employed to be miniftring fpirits, to minifter
to the heirs of falvation. It would therefore be his
chief delight to efpoufe and promote their caufe,
and to employ all his talents and influence in
fpreading the favour and knowledge of the name
of Jefus, which is the only and effectual means of
bringing finners out of bondage and darknefs, into
the glorious liberty of the fons of God.

Laftly, Though his zeal for the glory of his
Lord would make him willing to continue here
till he had finifhed the work given him to do, he
would, I am perfuaded, look forward with defire
to the appointed moment of his recall, that he
might be freed from beholding and mixing with
the fin and vanity of thofe who know not God,
render his account with joy, and be welcomed to
heaven, with a Well done good and faithful fervant. Surely he would long for this, as a labourer
for the fetting fun; and would not form any connection with the things of time, which fhould
prompt him to wifh his removal protracted for a
fingle hour beyond the period of his prefcribed
fervice.

Alas, why am not I more like an angel! My
views in my better judgement are the fame. My
motives and obligations are even ftronger: an angel is not fo deeply indebted to the grace of God,
as a believing finner, who was once upon the brink
of deftruction, has been redeemed with blood, and
might juftly have been, before now, fhut up with
the powers of darknefs without hope! Yet the
mereft trifles are fufficient to debafe my views,
damp my activity, and impede my endeavours in
                                                    the

the Lord's fervice, though I profefs to have no
other end or defire which can make a continuance
in life worthy my wifh.

I am, &c.

L E T T E R   XXI.

My Lord,   *November —* 1775.

*D*UM *loquimur tempus fugit.* In the midft of
the hurries and changes of this unfettled ftate,
we glide along fwiftly towards an unchangeable
world, and fhall foon have as little connection with
the fcenes we are now paffing through, as we have
with what happened before the flood. All that appears great and interefting in the prefent life, abftracted from its influence upon our internal character, and our everlafting allotment, will foon be
as unreal as the vifions of the night. This we
know and confefs ; but though our judgements are
convinced, it is feldom our hearts are duly affected
by the thought. And while I find it eafy to write
in this moralizing ftrain, I feel myfelf difpofed to
be ferioufly engaged about trifles, and trifling in
the moft ferious concerns, as if I believed the very
contrary. It is with good reafon the Lord challenges, as his own prerogative, the full knowledge
of the deceitfulnefs, defperate wickednefs, and latent depths of the human heart, which is capable
of making even his own people fo fhamefully inconfiftent with themfelves, and with their acknowledged principles.

I find that, when I have fomething agreeable in
expectation, (fuppofe for inftance it were a few
hours converfation with your Lordfhip), my imagination.

gination paints and prepares the fcene beforehand;
hurries me over the intervening fpace of time, as
though it were a ufelefs blank, and anticipates the
pleafure I propofe. Many of my thoughts of this
kind are mere waking dreams; for perhaps the
opportunity I am eagerly waiting for never happens, but is fwallowed up by fome unforefeen difappointment; or if not, fomething from within or
without prevents its anfwering the idea I had formed
of it. Nor does my fancy confine itfelf within the
narrow limits of probabilities; it can bufy itfelf as
eagerly in ranging after chimæras and impoffibi-
lities, and engage my attention to the ideal purfuit
of things which are never likely to happen. In
thefe refpects my imagination travels with wings;
fo that if the wildnefs, the multiplicity, the variety
of the phantoms which pafs through my mind in
the fpace of a winter's day, were known to my
fellow-creatures, they would probably deem me,
as I am often ready to deem myfelf, but a more
fober and harmlefs kind of lunatic. But if I endeavour to put this active roving power in a right
track, and to reprefent to myfelf thofe fcenes,
which though not yet prefent, I know will foon be
realifed, and have a greatnefs, which the moft enlarged exercife of my powers cannot comprehend:
if I would fix my thoughts upon the hour of death,
the end of the world, the coming of the Judge, or
fimilar fubjects; then my imagination is prefently
tame, cold, and jaded, travels very flowly, and is
foon wearied in the road of truth; though in the
fairy fields of uncertainty and folly it can fkip from
mountain to mountain. Mr Addifon fuppofes,
that the imagination alone, as it can be differently
affected, is capable of making us either inconcei-
vably happy or miferable. I am fure it is capable
of making us miferable, though I believe it feldom
gives us much pleafure, but fuch as is to be found

in

in a fool's paradife.   But I am fure, were my outward life and conduct perfectly free from blame,
the diforders and defilement of my imagination are
fufficient to conftitute me a chief finner, in the fight
of him to whom the thoughts and intents of the
heart are continually open, and who is of purer
eyes than to behold iniquity.

Upon this head I cannot but lament how univerfally almoft, education is fuited, and as it were defigned, to add to the ftimulus of depraved nature.
A cultivated imagination is commended and fought
after as a very defirable talent, though it feldom
means more than the poffeffion of a large ftock of
other people's dreams and fables, with a certain
quicknefs in compounding them, enlarging upon
them, and exceeding them by inventions of our
own.   Poets, painters, and even hiftorians, are employed to affift us from our early years, in forming
an habitual relifh for fhadows and colourings,
which both indifpofe for the fearch of truth, and
even unfit us for its reception, unlefs propofed juft
in our own way.   The beft effect of the Belles
Lettres upon the imagination feems generally expreffed by the word Tafte.   And what is this tafte,
but a certain difpofition which loves to be hu-
moured, foothed, and flattered, and which can
hardly receive or bear the moft important truths,
if they be not decorated and fet off with fuch a delicacy and addrefs as tafte requires.   I fay *the moft
important truths;* becaufe truths of a fecular importance ftrike fo clofely upon the fenfes, that the
decifion of tafte perhaps is not waited for.   Thus,
if a man be informed of the birth of his child, or
that his houfe is on fire, the meffage takes up his
thoughts, and he is feldom much difgufted with
the manner in which it is delivered.   But what an
infuperable bar is the refined tafte of many, to
their profiting by the preaching of the gofpel, or
even

even to their hearing it. Though the fubject of a difcourfe be weighty, and fome juft reprefentation given of the evil of fin, the worth of the foul, and the love of Chrift; yet, if there be fomething amifs in the elocution, language, or manner of the preacher, people of tafte muft be poffeffed, in a good meafure, of grace likewife, if they can hear him with tolerable patience. And perhaps three fourths of thofe who are accounted the moft fenfible and judicious in the auditory, will remember little about the fermon, but the tone of the voice, the aukwardnefs of the attitude, the obfolete expreffions, and the like; while the poor and fimple, not being encumbered with this hurtful accomplifhment, receive the meffenger as the Lord's fervant, and the truth as the Lord's word, and are comforted and edified. But I ftop. Some people would fay, that I muft fuppofe your Lordfhip to have but little tafte, or elfe much grace, or I fhould not venture to trouble you with fuch letters as mine.

　　I am, &c.

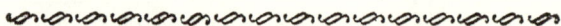

LETTER XXII.

My Lord,

THE apoftle fpeaks of a *bleffednefs*, which it is the defign of the gofpel to impart to thofe who receive it. The Galatians once had it, and fpoke of it. The apoftle reminds them of their lofs, which is left upon record as a warning to us. His expreffion has led me fometimes to confider wherein a Chriftian's prefent bleffednefs confifts.—I mean that which is attainable in this ftate of trial, and
the

the fenfe and exercife of which may be, and too
often is, fufpended and taken from us. It is a
bleffednefs which, if we fpeak of man in a natural
ftate, his eye hath not feen, nor his ear heard fo
as to underftand it, nor can the idea of it arife in
his heart. It is no way dependent upon outward
circumftances. Profperity cannot impart it, preferve or fupply the want of it ; nor can adverfity
put it out of our reach. The wife cannot acquire
it by dint of fuperior abilities ; nor fhall the fimple
mifs it for want of capacity.

The ftate of true believers, compared with that
of others, is always *bleffed*. If they are born from
above, and united to Jefus, they are delivered from
condemnation, and are heirs of eternal life, and
may therefore well be accounted happy. But I
confider now, not their harveft but their firft
fruits ; not their portion in reverfion, but the *earneft* attainable in this life ; not what they *fhall* be
in heaven, but what, in an humble attendance upon the Lord, they *may be* while upon earth. There
is even at prefent a prize of our high calling fet
before us. It is much to be defired, that we had
fuch a fenfe of its value as might prompt us fo to
run that we might obtain. I have thought this
bleffednefs may be comprifed in five particulars,
though, in order to take a fuccinct view of the
fubject, fome of thefe might be branched out into
feveral others ; but I would not by too many fub-
divifions give my letter the air of a fermon.

In the firft place, a clear, well-grounded, habitual perfuafion of our acceptance in the Beloved
is attainable ; and though we may be fafe, we cannot be faid to enjoy bleffednefs without it. To be
in a ftate of fufpence and uncertainty in a point of
fo great importance, is painful ; and the Lord has
accordingly provided, that his people may have
ftrong confolation on this head. They are bleffed,
therefore,

therefore, who have such views of the power, grace, and suitableness of Jesus, and the certainty and security of redemption in him, together with such a consciousness that they have anchored their hopes, and ventured their all upon his person, work, and promise, as furnishes them with a ready answer to all the cavils of unbelief and Satan, in the apostle's manner, Rom. viii. 31.—37. That Paul could thus challenge and triumph over all charges and enemies, was not an appendage of his office as an apostle, but a part of his experience as a believer; and it lies equally open to us: for we have the same gospel and the same promises as he had; nor is the efficacy of the holy Spirit's teaching, a whit weakened by length of time. But many stop short of this. They have a hope, but it rather springs from their frames and feelings, than from a spiritual apprehension of the Redeemer's engagements and fulness, and therefore fluctuates and changes like the weather. Could they be persuaded to pray with earnestness and importunity, as the Apostle prays for them, Ephes. i. 17. 18. and iii. 16. 19.; they would find a blessedness which they have not yet known; for it is said, " Ask, and ye " shall receive."—And it is said likewise, " Ye re- " ceive not, because ye ask not."

Could this privilege be enjoyed singly, the natural man would have no objection to it. He would (as he thinks) be pleased to know he should be saved at last, provided that while here he might live in his sins. But the believer will not, cannot think himself blessed, unless he has likewise a conscience void of offence. This was the Apostle's daily exercise, though no one was farther from a legal spirit, or more dependent upon Jesus for acceptance. But if we live in any known sin, or allow ourselves in the customary omission of any known duty, supposing it possible, in such a case,

to preferve a fenfe of our acceptance, (which can
hardly be fuppofed ; for if the Spirit be grieved,
our evidences decline of courfe), yet we could not
be eafy.   If a traveller was abfolutely fure of reaching his journey's end in fafety; yet if he walked
with a thorn in his foot, he muft take every ftep in
pain.   Such a thorn will be felt in the confcience,
till we are favoured with a fimplicity of heart, and
made willing in all things, great or fmall, to yield
obedience to the authority of the Lord's precepts,
and make them the ftanding rule of our conduct,
without wilfully admitting a fingle exception.   At
the beft, we fhall be confcious of innumerable fhort-
comings, and fhameful defilement ; but thefe things
will not break our peace, if our hearts are upright.
But if we trifle with light, and connive at what we
know to be wrong, we fhall be weak, reftlefs, and
uncomfortable.   How many, who we would hope
are the children of the King, are lean from day to
day, becaufe fome right-hand or right-eye evil,
which they cannot perfuade themfelves to part with,
keeps them halting between two opinions ; and they
are as diftant from happinefs, as they are from the
poffibility of reconciling the incompatible fervices
of God and the world.   But happy indeed is he
who condemneth not himfelf in that thing which he
alloweth.

Real communion with the Lord, in his appointed
means of grace, is likewife an important branch of
this bleffednefs.   They were inftituted for this end,
and are fufficient, by virtue of his power and Spirit, to anfwer it.   I do not believe this enjoyment
will be always equal.   But I believe a comfortable
fenfe of it, in fome meafure, is generally attainable.   To read the fcripture, not as an attorney
may read a will, merely to know the fenfe ; but as
the heir reads it, as a defcription and proof of his
intereft : To hear the gofpel, as the voice of our
                                            Beloved,

Beloved, fo as to have little leifure either for admiring the abilities, or cenfuring the defects of the
preacher; and, in prayer, to feel a liberty of pour-
ing out our hearts before the Lord, to behold fome
glances of his goodnefs paffing before us, and to
breathe forth before him the tempers of a child,
the fpirit of adoption: And thus, by beholding his
glory, to be conformed more and more to his image,
and to renew our ftrength, by drawing water out
of the wells of falvation: Herein is bleffednefs.
They who have tafted it can fay, it is good for me
to draw nigh to God. The foul thus refrefhed by
the water of life, is preferved from thirfting after
the vanities of the world; thus inftructed in the
fanctuary, comes down from the mount filled with
heavenly wifdom, anointed with a holy unction,
and thereby qualified to judge, fpeak, and act in
character, in all the relations and occafions of fecular life. In this way, befides the pleafure, a fpiritual tafte is acquired, fomething analogous to the
meaning of the word tafte when applied to mufic
or good breeding, by which difcords and impro-
prieties are obferved and avoided, as it were by in-
ftinct, and what is right is felt and followed, not
fo much by the force of rules, as by a habit infenfibly acquired, and in which the fubftance of all
neceffary rules are, if I may fo fay, digefted. O
that I knew more of this bleffednefs, and more of
its effects!

Another branch of bleffednefs, is a power of re-
pofing ourfelves and our concerns upon the Lord's
faithfulnefs and care; and may be confidered in
two refpects: A reliance upon him that he will
furely provide for us, guide us, protect us, be our
help in trouble, our fhield in danger; fo that however poor, weak, and defencelefs in ourfelves, we
may rejoice in his all-fufficiency as our own;—and
farther, in confequence of this, a peaceful, humble
fubmiffion

fubmiffion to his will, under all events which, upon their firft impreffion, are contrary to our own
views and defires. Surely, in a world like this,
where every thing is uncertain, where we are expofed to trials on every hand, and know not but a
fingle hour may bring forth fomething painful, yea
dreadful to our natural fenfations, there can be no
bleffednefs, but fo far as we are thus enabled to
entruft and refign all to the direction and faithfulnefs of the Lord our fhepherd. For want of more
of this fpirit, multitudes of profeffing Chriftians
perplex and wound themfelves, and difhonour their
high calling, by continual anxieties, alarms, and
complaints. They think nothing fafe under the
Lord's keeping, unlefs their own eye is likewife upon it ; and are feldom fatisfied with any of his difpenfations : for though he gratify their defires in
nine inftances, a refufal in the tenth fpoils the relifh of all, and they fhew the truths of the gofpel
can afford them little comfort, if felf is croffed.
But bleffed is the man who trufteth in the Lord,
and whofe hope the Lord is. He fhall not be afraid
of evil-tidings : he fhall be kept in perfect peace,
though the earth be moved, and the mountains caft
into the midft of the fea.

The paper admonifhes me it is time to relieve
your Lordfhip.—And I have not room to detain
you long upon the fifth particular. It belongs to a
believer's bleffednefs, to feel his fpirit chearful and
active for the Lord's fervice, in the world. For to
what other end fhould he wifh to live ? If he
thought of himfelf only, it would be better to depart and be with Jefus immediately. But he is a
debtor to his grace and love ; and though ftrictly
he can make no returns,—yet he longs to fhew his
thankfulnefs : and if the Lord give him a heart to
redeem his time, to devote his ftrength and influence, and lay himfelf out for his fervice,—that he
may

may be inftrumental in promoting his caufe, in comforting his people,—or enable him to let his light fhine before men, that his God and Father may be honoured ;—he will account it bleffednefs. This is indeed the great end of life, and he knows it will evidently appear fo at the approach of death; and therefore, while others are cumbered about many things, he efteems this the one thing needful.

I remain, my Lord, &c.

❧❧❧❧❧❧❧❧❧❧❧❧❧❧❧❧❧❧❧

LETTER XXIII.

My Lord,   *July* — 1776.

THat I may not weary you by a preamble, I oblige myfelf to take the turn of my letter from fome paffage of fcripture ; and I fix upon that which juft now occurred to my thoughts, a claufe in that pattern of prayer which he who beft knows our ftate, has been pleafed to leave for the inftruction of his people in their great concern of waiting at his throne of grace, Matth. vi. 13.—" And " lead us not into temptation." This petition is feafonable at all times, and to all perfons who have any right knowledge of themfelves, or their fpiritual calling.

The word *temptation*, taken at large, includes every kind of trial. To tempt is to try or prove. In this fenfe, it is faid, the Lord tempted Abraham : that is, he tried him; for God cannot tempt to evil. He propofed fuch an act of obedience to him, as was a teft of his faith, love, dependence, and integrity. Thus, all our afflictions, under his gracious management, are appointed to prove, manifeft, exercife, and purify the graces of his children.

dren. And not afflictions only ; prosperity likewise
is a state of temptation : and many who have endured
sharp sufferings, and came off honourably, have been
afterwards greatly hurt and ensnared by prosperity.
To this purpose the histories of David and Hezekiah
are in point. But by temptation we more frequently understand the wiles and force which Satan
employs in assaulting our peace, or spreading snares
for our feet. He is always practising against us,
either directly and from himself, by the access he
has to our hearts, or mediately, by the influence
he has over the men and the things of this world.
The words which follow confirm this sense,—
" Lead us not into temptation ; but deliver us from
" evil," απο του πονηρου from the *evil one,* as it
might be properly rendered here, and in 1 John, v.
19. The subtilty and power of this adversary are
very great : he is an over-match for us ; and we
have no hope of safety but in the Lord's protection.
Satan's action upon the heart may be illustrated by
the action of the wind upon the sea. The sea sometimes appears smooth ; but it is always disposed to
swell and rage, and to obey the impulse of every
storm. Thus, the heart may be sometimes quiet ;
but the wind of temptation will awaken and rouse
it in a moment : for it is essential to our depraved
nature to be unstable and yielding as the water ;
and when it is under the impression of the enemy,
its violence can only be controuled by him, who
says to the raging sea, " Be still, and here shall thy
" proud waves be stayed." The branches of temptation are almost innumerable ; but the principal
may be reduced to the several faculties of the soul
(as we commonly speak) to which they are more directly suited.

He has temptations for the understanding. He
can blind the mind with prejudices and false rea-
sonings, and ply it with arguments for infidelity,

till the moft obvious truths become queftionable.
Even where the gofpel has been received, he can
infinuate error, which for the fuddennefs and ma-
lignity of its effects may be properly compared to
poifon.   A healthy man may be poifoned in a moment; and if he be, the baneful drug is ufually mixed with his food.   Many who for a while feemed
to be found in the faith, have had their judgements
ftrongly and ftrangely perverted, and prevailed upon
to renounce and oppofe the truths they once prized
and defended.   Such inftances are ftriking proofs
of human weaknefs, and loud calls to watchfulnefs and dependence, and to beware of leaning to
our underftandings.   For thefe purpofes he employs both preachers and authors, who, by fine
words and fair fpeeches, beguile the hearts of the
unwary.   And, by his immediate influence upon
the mind, he is able (if the Lord permits him) to
entangle thofe who are providentially placed out of
the reach of corrupt and defigning men.

He tempts the confcience.   By working upon
the unbelief of our hearts, and darkening the glory
of the gofpel, he can hold down the foul to the
number, weight, and aggravation of its fins, fo that
it fhall not be able to look up to Jefus, nor draw
any comfort from his blood, promifes, and grace.
How many go burdened in this manner, feeking
relief from duties, and perhaps fpending their
ftrength in things not commanded, though they
hear, and perhaps acknowledge the gofpel? Nor are
the wifeft and moft eftablifhed able to withftand his
affaults, if the Lord withdraw and give him leave
to employ his power and fubtilty unreftrained. The
gofpel affords fufficient ground for an abiding affurance of hope; nor fhould we reft fatisfied without it.   However, the poffeffion and prefervation
of this privilege depends upon the Lord's prefence
with the foul, and his fhielding us from Satan's at-
tacks;

tacks; for I am perfuaded he is able to fift and ſhake the ſtrongeſt believer upon earth.

He has likewiſe temptations ſuited to the will. Jeſus makes his people willing in the day of his power; yet there is a contrary principle remaining within them, of which Satan knows how to avail himſelf. There are occaſions in which he almoſt prevails to ſet ſelf again upon the throne, as Dagon was raiſed after he had fallen before the ark. How elſe ſhould any who have taſted that the Lord is gracious, give way to a repining ſpirit, account his diſpenſations hard, or his precepts too ſtrict, ſo as to ſhrink from their obſervance through the fear of men, or a regard to their worldly intereſt?

Farther, he has ſnares for the affections. In managing theſe he gains a great advantage from our ſituation in a world that knows not God. The ſcripture gives Satan the title of God of this world; and believers learn, by painful experience, how great his power is in and over the perſons and things of it. So that to be ſtedfaſt in wiſdom's ways, requires unremitted efforts, like preſſing through a crowd, or ſwimming againſt a ſtream. How hard is it to live in the midſt of pitch and not be defiled? The air of the world is infectious. Our buſineſs and unavoidable connections are ſo interwoven with occaſions of ſin, and there is ſo much in our hearts ſuited to them, that unleſs we are inceſſantly upheld by almighty ſtrength, we cannot ſtand a day or an hour. Paſt victories afford us no greater ſecurity than they did Samſon, who was ſhamefully ſurpriſed by enemies whom he had formerly conquered. Nor are we only tempted by compliances that are evil in themſelves. With reſpect to theſe, perhaps, conſcience may be awake, and we ſtand upon our guard: but we are ſtill upon Satan's ground; and while he may ſeem to allow himſelf defeated, he can dexterouſly change his method,

and

and come upon us where we do not fuſpect him.
For *Perimus in licitis.* Perhaps our greateſt danger ariſes from things in themſelves lawful. He
can tempt us by our neareſt and deareſt friend, and
pervert every bleſſing of a kind Providence into an
occaſion of drawing our hearts from the Giver;
yea, ſpiritual bleſſings, gifts, comforts, and even
graces, are ſometimes the engines by which he prac-
tiſes againſt us, to fill us with vain confidence and
ſelf-ſufficiency, or to lull us into formality and in-
dolence.

That wonderful power which we call the imagination, is, I ſuppoſe, rather the medium of the
ſoul's perceptions during its preſent ſtate of union
with the body, than a ſpiritual faculty, ſtrictly
ſpeaking; but it partakes largely of that depravity
which ſin has brought upon our whole frame, and
affords Satan an avenue for aſſaulting us with the
moſt terrifying, if not the moſt dangerous of his
temptations. At the beſt we have but an indifferent
command over it. We cannot, by an act of our
own will, exclude a thouſand painful, wild, inconſiſtent, and hurtful ideas, which are ever ready to
obtrude themſelves upon our minds; and a ſlight
alteration in the animal ſyſtem, in the motion of
the blood or nervous ſpirits, is ſufficient to withdraw it wholly from our dominion, and to leave
us like a city without walls or gates, expoſed to the
incurſion of our enemy. We are fearfully and
wonderfully made; and, with all our boaſted
knowledge of other things, can form no conception of what is ſo vaſtly intereſting to us, the my-
ſterious connection between ſoul and body, and
the manner in which they are mutually affected by
each other. The effects we too ſenſibly feel. The
wiſeſt of men would be accounted fools or mad,
were they to expreſs in words a ſmall part of what
paſſes within them; and it would appear that much

of

of the foberest life is little better than a waking
dream : but how dreadful are the confequences when
the Lord permits fome hidden pin in the human machine to be altered ! Immediately a door flies open,
which no hand but his can fhut, and the enemy
pours in, like a flood, falfehood and horror, and
the blacknefs of darknefs ; the judgement is borne
down and difabled, and the moft diftreffing illu-
fions feize us with all the apparent force of evidence and demonftration.   When this is the cafe
in a certain degree, we call it diftraction ; but there
are various degrees of it, which leave a perfon in the
poffeffion of his fenfes, as to the things of common
life, and yet are fufficient, with refpect to his fpiritual concerns, to fhake the very foundations of
his hope, and deprive him of all peace and comfort, and make him a terror to himfelf.   All the
Lord's people are not called to navigate in thefe
deep waters of foul diftrefs ; but all are liable. Ah !
if we knew what fome fuffer, the *Horribilia de Deo,
et Terribilia de Fide*, which excruciate the minds of
thofe over whom Satan is permitted to tyrannize
in this way, furely we fhould be more earneft and
frequent in praying, "Lead us not into temptation." From fome little fenfe I have of the malice
and fubtilty of our fpiritual enemies, and the weaknefs of thofe barriers which we have to prevent
their affaults, I am fully perfuaded that nothing
lefs than the continual exertion of that almighty
power which preferves the ftars in their orbits, can
maintain our peace of mind for an hour or a minute. In this view, all comparative difference in
external fituation feems to be annihilated ; for as
the Lord's prefence can make his people happy in
a dungeon ; fo there are temptations, which, if we
felt them, would inftantly render us incapable of
receiving a moment's fatisfaction from an affemblage of all earthly bleffings, and make the com-

pany of our deareſt friends taſtelefs, if not infupportable.

Ah ! how little do the gay and the buſy think of
theſe things ! How little indeed do they think of
them who profefs to believe them ! How faint is
the ſenſe of our obligations to *him*, who freely
ſubmitted to the fierceſt onfets of the powers of
darkneſs, to free us from the puniſhment due to our
ſins ; otherwiſe we muſt have been for ever ſhut up
with thoſe miſerable and mercileſs ſpirits, who delight in our torment, and who, even in the preſent
ſtate, if they get accefs to our minds, can make our
exiſtence a burden !

But our Lord, who knows and confiders our
weakneſs, of which we are ſo little aware, allows
and directs us to pray, " Lead us not into temptation." We are not to expect an abſolute freedom
from temptation ; we are called to be ſoldiers, and
muſt ſometimes meet with enemies, and perhaps
with wounds : yet confidering this prayer as provided by him, who knows what we are, and where
we are, it may afford us both inſtruction and confolation.

It calls to a conſtant reflection upon our own
weakneſs. Believers, eſpecially young ones, are
prone to reſt too much in grace received. They
feel their hearts warm ; and, like Peter, are ready
to pleaſe themſelves with thinking how they would
act in ſuch or ſuch a ſtate of trial. It is as if the
Lord had ſaid, Poor worms, be not high-minded,
but fear and pray, that, if it may be, you may be
kept from learning, by bitter experience, how weak
your ſuppoſed ſtrength is. It ſweetly intimates, that
all our ways, and all our enemies, are in the hands
of our great Shepherd. He knows our path. We
are ſhort-ſighted, and cannot tell what an hour may
bring forth : but we are under his protection ; and
if we depend upon him, we need not be anxiouſly
                                                    afraid.

afraid. He will be faithful to the truft we repofe
in him, and will fuffer no temptation to overtake us,
but what he will fupport us under and bring us
through. But it becomes us to beware of fecurity
and prefumption, to keep our eyes upon him, and
not to think ourfelves fafe a moment longer than
our fpirits feel and breathe the meaning of this petition.

It implies, likewife, the duty of watchfulnefs
on our part, as our Lord joins them elfewhere,
" Watch and pray." If we defire not to be led into
temptation, furely we are not to run into it. If we
wifh to be preferved from error, we are to guard
againft a curious and reafoning fpirit. If we
would preferve peace of confcience, we muft beware of trifling with the light and motions of the
Holy Spirit; for without his affiftance we cannot
maintain faith in exercife. If we would not be
enfnared by the men of the world, we are to keep
at a proper diftance from them. The lefs we have
to do with them the better, excepting fo far as the
providence of God makes it our duty in the difcharge of our callings and relations, and taking
opportunities of doing them good. And though
we cannot wholly fhut Satan out of our imaginations, we fhould be cautious that we do not wilfully provide fuel for his flame; but intreat the
Lord to fet a watch upon our eyes and our ears,
and to teach us to reject the firft motions and the
fmalleft appearance of evil.

I have been fo intent upon my fubject, that I
have once and again forgot I was writing to your
Lordfhip, otherwife I fhould not have let my
lucubration run to fo great a length, which I certainly did not intend when I began. I fhall not add
to this fault, by making an apology. I have touched upon a topic of great importance to myfelf. I
am one among many who have fuffered greatly for

E 4   want

want of paying more attention to my need of this prayer. O that I could be wiser hereafter, and always act and speak as knowing that I am always upon a field of battle, and beset by legions!

I am, with great respect, &c.

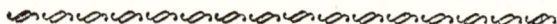

LETTER XXIV.

My Lord,   *September —* 1776.

Without any preamble, I purpose now to wait on your Lordship, with a few thoughts on the meaning of that name which first obtained at Antioch, in other words, what it is to be a Christian? What are the effects, which (making allowance for the unavoidable infirmities attending upon the present state of mortality) may be expected from a real experimental knowledge of the gospel? I would not insinuate that none are Christians who do not come up to the character I would describe; for then I fear I should unchristian myself: but only to consider what the scripture encourages us to aim at as the prize of our high calling in this life. It is generally allowed and lamented, that we are too apt to live below our privileges, and to stop short of what the spirit and the promises of the gospel point out to us as attainable.

Mr Pope's admired line, "An honest man's the " nobleft work of God," may be admitted as a truth, when rightly explained. A Christian is the nobleft work of God in this visible world, and bears a much brighter impression of his glory and goodness than the sun in the firmament; and none but a Christian can be strictly and properly honeft: all others are too much under the power of self, to do
universally

univerfally to others as they would others fhould do unto them; and nothing but an uniform conduct upon this principle deferves the name of honefty.

The Chriftian is a new creature, born and taught from above. He has been convinced of his guilt and mifery as a finner, has fled for refuge to the hope fet before him, has feen the Son and believed on him: his natural prejudices againft the glory and grace of God's falvation have been fubdued and filenced by almighty power; he has accepted the Beloved, and is made acceptable in him: He now knows the Lord; has renounced the confufed, diftant, uncomfortable notions he once formed of God; and beholds him in Chrift, who is the way, the truth, and the life, the only door by which we can enter to any true fatisfying knowledge of God, or communion with him. But he fees God in Chrift, reconciled, a Father, a Saviour, and a Friend, who has freely forgiven him all his fins, and given him the fpirit of adoption: he is now no longer a fervant, much lefs a ftranger, but a fon; and becaufe a fon, an heir already interefted in all the promifes, admitted to the throne of grace, and an affured expectant of eternal glory. The gofpel is defigned to give us not only a peradventure or a probability, but a certainty both of our acceptance and our perfeverance, till death fhall be fwallowed up in life. And though many are fadly fluctuating and perplexed upon this head, and perhaps all are fo for a feafon; yet there are thofe who can fay, we know that we are of God; and therefore they are ftedfaft and unmoveable in his way; becaufe they are confident that their labour fhall not be in vain, but that when they fhall be abfent from the body, they fhall be prefent with their Lord. This is the ftate of the advanced experienced Chriftian, who being enabled to make

E 5   his

his profeſſion the chief buſineſs of his life, is ſtrong
in the Lord, and in the power of his might.
Every one who has this hope in Chriſt, purifieth
himſelf, even as he is pure. I would now attempt
a ſketch of the Chriſtian's temper, formed upon
theſe principles and hopes, under the leading
branches of its exerciſe, reſpecting God, himſelf,
and his fellow-creatures.

The Chriſtian's temper Godward is evidenced
by *humility.* He has received from Gethſemane
and Golgotha ſuch a ſenſe of the evil of ſin, and
of the holineſs of God, combined with his match-
leſs love to ſinners, as has deeply penetrated his
heart; he has an affecting remembrance of the
ſtate of rebellion and enmity in which he once
lived againſt this holy and good God; and he has
a quick perception of the defilements and defects
which ſtill debaſe his beſt ſervices. His mouth is
therefore ſtopped as to boaſting; he is vile in his
own eyes, and is filled with wonder, that the Lord
ſhould viſit ſuch a ſinner with ſuch a ſalvation.
He ſees ſo vaſt a diſproportion between the obligations he is under to grace, and the returns he
makes, that he is diſpoſed, yea, conſtrained, to
adopt the apoſtle's words without affectation, and
to account himſelf leſs than the leaſt of all ſaints;
and knowing his own *heart,* while he ſees only the
outſide of others, he is not eaſily perſuaded there
can be a believer upon earth ſo faint, ſo unfruitful,
ſo unworthy as himſelf. Yet, though abaſed, he
is not diſcouraged, for he enjoys *peace.* The dignity, offices, blood, righteouſneſs, faithfulneſs, and
compaſſion of the Redeemer, in whom he reſts,
truſts, and lives, for wiſdom, righteouſneſs, ſanc-
tification, and redemption, are adequate to all his
wants and wiſhes, provide him with an anſwer to
every objection, and give him no leſs confidence in
God, than if he were ſinleſs as an angel; For he

fees, that though fin has abounded in him, grace
has much more abounded in Jefus. With refpect
to the paft, all things are become new ; with refpect to the prefent and future, he leans upon an
Almighty arm, and relies upon the word and
power which made and upholds the heavens and
the earth. Though he feels himfelf unworthy of
the fmalleft mercies, he claims and expects the
greateft bleffings that God can beftow ; and being
rooted and grounded in the knowledge and love
of Chrift, his peace abides, and is not greatly affected, either by the variation of his own frames,
or the changes of God's difpenfations towards him
while here. With fuch a fenfe of himfelf, fuch
a heart-felt peace and heavenly hope, how can his
fpirit but breathe *love* to his God and Saviour ? It
is indeed the perfection of his character and happinefs, that his foul is united by love to the chief
good. The love of Chrift is the joy of his heart,
and the fpring of his obedience. With his Saviour's
prefence, he finds a heaven begun upon earth ; and
without it, all the other glories of the heavenly
ftate would not content him. The excellence of
Chrift, his love to finners, efpecially his dying love ;
his love to himfelf in feeking and faving him when
loft, faving him to the uttermoft—But I muft ftop.
—Your Lordfhip can better conceive than I can
defcribe, how and why Jefus is dear to the heart
that knows him. That part of the Chriftian's life
which is not employed in the active fervice of his
Lord, is chiefly fpent in feeking and maintaining
communion with him. For this he plies the throne,
and ftudies the word of grace, and frequents the
ordinances, where the Lord has promifed to meet
with his people. Thefe are his golden hours ; and,
when thus employed, how poor and trivial does
all that the world calls great and important appear
in his eyes ! Yea, he is folicitous to keep up an

E 6   intercourfe.

intercourse of heart with his Beloved in his busiest scenes; and so far as he can succeed, it alleviates all his labours, and sweetens all his troubles. And when he is neither communing with his Lord, nor acting for him, he accounts his time lost, and is ashamed and grieved. The truth of his love is manifested by *submission*. This is twofold, and absolute and without reserve in each.—He submits to his revealed will, as made known to him by precept, and by his own example. He aims to tread in his Saviour's footsteps, and makes conscience of *all* his commandments, without exception and without hesitation. Again, he submits to his providential will: he yields to his sovereignty, acquiesces in his wisdom; he knows he has no *right* to complain of any thing, because he is a sinner; and he has no *reason*, because he is sure the Lord does all things well. Therefore this submission is not forced, but is an act of *trust*. He knows he is not more unworthy than he is unable to chuse for himself, and therefore rejoices that the Lord has undertaken to manage for him; and were he compelled to make his own choice, he could only chuse, that all his concerns should remain in that hand to which he has already committed them. And thus he judges of *public* as well as of his personal affairs. He cannot be an unaffected spectator of national sins, nor without apprehension of their deserved consequences; he feels, and almost trembles for others, but he himself dwells under the shadow of the Almighty, in a sanctuary that cannot be forced; and therefore, should he see the earth shaken, and the mountains cast into the midst of the sea, his heart would not be greatly moved, for God is his refuge. The Lord reigns. He sees his Saviour's hands directing every dark appearance, and over-ruling all to the accomplishment of his own great purposes: this satisfies him; and though
the

the winds and waves fhould be high, he can venture his own little bark in the ftorm, for he has an infallible and almighty pilot on board with him. And indeed, why fhould he fear when he has nothing to lofe? His beft concerns are fafe; and other things he holds as gifts from his Lord, to whofe call he is ready to refign them, in whatever way he pleafes; well knowing, that creatures and inftruments cannot of themfelves touch a hair of his head without the Lord's permiffion, and that if he does permit them, it muft be for the beft.

I might enlarge farther.—But I fhall proceed to confider the Chriftian's temper refpecting himfelf. He lives godly and *foberly*. By fobriety we mean more than that he is not a drunkard; his tempers toward God of courfe form him to a moderation in all temporal things. He is not fcrupulous or fuperftitious; he underftands the liberty of the gofpel, that every creature of God is good if it be received with thankfgiving: He does not aim at being needlefsly fingular, nor practife felf-devifed aufterities. The Chriftian is neither a Stoic nor a Cynic; yet he finds daily caufe for watchfulnefs and reftraint. Satan will not often tempt a believer to grofs crimes: our greateft fnares and foreft conflicts are ufually found in things lawful in themfelves, but hurtful to us by their abufe, engroffing too much of our time, or of our hearts, or fomehow indifpofing us for communion with the Lord. The Chriftian will be jealous of any thing that might entangle his affections, damp his zeal, or ftraiten him in his opportunities of ferving his Saviour. He is likewife content with his fituation, becaufe the Lord chufes it for him; his fpirit is not eager for additions and alterations in his circumftances. If Divine Providence points out and leads to a change, he is ready to follow, though it fhould be what the world would call from a better

to a worfe; for he is a pilgrim and a ftranger
here, and a citizen of heaven. As people of fortune fometimes, in travelling, fubmit chearfully to
inconvenient accommodations, very different from
their homes, and comfort themfelves with thinking
they are not always to live fo; fo the Chriftian is
not greatly folicitous about externals. If he has
them, he will ufe them moderately If he has but
little of them, he can make a good fhift without
them; he is but upon a journey, and will foon be
at home. If he be rich, experience confirms our
Lord's words, Luke, xii. 15 ; and fatisfies him,
that a large room, a crowd of fervants, and twenty
difhes upon his table, add nothing to the real happinefs of life. Therefore he will not have his
heart fet upon fuch things. If he be in a humbler
ftate, he is more difpofed to pity than to envy
thofe above him; for he judges they muft have
many incumbrances from which he is freed. However, the will of God, and the light of his countenance, are the chief things the Chriftian, whether rich or poor, regards; and therefore his moderation is made known unto all men.

A third branch of the Chriftian's temper refpects
his fellow-creatures. And here, methinks, if I
had not filled a fheet already, I could enlarge with
pleafure. We have in this degenerate day, among
thofe who claim and are allowed the name of
Chriftian, too many of a narrow, felfifh, merce-
nary fpirit; but in the beginning it was not fo.
The gofpel is defigned to cure fuch a fpirit, but
gives no indulgence to it. A Chriftian has the
mind of Chrift, who went about doing good, who
makes his fun to fhine upon the good and the evil,
and fendeth rain on the juft and the unjuft. His
Lord's example forms him to the habit of diffufive
benevolence; he breathes a fpirit of good-will to
mankind, and rejoices in every opportunity of
being

being ufeful to the fouls and bodies of others, without refpect to parties or interefts. He commiferates, and would if poffible alleviate, the miferies of all around him; and if his actual fervices are reftrained by want of ability, yet all fhare in his fympathy and prayers. Acting in the fpirit of his mafter, he frequently meets with a meafure of the like treatment; but if his good is requited with evil, he labours to overcome evil with good. He feels himfelf a finner, and needs much forgivenefs : this makes him ready to forgive. He is not haughty, captious, eafily offended, or hard to be reconciled; for at the feet of Jefus he has learned meeknefs; and when he meets with unkindnefs or injuftice, he confiders, that though he has not deferved fuch things from men, they are inftruments employed by his heavenly Father, (from whom he has deferved to fuffer much more), for his humiliation and chaftifement; and is therefore more concerned for their fins than for his own fufferings, and prays, after the pattern of his Saviour, " Father, forgive them, for they know not " what they do." He knows he is fallible; therefore cannot be pofitive. He knows he is frail; and therefore dares not be cenforious. As a member of fociety, he is juft, punctual in the difcharge of every relative duty, faithful to his engagements and promifes, rendering to all their dues, obedient to lawful authority, and acting to all men according to the golden rule, of doing as he would be done by. His conduct is fimple, devoid of artifice, and confiftent, attending to every branch of duty; and in the clofet, the family, the church, and in the tranfactions of common life, he is the fame man; for in every circumftance he ferves the Lord, and aims to maintain a confcience void of offence in his fight. No fmall part of the beauty of his profeffion in the fight of men, confifts in the due

government

government of his tongue. The law of truth, and kindnefs, and purity, is upon his lips. He abhors lying; and is fo far from inventing a flander, that he will not repeat a report to the difadvantage of his neighbour, however true, without a proper call. His converfe is chearful, but inoffenfive; and he will no more wound another with his wit (if he has a talent that way) than with a knife. His fpeech is with grace, feafoned with falt, and fuited to promote the peace and edification of all around him.

Such is the Chriftian in civil life; but though he loves all mankind, he ftands in a nearer relation, and bears an efpecial brotherly love, to all who are partakers of the faith and hope of the golpel. This regard is not confined within the pale of a denomination, but extended to all who love the Lord Jefus Chrift in fincerity. He calls no man mafter himfelf; nor does he wifh to impofe a Shibboleth of his own upon others. He rejoices in the image of God, where-ever he fees it, and in the work of God, where-ever it is carried on. Though tenacious of the truths which the Lord has taught him, his heart is open to thofe who differ from him in lefs effential points, and allows to others that right of private judgement which he claims for himfelf, and is difpofed to hold communion in love with all who hold the head. He cannot indeed countenance thofe who fet afide the one foundation which God has laid in Zion, and maintain errors derogatory to the honour of his Saviour, or fubverfive of the faith and experience of his people; yet he wifhes well to their perfons, pities and prays for them, and is ready in meeknefs to inftruct them that oppofe: but there is no bitternefs in his zeal, being fenfible that raillery and invective are difhonourable to the caufe of truth, and quite unfuitable in the mouth of a finner, who owes all that diftinguifhes him

from

from the vileft of men to the free grace of God.
In a word, he is influenced by the wifdom from
above, which, as it is pure, is likewife peaceable,
gentle, and eafy to be intreated, full of mercy and
good works, without partiality, and without hypocrify.

I muft juft recur to my firft head, and obferve,
that with this fpirit and deportment, the Chriftian,
while he is enabled to maintain a confcience void of
offence towards God and man, is ftill fenfible and
mindful of indwelling fin : he has his eye more upon his rule than upon his attainments ; and therefore finds and confeffes, that in every thing he comes
exceedingly fhort, and that his beft fervices are not
only defective, but defiled : He accounts himfelf an
unprofitable fervant, is abafed in his own eyes, and
derives all his hope and comfort, as well as his
ftrength, from Jefus, whom he has known, received,
and trufted, to whom he has committed his foul, in
whom he rejoices, and worfhips God in the fpirit,
renouncing all confidence in the flefh, and efteem-
ing all things as lofs, for the excellency of the
knowledge of Chrift Jefus his Lord.

If I have lately been rather tardy in making my
payments to your Lordfhip, I have proportionably
increafed the quantity. It is high time I fhould now
relieve your patience. I hope I long to be a Chriftian indeed ; and I hope this hafty exemplification
of my wifhes will anfwer to your Lordfhip's experience better than I fear it does to my own. May
I beg a remembrance in your prayers, that he
who has given me to will and defire, may work in
me to be and to do according to his own good
pleafure.

I am, &c.

L E T-

L E T T E R   XXV.

My Lord,   *November* — 1776.

MY London journey, which prevented my writing in October, made me amends by an opportunity of waiting upon your Lordfhip in perfon. Such feafons are not only pleafant at the time,
but afford me pleafure in the review.—I could have
wifhed the half-hour we were together by ourfelves
prolonged to half a day. The fubject your Lordfhip was pleafed to fuggeft has been often upon my
mind; and glad fhould I be, were I able to offer
you any thing fatisfactory upon it. There is no
doubt but firft religious impreffions are ufually
mingled with much of a legal fpirit; and that confcience at fuch a time is not only tender, but mif-
informed and fcrupulous : and I believe, as your
Lordfhip intimated, that when the mind is more
enlightened, and we feel a liberty from many fet-
ters we had impofed upon ourfelves, we are in danger of verging too far towards the other extreme.
It feems to me that no one perfon can adjuft the
medium, and draw the line exactly for another.
There are fo many particulars in every fituation, of
which a ftranger cannot be a competent judge, and
the beft human advices and models are mixed with
fuch defects, that it is not *right* to expect others to
be abfolutely guided by our rules, nor is it *fafe*
for us implicitly to adopt the decifions or practices
of others. But the fcripture undoubtedly furnifhes
fufficient and infallible rules for every perfon, however circumftanced; and the throne of grace is appointed for us to wait upon the Lord for the beft
expofition of his precepts. Thus David often prays
to be led in the right way, in the path of judge-
                                              ment.

ment.   By frequent prayer, and clofe acquaintance
with the fcripture, and an habitual attention to the
frame of our hearts, there is a certain delicacy of
fpiritual tafte and difcernment to be acquired, which
renders a nice difquifition concerning the nature
and limits of the Adiaphora, as they are called, or
how near we may go to the utmoft bounds of what
is right, without being wrong, quite unneceffary.
Love is the cleareft and moft perfuafive cafuift; and
when our love to the Lord is in lively exercife, and
the rule of his word is in our eye, we feldom make
great miftakes.   And I believe the overdoings of a
young convert, proceeding from an honeft fimplicity of heart, and a defire of pleafing the Lord, are
more acceptable in his fight than a certain coolnefs
of conduct, which frequently takes place afterward,
when we are apt to look back with pity upon our
former weaknefs, and fecretly to applaud ourfelves
for our prefent greater attainments in knowledge,
though perhaps (alas that it fhould ever be fo !) we
may have loft as much in warmth as we have gained
in light.

From the time we know the Lord, and are bound
to him by the cords of love and gratitude, the two
chief points we fhould have in our view, I apprehend, are, to maintain communion with him in
our own fouls, and to glorify him in the fight of
men.   Agreeable to thefe views, though the fcripture does not enumerate or decide, *totidem verbis*,
for or againft many things which fome plead for,
and others condemn ; yet it furnifhes us with fome
general canons, which, if rightly applied, will perhaps go a good way towards fettling the debate, at
leaft to the fatisfaction of thofe who would rather
pleafe God than man.   Some of thefe canons I
will juft mark to your Lordfhip ;—Rom. xii. 1. 2. ;
1 Cor. viii. 13. and x. 31. ; 2 Cor. vi. 17. ; Ephef.
iv. 30. ; Ephef. v. 11. 15. 16. ; 1 Theff. v. 22. ; E-
phef.

phef. vi. 18.; to which I may add, as fuitable to the
prefent times, If. xxii. 12. Luke, xxi. 34. I apprehend the fpirit of thefe and fimilar paffages of fcripture (for it would be eafy to adduce a larger number)
will bring a Chriftian under fuch reftrictions as follow.

To avoid and forbear, for his own fake, whatever has a tendency to damp and indifpofe his fpirit
in attendance upon the means of grace ; for fuch
things, if they be not condemned as finful *per fe*,
if they be not abfolutely unlawful, yea though they
be, when duly regulated, lawful and right, (for
often our chief fnares are entwined with our bleffings) ; yet if they have a repeated and evident tendency to deaden our hearts to divine things, of
which each perfon's experience muft determine,
there muft be fomething in them, either in feafon,
meafure, or circumftance, wrong to us ; and let
them promife what they will, they do but rob us
of our gold to pay us with counters. For the light
of God's countenance, and an open chearfulnefs of
fpirit in walking with him in private, is our chief
joy ; and we muft be already greatly hurt, if any
thing can be purfued, allowed, or refted in, as a
tolerable fubftitute for it.

For the fake of the church, and the influence
example may have upon his fellow-Chriftians, the
law of charity and prudence will often require a believer to abftain from fome things, not becaufe they
are unlawful, but inexpedient. Thus the Apoftle,
though ftrenuous for the *right* of his Chriftian liberty, would have abridged himfelf of the *ufe*, fo
as to eat no meat, rather than offend a weak bro-
ther, rather than miflead him to act againft the prefent light of his confcience. Upon this principle,
if I could, without hurt to myfelf, attend fome public amufements, as a concert or oratorio, and return from thence with a warm heart to my clofet,
(the

(the poffibility of which in my own cafe I greatly queftion) ; yet I fhould think it my duty to forbear, left fome weaker than myfelf fhould be encouraged by me to make the like experiment, though in their own minds they might fear it was wrong, and have no other reafon to think it lawful but be-caufe I did it : in which cafe I fhould fufpect, that though I received no harm, they would. And I have known and converfed with fome who I fear have made fhipwreck of their profeffion, who have dated their firft decline from imitating others, whom they thought wifer and better than them-felves, in fuch kind of compliances. And it feems that an obligation to this fort of felf-denial rifes and is ftrengthened in proportion to the weight and influence of our characters. Were I in private life, I do not know that I fhould think it finful to kill a partridge or a hare ; but, as a minifter, I no more dare do it than I dare join in a drunken fro-lic, becaufe I know it would give offence to fome, and be pleaded for as a licence by others.

There is a duty, and a charity likewife, which we owe to the world at large, as well as a faithfulnefs to God and his grace, in our neceffary converfe among them. This feems to require, that though we fhould not be needlefsly fingular, yet, for their inftruction, and for the honour of our Lord and Mafter, we fhould keep up a certain kind of fingu-larity, and fhew ourfelves called to be a feparated people : That though the providence of God has given us callings and relations to fill up, (in which we cannot be too exact), yet we are not of the world, but belong to another community, and act from other principles, by other rules, and to other ends, than the generality of thofe about us. I have obferved, that the world will often leave profeffors in quiet poffeffion of their notions and fentiments, and places of worfhip, provided they will not be

too

too ſtiff in the matter of conformity with their more general cuſtoms and amuſements.—But I fear many of them have had their prejudices ſtrengthened a-gainſt our holy religion by ſuch compliances, and have thought that if there were ſuch joy and com-fort to be found in the ways of God as they hear from our pulpits, profeſſors would not, in ſuch numbers, and ſo often, run amongſt them to beg a relief from the burden of time hanging upon their hands. As our Lord Jeſus is the great repreſenta-tive of his people in heaven, he does them the ho-nour to continue a ſucceſſion of them as his repre-ſentatives upon earth. Happy are they who are favoured with moſt of the holy unction, and beſt enabled to manifeſt to all around them, by their ſpirit, tempers, and converſation, what is the pro-per deſign and genuine effect of his goſpel upon the hearts of ſinners.

In our way of little life in the country, ſerious people often complain of the ſnares they meet with from worldly people, and yet they muſt mix with them to get a livelihood. I adviſe them, if they can, to do their buſineſs with the world as they do it in the rain. If their buſineſs calls them abroad, they will not leave it undone for fear of being a little wet; but then, when it is done, they pre-ſently ſeek ſhelter, and will not ſtand in the rain for pleaſure : So providential and neceſſary calls of duty, that lead us into the world, will not hurt us, if we find the ſpirit of the world unpleaſant, and are glad to retire from it, and keep out of it as much as our relative duties will permit. That which is our croſs is not ſo likely to be our ſnare; but if that ſpirit, which we ſhould always watch and pray againſt, infects and aſſimilates our minds to itſelf, then we are ſure to ſuffer loſs, and act below the dignity of our profeſſion.

The value of time is likewiſe to be taken into the
account.

account.—It is a precious talent, and our Chriſtian profeſſion opens a wide field for the due improvement of it. Much of it has been already loſt, and therefore we are exhorted to redeem it. I think many things which cuſtom pleads for will be excluded from a ſuitableneſs to a Chriſtian, for this one reaſon, that they are not conſiſtent with the ſimpleſt notion of the redemption of time. It is generally ſaid we need relaxation; I allow it in a ſenſe; the Lord himſelf has provided it; and becauſe our ſpirits are too weak to be always upon the wing in meditation and prayer, he has appointed to all men, from the King downwards, ſomething to do in a ſecular way. The poor are to labour, the rich are not exempted from ſomething equivalent. And when every thing of this ſort in each perſon's ſituation is properly attended to, I apprehend, if the heart be alive and in a right ſtate, ſpiritual concernments will preſent themſelves, as affording the nobleſt, ſweeteſt, and moſt intereſting relaxation from the cares and buſineſs of life; as, on the other hand, that buſineſs will be the beſt relaxation, and unbending of the mind from religious exerciſes; and between the two, perhaps there ought to be but little mere leiſure time. A life *in this ſenſe,* divided between God and the world, is deſirable;— when one part of it is ſpent in retirement, ſeeking after and converſing with him whom our ſouls love; and the other part of it employed in active ſervices for the good of our family, friends, the church, and ſociety, for his ſake. Every hour which does not fall in with one or other of theſe views, I apprehend is loſt time.

The day in which we live ſeems likewiſe to call for ſomething of a peculiar ſpirit in the Lord's people. It is a day of abounding ſin, and I fear a day of impending judgement. The world, as it was in the days of Noah and Lot, is ſecure. We are
ſoon

foon to have a day of apparent humiliation ; but
the juft caufes for it are not confined to one day,
but will fubfift and too probably increafe every day.
If I am not miftaken in the figns of the times, there
never was, within the annals of the Englifh hiftory,
a period in which the fpirit and employment defcribed Ezek. ix. 4. could be more fuitable than the
prefent. The Lord calls for mourning and weep-
ing, but the words of many are ftout againft him ;
new fpecies of diffipation are invented almoft daily,
and the language of thofe who bear the greateft
fway in what is called the polite circle, I mean the
interpretative language of their hearts, is like that
of the rebellious Jews, Jer. xliv. 16. 17. &c. As
for the word which thou haft fpoken, we will not
hearken unto thee at all.—In fhort, things are coming to a point, and it feems to be almoft putting
to the vote whether the Lord or Baal be God. In
this ftate of affairs, methinks, we cannot be too explicit in avowing our attachment to the Lord, nor
too careful in avoiding an improper correfpondence
with thofe who are in confederacy againft him.
We know not how foon we may greatly need that
mark of providential protection which is reftrained
to thofe who figh and cry for our abominations.
Upon the whole, it appears to me, that it is more
honourable, comfortable, and fafe, (if we cannot
exactly hit the golden mean), to be thought by
fome too fcrupulous and precife, than actually to
be found too compliant with thofe things which,
if not abfolutely contrary to a divine commandment, are hardly compatible with the genius of the
gofpel, or conformable to the mind that was in
Chrift Jefus, which ought alfo to be in his people.
The places and amufements which the world frequent and admire, where occafions and temptations
to fin are cultivated, where the law of what is called good-breeding is the only law which may not be
violated

violated with impunity, where finful paffions are provoked and indulged, where the fear of God is fo little known or regarded, that thofe who do fear him muft hold their tongues though they fhould hear his name blafphemed, can hardly be a Chriftian's voluntary chofen ground. Yet I fear thefe characters will apply to every kind of polite amufement or affembly in the kingdom.

As to family-connections, I cannot think we are bound to break or flight them. But as believers and their friends often live as it were in two elements, there is a mutual awkwardnefs, which makes their interviews rather dry and tedious.—But upon that account they are lefs frequent than they would otherwife be, which feems an advantage. Both fides keep up returns of civility and affection; but as they cannot unite in fentiment and leading inclination, they will not contrive to be very often together, except there is fomething confiderable given up by one or the other; and I think Chriftians ought to be very cautious what conceffions they make upon this account. But, as I faid at the beginning, no general pofitive rules can be laid down.

I have fimply given your Lordfhip fuch thoughts as have occurred to me while writing, without ftudy, and without coherence. I dare not be dogmatical; but I think what I have written is agreeable both to particular texts and to the general tenor of fcripture. I fubmit it to your judgement.

I am, &c.

L E T T E R   XXVI.

My Lord,   *July* — 1777.

I Owe your Lordſhip a quire of letters for the favour and pleaſure of your late viſit; and therefore I muſt begin and write away.

I have lately read Robertſon's Hiſtory of Charles
V. which, like moſt other hiſtories, I conſider as
a comment upon thoſe paſſages of ſcripture which
teach us the depravity of man, the deceitfulneſs of
the heart, the ruinous effects of ſin, and the powerful, though ſecret rule of Divine Providence, moving, directing, controuling the deſigns and actions
of men, with an unerring hand, to the accompliſh-
ment of his own purpoſes, both of mercy and
judgement.   Without the clue and the light which
the word of God affords, the hiſtory of mankind,
of any, of every age, only preſents to view a laby-
rinth and a chaos; a detail of wickedneſs and miſe-
ry to make us tremble, and a confuſed jumble of
interfering incidents, as deſtitute of ſtability, connection, or order, as the clouds which fly over our
heads.   In this view, *Delirant reges, plectuntur A-
chivi*, may ſerve as a motto to all the hiſtories I
have ſeen.   But with the ſcripture key, all is plain,
all is inſtructive.   Then I ſee, verily there is a God
who governs the earth, who pours contempt upon princes, takes the wiſe in their own craftineſs,
over-rules the wrath and pride of man, to bring
his own deſigns to paſs, and reſtrains all that is not
neceſſary to that end; blaſting the beſt-concerted
enterpriſes at one time, by means apparently ſlight,
and altogether unexpected, and at other times producing the moſt important events, from inſtru-
ments and circumſtances which are at firſt thought
                                                    too

too feeble and trivial to deferve notice. I fhould like
to fee a writer of Dr Robertfon's abilities give us a
hiftory upon this plan; but I think his reflections of
this fort are too general, too cold, and too few. ——
What an empty phantom do the great men of the
world purfue, while they wage war with the peace
of mankind, and butcher (in the courfe of their
lives) perhaps hundreds of thoufands, to maintain
the fhadow of authority over diftant nations, whom
they can reach with no other influence than that
of oppreffion and devaftation! But when we confider thofe who are facrificed to their ambition, as
juftly fuffering for their fins, then heroes and conquerors appear in their proper light, and worthy
to be claffed with earthquakes and peftilences, as
inftruments of divine vengeance. So many cares,
fo much pains, fo many mifchiefs,—merely to fupport the idea a worm has formed of his own grandeur, is a proof that man by nature is not only
depraved, but infatuated. Permit me to prefent
my thoughts to more advantage in the words of M.
Nicole: ——

" Un Grand dans fon idée n'eft pas un feul
" homme; c'eft un homme environné de tous
" ceux qui font à lui, et qui s'imagine avoir autant
" de bras qu'ils en ont tous enfemble, parce qu'il
" en difpofe et qu'il les remue. Un General d'ar-
" mée fe reprefente toujours à lui-même, au mi-
" lieu de tous fes foldats. Ainfi chacun tâche
" d'occuper le plus de place qu'il peut dans fon
" imagination, et l'on ne fe pouffe, et ne s'agrandit
" dans le monde, que pour augmentir l'idée que
" chacun fe forme de foi-même. Voilà le but de
" tous les deffeins ambitieux des hommes! Alex-
" andre et Cæfar n'ont point eu d'autre vûe dans
" toutes leurs batailles que celle-là. Et fi l'on de-
" mande pourquoi le Grand Seigneur a fait depuis
" peu perir cent mille hommes devant Candie, on

F 2   " peut

" peut repondre furement, que ce n'eft que pour
" attacher encore à cette image interieure qu'il a
" de lui-même, le titre de Conquerant *."

How awful is the cafe of thofe who live and die
in fuch a fpirit, and who have multiplied miferies
upon their fellow-creatures, in order to fupport and
feed it! Perhaps they may, upon their entrance on
another ftate, be accofted by multitudes, to the purport of that farcaftical language in the Prophet's
fublime ode of triumph over the King of Babylon,
If. xiv. 5.—17.

> *Hic eft, quem fuga, quem pavor*
> *Præceffit ? hic, quem terricolis gravem*
> *Strages fecuta eft, vaftitafque ? hic*
> *Attoniti fpoliator orbis ?*

But though the effects of this principle of felf
are more extenfive and calamitous, in proportion as
thofe who are governed by it are more elevated,
the principle itfelf is deep-rooted in every heart,
and is the fpring of every action, till grace infufes
a new principle, and felf, like Dagon, falls before
the Lord of hofts. Great and fmall are but relative
terms; and the paffions of difcontent, pride, and
envy, which, in the breaft of a potentate, are fe-
verely felt by one half of Europe, exert themfelves
with equal ftrength in the heart of a peafant, though,
for want of materials and opportunities, their operations are confined within narrow bounds. We
are fallen into a ftate of grofs idolatry, and felf is
the idol we worfhip.

I am, &c.

* Effais de Morale, vol. 1.

EIGHT

EIGHT

LETTERS

TO THE

REVEREND MR S——.

LETTER I.

Dear Sir,   *June* 23. 1775.

I Have met with interruptions till now, or you would have heard from me fooner. My thoughts have run much upon the fubject of your laft, becaufe I perceive it has a near connection with your peace. Your integrity greatly pleafes me ; far be it from me to fhake the *principle* of your conduct ; yet, in the application, I think there is a poffibility of carrying your exceptions too far

From the account you give me of your fentiments, I cannot but wonder you find it fo difficult to accede to the Athanafian Creed, when it feems to me you believe and avow what that creed chiefly fets forth. *The doctrine of the Trinity,* fome explication of the terms being fubjoined, is the Catholic Faith without the belief of which a man cannot be faved. This damnatory claufe feems to me proved by Mark, xvi. 16. " He that believeth fhall be " faved," &c. The object of faith muft be *truth*. The doctrine of the deity of Chrift, and of the Holy Spirit, in union with the Father, fo that they are not three Gods, but one God, is not merely a propofition expreffed in words, to which our affent is required, but is abfolutely neceffary to be known ; fince without it no one truth refpecting falvation can be rightly underftood, no one promife duly believed, no one duty fpiritually performed. I take it for granted, that this doctrine muft appear irrational and abfurd in the eye of reafon, if by reafon we mean the reafon of man in his fallen ftate, before it is corrected and enlightened by an heavenly

F 4   teacher,

teacher. No man can fay Jefus is Lord, but by
the Holy Ghoft. I believe with you, that a man
may be faved who never heard of the creed, who
never read any book but the New Teftament, or
perhaps a fingle Evangelift; but he muft be taught
of God the things that accompany falvation, or I
do not think he can be faved. *The mercies of God
in Chrift* will not fave any, (as I apprehend), but
according to the method revealed in his word, that
is, thofe who are truly partakers of faith and holinefs. For as the religion of the New Teftament
afcribes all power to God, and confiders all goodnefs in us as the effect of his communication, we
being by nature deftitute of fpiritual life or light;
fo thofe whom God himfelf is pleafed to teach, will
infallibly attain the knowledge of all that they are
concerned to know. This teaching you are waiting for, and it fhall be given you; yea the Lord,
I truft, has begun to teach you already: but if
you confider yourfelf as a learner, and that it is
poffible, under the Spirit's increafing illumination,
you may hereafter adopt fome things which at prefent you cannot approve, I fhould think it too early as yet to prefcribe to yourfelf rules and deter-
minations for the government of your future life.
Should the will of God appoint you a new path for
fervice, he may, fooner than you are aware, quiet
your mind, and enable you to fubfcribe with as
full a perfuafion of mind, as you now object to
fubfcription. If it depended upon me, I could
be content that the creed fhould reft at the bottom
of the fea, rather than embarrafs a fingle perfon of
your difpofition. Nor am I a warm ftickler for
fubfcription in itfelf; but fomething of this kind
feems neceffary upon the fuppofition of an eftablifhment.

When I think of an inclofure, fome hedge, wall,
bank, ditch, &c. is of courfe included in my idea;
for

for who can conceive of an inclofure without a boundary ? So, in a national church, there muſt be, I apprehend, ſomething marked out, the approbation or refuſal of which will determine who do or do not belong to it : And for this purpoſe articles of ſome kind ſeem not improper. You think it would be better to have theſe articles in ſcriptural expreſſions. But if it be lawful to endeavour to exclude from our pulpits men who hold ſentiments the moſt repugnant to the truth, I wiſh you to conſider, whether this can be in any meaſure ſecured by articles in which the ſcripture-doctrines are not explained and ſtated, as well as expreſſed. This propoſal is ſtrenuouſly pleaded for by many in our day, upon views very different from yours. The Socinians, for inſtance, would readily ſubſcribe a ſcriptural declaration of the high prieſthood, atonement, and interceſſion of Chriſt, (while they are allowed to put their own ſenſe upon the terms); though the ſenſe they maintain be utterly inconſiſtent with what thoſe who are enlightened by the Holy Spirit learn from the ſame expreſſions.

I acknowledge, indeed, that the end is not anſwered by the preſent method ; ſince there are too many, like the perſon you mention, who would eaſily ſubſcribe 900 articles, rather than baulk his preferment : yet the profligacy of ſome ſeems to be no juſt reaſon why the church, why any church, ſhould not be at liberty to define the terms upon which they will accept members or teachers, or why conſcientious perſons ſhould object to theſe terms, (if they think them agreeable to the truth), merely becauſe they are not expreſſed in the preciſe words of ſcripture. If allowance may be made for human infirmity in the *Liturgy*, I ſee not why the *Articles* may not be intitled to the ſame privilege. For it ſeems requiſite that we ſhould be as well ſatisfied with the expreſſions we uſe with our lips, in frequent ſo-

lemn prayer to God, as in what we fubfcribe with
our hands. I am perfuaded that the leaders of the
Affociation at the Feathers Tavern, fome of them
at leaft, though they begin with the affair of fubfcription, would not (if they might have their wifh)
ftop there, but would go on with their projected
reform, till they had overturned the Liturgy alfo,
or at leaft weeded it from every expreffion that bears
teftimony to the deity of the Saviour, and the efficacious influence of the Holy Spirit. I blefs God
that you are far otherwife minded.

   I hope, however, though you fhould not think
yourfelf at liberty to repeat your fubfcription, the
Lord will make you comfortable and ufeful in your
prefent rank as a curate. Preferment is not neceffary, either to our peace or ufefulnefs. We may
live and die contentedly, without the honours and
emoluments which afpiring men thirft after, if he
be pleafed to honour us with a difpenfation to
preach *his* gofpel, and to crown our endeavours
with a bleffing. He that winneth fouls is wife ;
wife in the choice of the higheft end he can propofe
to himfelf in this life, wife in the improvement of
the only means by which this defirable end can
be attained. Where-ever we caft our eyes, the
bulk of the people are ignorant, immoral, carelefs.
They live without God in the world ; they are neither awed by his authority, or affected by his
goodnefs, or enabled to truft to his promifes, or
difpofed to aim at his glory. If, perhaps, they
have a ferious interval, or fome comparative fobriety of character, they ground their hopes upon
their own doings, endeavours, or purpofes; and
treat the inexpreffible love of God revealed in
Chrift, and the gofpel method of falvation by faith
in his name, with neglect, often with contempt.
They have preachers, whom perhaps they hear
with fome pleafure, becaufe they neither alarm
                                        their

their confciences by infifting on the fpirituality and
fanction of the divine law, nor offend their pride
by publifhing the humiliating doctrines of that gofpel, which is the power of God through faith unto
falvation.   Therefore what they do fpeak, they
fpeak in vain; the world grows worfe and worfe
under their inftructions; infidelity and profligacy
abound more and more; for God will own no
other doctrine but what the apoftle calls the truth
as it is in Jefus; that doctrine which drives the
finner from all his vain pleas, and points out the
Lord Jefus Chrift as the only ground of hope, the
fupreme object of defire, as appointed of God, to
be wifdom, righteoufnefs, fanctification, and redemption, to all who believe in his name.   When
minifters themfelves are convinced of fin, and feel
the neceffity of an Almighty Saviour, they prefently account their former gain but lofs, and determine, with the apoftle, to know nothing but
Jefus Chrift, and him crucified.   In proportion as
they do this, they are fure to be wondered at,
laughed at, and railed at, if the providence of God,
and the conftitution of their country, fecure them
from feverer treatment.—But they have this inva-
luable compenfation, that they no longer fpeak
without effect.   In a greater or lefs degree a change
takes place in their auditories:—the blind receive
their fight, the deaf hear, the lepers are cleanfed;
—finners are turned from darknefs to light, and
from the power of Satan to God;—finful practices
are forfaken; and a new courfe of life in the converts, evidences that they have not followed cunningly devifed fables, or taken up with uncertain
notions; but that God has indeed quickened them
by his Spirit, and given them an underftanding to
know him that is true.   The preachers, likewife,
while they attempt to teach others, are taught
themfelves: A bleffing defcends upon their ftudies.
F 6   and

and labours, upon their perufal of the fcripture, upon their attention to what paffes within them and around them : The events of every day contribute to throw light upon the word of God; their views of divine truth grow more enlarged, connected, and comprehenfive ; many difficulties which perplexed them at their firft fetting out, trouble them no more ; the God whom they ferve, and on whom they wait, reveals to them thofe great things, which, though plainly expreffed in the letter of the fcripture, cannot be underftood and realifed without divine teaching, 1 Cor. ii. 9. to 15. Thus they go on from ftrength to ftrength, hard things become eafy, and a divine light fhines upon their paths. Oppofition from men perhaps may increafe : they may expect to be reprefented as thofe who turn the world upfide down; the cry μεγαλη η Αρτεμις * will be raifed againft them, the gates of the temple of preferment will be feldom open to them ; but they will have the unfpeakable confolation of applying to themfelves thofe lively words of the apoftle, ως λυπωμενοι, και δε χαιροντες· ως π[ω]χοι, πολλως δε πλωτιζοντες· ως μηδεν εχοντες, και παντα κατεχοντες. †

It is the ftrain of evident fincerity which runs through your letters, that gives me a pleafing confidence the Lord is with you. A difinterefted defire of knowing the truth, with a willingnefs to follow it through all difadvantages, is a preparation of the heart which only God can give. He has directed you to the right method, fearching the fcripture with prayer. Go on, and may his bleffing attend you. You may fee from what I have written above, what is the defire of my heart for you. But I am not impatient. Follow your hea-

* Great is Diana.   † 2 Cor. vi. 10.

venly

venly leader, and in his own time and manner he
will make your way plain. I have travelled the
path before you, I fee what you yet want, I cannot
impart it to you, but he can, and I truft he will.
It will rejoice my foul to be any way affiitant to
you; but I am afraid I fhould not afford you much,
either profit or fatisfaction, by entering upon a dry
defence of creeds and articles.

The truths of fcripture are not like mathematical
theorems, which prefent exactly the fame ideas to
every perfon who underftands the terms. The
word of God is compared to a mirror, 2 Cor. iii.
18.; but it is a mirror in which the longer we
look, the more we fee; the view will be ftill growing upon us; and ftill we fhall fee but in part
while on this fide eternity. When our Lord pro-
nounced Peter bleffed, declaring he had learnt that
which flefh and blood could not have taught him,
yet Peter was at that time much in the dark. The
fufferings and death of Jefus, though the only and
neceffary means of his falvation, were an offence
to him. But he lived to glory in what he once
could not bear to hear of. Peter had received
grace to love the Lord Jefus, to follow him, to
venture all, and to forfake all for him: thefe firft
good difpofitions were of God, and they led to further advances. So it is ftill. By nature, felf rules
in the heart; when this idol is brought low, and
we are truly willing to be the Lord's, and to apply
to him for ftrength and direction, that we may
ferve him, the good work is begun; for it is a
truth that holds univerfally and without exception,
a man can receive nothing except it be *given* him
from heaven. The Lord firft *finds* us when we
are thinking of fomething elfe, Ifaiah, lxv. 1.; and
then we begin to feek him in good earneft, and he
has promifed to be *found* of us. People may, by
induftry

industry and natural abilities, make themselves ma-
sters of the external evidences of Christianity, and
have much to say for and against different schemes
and systems of sentiments; but all this while the
heart remains untouched. True religion is not a
science of the head, so much as an inward and
heart-felt perception, which casts down imaginations, and every υψωμα that exalteth itself in the
mind, and brings every thought into a sweet and
willing subjection to Christ by *faith*. Here the
learned have no real advantage above the ignorant;
both see when the eyes of the understanding are
enlightened; till then both are equally blind. And
the first lesson in the school of Christ is to become
a little child, sitting simply at his feet, that we may
be made wise unto salvation.

I was not only prevented beginning my letter so
soon as I wished, but have been unusually interrupted since I began it. Often, as soon as I could
well take the pen in hand, I have been called away
to attend company and intervening business. Tho'
I persuade myself, after what I have formerly said,
you will put a favourable construction upon my
delay, yet it has given me some pain. I set a great
value upon your offer of friendship, which I trust
will not be interrupted on either side, by the
freedom with which we mutually express our difference of sentiments, when we are constrained to
differ. You please me with intrusting me with the
first rough draught of your thoughts; and you
may easily perceive by my manner of writing, that
I place equal confidence in your candour. I shall
be glad to exchange letters as often as it suits us,
without constraint, ceremony, or apology; and
may he who is always present with our hearts make
our correspondence useful. I pray God to be your
sun and shield, your light and strength, to guide
                                                    you

you with his eye, to comfort you with his gracious prefence in your own foul, and to make you an happy inftrument of comforting many.

I am, &c.

LETTER II.

My dear Friend,   *July* 14. 1775.

I Gladly adopt your addrefs, and can affure you that the interchange of every letter unites my heart more clofely to you. I am glad to find that your views of articles and creeds are not likely to hinder you from going forward in your prefent fituation; and if, without contracting your ufefulnefs, they only prove a bar to your preferment, I am fure it will be no grief of mind to you at the hour of death, or the day of judgement, that you were enabled to follow the dictates of confcience, in oppofition to all the pleas of cuftom or intereft. Since, therefore, I have no defire of fhaking your refolves, may we not drop this fubject entirely? For indeed I act but an awkward part in it, being by no means myfelf an admirer of articles and creeds, or difpofed to be a warm advocate for church power. The propriety of our national eftablifhment, or of any other, is what I have not much to do with; I found it as it is, nor have I influence to alter it were I willing. The queftion in which I was concerned was fimply, Whether I, *rebus fic ftantibus,* could fubmit to it, fo as confcientioufly to take a defignation to the miniftry under it? I thought I could; I accordingly did, and I am thankful that I never have feen caufe to repent it.

You

You feem gently to charge me with a want of candour in what I obferved or apprehended concerning the gentlemen of the Feathers Tavern. If I miftake not, (for I retain no copies of my letters), I expreffed myfelf with a double reftriction, by firft faying the *leaders* of that fociety, and then adding, or *fome of them at leaft.* I apprehend your candour will hardly lead you to fuppofe, that there are *none* amongft them who would pull down the whole fabric, (that is, I mean fo far as it croffes the Socinian fcheme), if it was left to their choice. I apprehend I may, without the leaft breach of candour, fuppofe that the exceptions which Mr Lindfay has made to the Liturgy are not peculiar to himfelf. It feems plain in his cafe, and from his own writings, that the mere removal of fubfcriptions, which is the immediate and oftenfible object of the clerical petition, could not have fatisfied *him*; and it is paft a doubt with me, that there are others of the clergy like-minded with him. Indeed I could wifh to be thought candid by *you*; though, I confefs, I am not a friend to that lukewarmnefs and indifference for truth, which bears the name of candour among many in the prefent day. I defire to maintain a fpirit of candour and benevolence to all men, to wifh them well, to do them every good office in my power, and to commend what appears to me commendable in a Socinian, as readily as in a Calvinift. But with fome people I can only go *ufque ad aras.* I muft judge of principles by the word of God, and of the tree by its fruit. I meddle with no man's final ftate; becaufe I know that he who is exalted to give repentance and remiffion of fins, can do it whenever, and to whomfoever he is pleafed: Yet I firmly believe, and I make no fcruple of proclaiming it, that fwearers, drunkards, adulterers, *continuing fuch*, cannot inherit the kingdom of God: and I look with no 'lefs compaffion upon

fome

some persons, whose characters in common life may be respectable, when I see them unhappily blinded by their own wisdom; and while they account themselves, and are accounted by many others, master-builders in Zion, rejecting the only foundation upon which a sinner's hope can be safely built.

I am far from thinking the Socinians all hypocrites, but I think they are all in a most dangerous error; nor do their principles exhibit to my view a whit more of the genuine fruits of Christianity than Deism itself. You say, " If they be sincere, and fail not for want of diligence in searching, I cannot help thinking, that God will not condemn them for an inevitable defect in their understandings." Indeed, my friend, I have such a low opinion of man in his depraved state, that I believe no one has real sincerity in religious matters till God bestows it; and when *he* makes a person sincere in his desires after truth, he will assuredly guide him to the possession of it in due time, as our Lord speaks, John, vi. 44. 45. To suppose that any persons can sincerely seek the way of salvation, and yet miss it through an inevitable defect of their understandings, would contradict the plain promises of the gospel, such as, Matth. vii. 7. 8. John, vii. 16. 17.; but to suppose that nothing is necessary to be known, which some persons who profess sincerity cannot receive, would be in effect to make the scripture a nose of wax, and open a wide door for scepticism. I am not a judge of the heart; but I may be sure, that whoever makes the foundation-stone a rock of offence, cannot be sincere in his inquiries. He may study the scripture accurately, but he brings his own preconceived sentiments with him, and instead of submitting them to the touchstone of truth, he makes them a rule by which he interprets. That they who lean to their own understandings

derftandings fhould ftumble and mifcarry, I cannot
wonder; for the fame God who has promifed to
fill the hungry with good things, has threatened
to fend the rich empty away. So Matth. xi. 25.
It is not through defect of underftanding, but a
want of fimplicity and humility, that fo many ftumble like the blind at noon-day, and can fee nothing
of thofe great truths which are written in the gofpel as with a fun-beam.

You with me to explain myfelf concerning the
doctrine of the Trinity. I will try, yet I know I
cannot, any farther than as he who taught me fhall
be pleafed to bear witnefs in your heart to what I
fay. My firft principle in religion is what the fcripture teaches me of the utter depravity of human
nature, in connection with the fpirituality and fanction of the law of God. I believe we are by nature
finners, by practice univerfally tranfgreffors; that
we are dead in trefpaffes and fins; and that the
bent of our natural fpirit is enmity againft the holinefs, government, and grace of God. Upon this
ground, I fee, feel, and acknowledge the neceffity
of fuch a falvation as the gofpel propofes, which, at
the fame time that it precludes boafting, and ftains
the pride of all human glory, affords encouragement to thofe who may be thought, or who may
think themfelves, the weakeft or the vileft of mankind. I believe, that whatever notions a perfon
may take up from education or fyftem, no one ever
did, or ever will, feel himfelf and own himfelf to be
fuch a loft, miferable, hateful finner, unlefs he be
powerfully and fupernaturally convinced by the
fpirit of God.—There is, when God pleafes, a certain light thrown into the foul, which differs not
merely in degree, but in kind, *toto genere*, from
any thing that can be effected or produced by moral
fuafion or argument. But (to take in another of
your queries) the Holy Spirit teaches or reveals no
new

new truths, either of doctrine or precept, but only
enables us to underftand what is already revealed in
the fcripture.   Here a change takes place, the perfon that was fpiritually blind begins to fee.   The
finner's character, as defcribed in the word of God,
he finds to be a defcription of himfelf ; that he is
afar off, a ftranger, a rebel ; that he has hitherto
lived in vain.   Now he begins to fee the neceffity
of an atonement, an advocate, a fhepherd, a com-
forter : he can no more truft to his own wifdom,
ftrength, and goodnefs ; but, accounting all his
former gain but lofs, for the excellency of the
knowledge of Chrift, he renounces every other refuge, and ventures his all upon the perfon, work,
and promife of the Redeemer.   In this way, I fay,
he will find the doctrine of the Trinity not only a
propofition, but a principle ; that is, from his own
wants and fituation he will have an abiding conviction, that the Son and Holy Spirit are God, and
muft be poffeffed of the attributes and powers of
Deity, to fupport the offices the fcriptures affign
them, and to deferve the confidence and worfhip
the fcriptures require to be placed in them, and
paid to them.   Without this awakened ftate of
mind, a divine, reputed orthodox, will blunder
wretchedly even in defending his own opinions.   I
have feen laboured defences of the Trinity, which
have given me not much more fatisfaction than I
fhould probably receive from a differtation upon
the rainbow compofed by a man blind from his
birth.   In effect, the knowledge of God cannot be
attained by ftudious difcuffion on our parts ; it muft
be by a revelation on his part, Matth. xi. 27. and
xvi. 17. ; a revelation, not objectively of new truth,
but fubjectively of new light in us.   Then he that
runs may read.   Perhaps you may not quite underftand my meaning, or not accede to my fentiment at prefent ; I have little doubt, however, but
the

the time is coming when you will. I believe the
Lord God has given *you* that fincerity, which he
never difappoints.

Far be it from me to arrogate infallibility to myfelf, or to any writer or preacher ; yet, bleffed be
God, I am not left to float up and down the uncertain tide of opinion, in thofe points wherein the
peace of my foul is nearly concerned. I know,
yea I infallibly know whom I have believed. I am
under no more doubt about the way of falvation
than of the way to London. I cannot be deceived,
becaufe the word of God cannot deceive me. It is
impoffible, however, for me to give you or any
perfon full fatisfaction concerning my evidence, becaufe it is of an experimental nature. Rev. ii. 17.
In general, it arifes from the views I have received
of the power, compaffion, and grace of Jefus, and
a confcioufnefs, that I, from a conviction of my fin
and mifery, have fled to him for refuge, intrufted
and devoted myfelf and my all to him. Since my
mind has been enlightened, every thing within me,
and every thing around me, confirms and explains
to me what I read in fcripture ; and though I have
reafon enough to diftruft my own judgement every
hour, yet I have no reafon to queftion the great
effentials, which the Lord himfelf hath taught me.

Befides a long letter, I fend you a great book.
A part of it (for I do not tafk you to read the
whole) may perhaps explain my meaning better
than I have leifure to do myfelf. I fet a high value
upon this book of Mr Halyburton's ; fo that unlefs
I could replace it with another, I know not if I
would part with it for its weight in gold. The
firft and longeft treatife is, in my judgement, a ma-
fter-piece ; but I would chiefly wifh you to perufe
the Effay concerning Faith, towards the clofe of
the book. I need not beg you to read it carefully,
and to read it all. The importance of the fubject,

its

its immediate connection with your inquiries, and the accuracy of the reasoning, will render the motive of *my request* unnecessary. I cannot style him a very elegant writer; and being a Scotsman, he abounds with the Scottish idiom. But you will prefer truth to ornament. I long to hear your opinion of it. It seems to me so adapted to some things that have passed between us as if written on purpose.

The Inquiry concerning Regeneration and Justification, which stands last in the book, I do not desire or even wish you to read; but if you should, and then think that you have read a speculation more curious than useful, I shall not contradict you. I think it must appear to you in that light; but it was bound up with the rest, and therefore could not stay behind: but I hope the Essay on Faith will please you.

I take great pleasure in your correspondence, still more in the thought of your friendship, which I hope to cultivate to the utmost, and to approve myself, sincerely and affectionately yours.

LETTER III.

My Dear Friend,   *August* 11. 1775.

NExt week I go to London, where I purpose (if nothing unforeseen prevents) to stay a month. Many things, which must necessarily be attended to before my departure, abridge me of that leisure which I could wish to employ in answering your last. However, I will spare you what I can. I thank you for yours. Your objections neither displease nor weary me.—While truth is the object of your inquiry, the more freedom you use with me
the

the better. Nor do they furprife me; for I have formerly made the like objections myfelf. I have ftood upon your ground, and I continue to hope you will one day ftand upon mine. As I have told you more than once, I do not mean to dictate to you, or to wifh you to receive any thing upon my *ipfe dixit*; but in the fimplicity of friendfhip, I will give you my thoughts from time to time upon the points you propofe, and leave the event to the divine blefling.

I am glad you do not account the Socinians mafter-builders. However, they efteem themfelves fo, and are fo efteemed, not only by a few (as you think) but by many. I fear Socinianifm fpreads rapidly amongft us, and bids fair to be the prevailing fcheme in this land, efpecially with thofe who profefs to be the thinking part. The term *Arminian*, as at prefent applied, is very indifcriminate, and takes in a great variety of perfons and fentiments, amongft whom, I believe, there are many who hold the fundamental truths of the gofpel, and live a life of faith in the Son of God. I am far from fuppofing that God will guide every *fincere* perfon exactly to adopt *all* my fentiments. But there are *fome* fentiments which I believe effential to the very ftate and character of a true Chriftian.—And thefe make him a Chriftian; not merely by being his acknowledged fentiments, but by a certain peculiar manner in which he poffeffes them. There is a certain important change takes place in the heart, by the operation of the Spirit of God, before the foundeft and moft orthodox fentiments can have their proper influence upon us. This work, or change, the fcripture defcribes by various names, each of which is defigned to teach us the marvellous effects it produces, and the almighty power by which it is produced. It is fometimes called a new-birth, John, iii. 3.; fometimes a new creature or new creation,

as

as 2 Cor. v. 17.; fometimes the caufing light to
fhine out of darknefs, 2 Cor. iv. 6.; fometimes
the opening the eyes of the blind, Acts. xxvi. 18.;
fometimes the raifing the dead to life, Ephef. ii. 5.
Till a perfon has experienced this change, he will
be at a lofs to form a right conception of it: but
it means, not being profelyted to an opinion, but
receiving a principle of divine life and light in the
foul.   And till this is received, the things of God,
the truths of the gofpel, cannot be rightly difcerned
or underftood, by the utmoft powers of fallen man,
who, with all his wifdom, reafon, and talents, is ftill
but what the Apoftle calls the natural man, till the
power of God vifits his heart, 1 Cor. ii. 14. This
work is fometimes wrought fuddenly, as in the cafe
of Lydia, Acts, xvi. 14.; at other times very gradually.   A perfon who before was a ftranger even
to the form of godlinefs, or at beft content with a
mere form—finds new thoughts arifing in his mind,
feels fome concern about his fins, fome defire to
pleafe God, fome fufpicions that all is not right —
He examines his views of religion, hopes the beft
of them, and yet cannot reft fatisfied in them. To-
day, perhaps, he thinks himfelf fixed; to-morrow
he will be all uncertainty. He inquires of others,
weighs, meafures, confiders, meets with fentiments
which he had not attended to, thinks them plau-
fible; but is prefently fhocked with objections or
fuppofed confequences, which he finds himfelf unable to remove.   As he goes on in his inquiry, his
difficulties increafe. New doubts arife in his mind;
even the fcriptures perplex him, and appear to affert contrary things. He would found the depths
of truth by the plummet of his reafon; but he finds
his line is too fhort. Yet even now the man is
under a guidance, which will at length lead him
right. The importance of the fubject takes up his
thoughts, and takes off the relifh he once had for
the

the things of the world. He reads, he prays, he
ftrives, he refolves; fometimes inward embarraffments and outward temptations bring him to his
wits end. He almoft wifhes to ftand where he is,
and inquire no more: But he cannot ftop.—At
length he begins to *feel* the inward depravity, which
he had before owned as an opinion; a fenfe of
fin and guilt cut him out new work. Here reafoning will ftand him in no ftead. This is a painful
change of mind; but it prepares the way for a
blefling. It filences fome objections better than a
thoufand arguments, it cuts the comb of his own
wifdom and attainments, it makes him weary of
working for life, and teaches him, in God's due
time, the meaning of that text, " To him that work-
" eth not, but believeth in him who juftifieth the
" ungodly, his faith is counted for righteoufnefs."
Then he learns, that fcriptural faith is a very different thing from a *rational affent* to the gofpel,—
that it is the immediate gift of God, Ephef. ii. 8. ;
the operation of God, Col. ii. 12. ; that Chrift is
not only the object, but the author and finifher of
faith, Heb. xii. 2. ; and that faith is not fo properly a part of that obedience we *owe to God*, as an
ineftimable benefit we *receive from him* for Chrift's
fake, Phil. i. 29. which is the medium of our juftification, Rom. v. 1. and the principle by which
we are united to Chrift (as the branch to the vine),
John, xvii. 21. I am well aware of the pains taken
to put a different fenfe upon thefe and other feemingly myfterious paffages of fcripture; but thus
far we fpeak that which we know, and teftify that
which we have feen. I have defcribed a path in
which I have known many led, and in which I have
walked myfelf.

The gofpel, my dear Sir, is a falvation appointed for thofe who are ready to perifh, and is not defigned to put them in a way to fave themfelves by
their

their own works. It fpeaks to us as condemned
already, and calls upon us to believe in a crucified
Saviour, that we may receive redemption through
his blood, even the forgivenefs of our fins.   And
the Spirit of God, by the gofpel, firft convinces us
of unbelief, fin, and mifery; and then, by revealing the things of Jefus to our minds, enables us, as
helplefs finners, to come to Chrift, to receive him,
to behold him, or, in other words, to believe in him,
and expect pardon, life, and grace from him; renouncing every hope and aim in which we once
refted, " and accounting all things lofs and dung
" for the excellency of the knowledge of Chrift,"
John, vi. 35.; Ifa. xlv. 22. with John, vi. 40.; Col.
ii. 6.   In fome of Omicron's letters you will find
my thoughts more at large upon thefe fubjects, than
I have now time to write them.   For a farther illuftration I refer you to the MSS. fent herewith.
The firft part, written in fhort-hand, does not fo
immediately concern our prefent point as the fecond, which you may read without a key.   It re-
lates to a matter of indifputable fact, concerning a
perfon with whom (as you will perceive) I was well
acquainted.   You may depend upon the truth of
every tittle.   I intruft it to you in the confidence
of friendfhip, and beg that it may not go out of
your hands, and that when you have perufed it,
you would return it, fealed up, by a fafe convey-
ance to my houfe.   You will fee in it the fentiments of a man of great learning, found reafoning,
an amiable and irreproachable character, and how
little he accounted of all thefe advantages, when
the Lord was pleafed to enlighten his mind.

Though we have not exactly the fame view of
human depravity, yet as we both agree to take our
meafure of it from the word of God, I truft we
fhall not always differ about it.   Adam was created
in the image of God, in righteoufnefs and true ho-

linefs, Ephef. iv. 24. This moral image, I believe,
was totally loft by fin. In that fenfe he died the
day, the moment he eat the forbidden fruit. God
was no longer his joy and delight ; he was averfe
from the thoughts of his prefence, and would (if
poffible) have hid himfelf from him. His natural
powers, though doubtlefs impaired, were not deftroyed. Man by nature is ftill capable of great
things. His underftanding, reafon, memory, imagination, &c. fufficiently proclaim that the hand
that made him is divine. He is, as Milton
fays of Beelzebub, majeftic though in ruins. He
can reafon, invent, and by application attain a
confiderable knowledge in natural things. The ex-
ertions of human genius, as fpecified in the characters of fome philofophers, poets, orators, &c.
are wonderful. But man cannot know, love, truft,
or ferve his Maker, unlefs he be renewed in the
fpirit of his mind. God has preferved in him likewife fome feelings of benevolence, pity, fome fenfe
of natural juftice and truth, &c. without which
there could be no fociety : but thefe, I apprehend,
are little more than inftincts, by which the world
is kept in fome fmall degree of order ; but, being
under the direction of pride and felf, do not deferve the name of virtue and goodnefs ; becaufe
the exercife of them does not fpring from a principle of love to God, nor is directed to his glory,
or regulated by the rule of his word, till a principle of grace is fuperadded. You think, I will
not fay, "that God, judicially in punifhment of
" one man's fin, added thefe corruptions to all his
" pofterity." Let us fuppofe, that the punifhment
annexed to eating the forbidden fruit, had been the
lofs of Adam's rational powers, and that he fhould
be degraded to the ftate and capacity of a brute.
In this condition, had he begotten children after
the fall in his own likenefs, his nature being previoufly

vioufly changed, they muft have been of courfe
brutes like himfelf; for he could not convey to
them thofe original powers which he had loft. Will
this illuftrate my meaning? Sin did not deprive
him of rationality, but of fpirituality. His nature
became earthly, fenfual, yea devilifh; and this fallen
nature, this carnal mind, which is enmity againft
God, which is not fubjeft to his law, neither indeed can be, Rom. viii. 7. we univerfally derive
from him. Look upon children; they prefently
fhew themfelves averfe from good, but exceedingly
propenfe to evil. This they can learn even without a mafter; but ten thoufand inftruftors and in-
ftruftions cannot inftil good into them, fo as to
teach them to love their Creator, unlefs a divine
power co-operates. Juft as it is with the earth,
which produces weeds fpontaneoufly; but if you
only fee a cabbage or an apple-tree, you are fure it
was planted or fown there, and did not fpring from
the foil. I know many hard queftions may be
ftarted upon this fubjeft; but the Lord in due
time will clear his own caufe, and vindicate his
own ways. I leave all difficulties with him. It is
fufficient for me that fcripture afferts, and experience proves, that it is thus in faft, Rom. iii.
9.—21. Job, xiv. 4. Thus we have not only for-
feited our happinefs by tranfgreffion, but are by
our depravity incapable of it, and have no more
defire or tafte for fuch a ftate as the fcripture defcribes heaven to be, than a man born deaf can have
for a concert of mufic. And therefore our Lord
declares, that except a man be born again, he not
only *fhall not*, but *cannot* fee the kingdom of God.
Hence a twofold neceffity of a Saviour—his blood
for the pardon of our fins—his life, fpirit, and
grace, to quicken our fouls, and form us anew for
himfelf, that we may feel his love, and fhew forth
his praife.

St

St Paul, before his converfion, was not fincere
in the fenfe I hope you to be : he thought himfelf
in the right, without doubt, as many have done
when they killed God's fervants, John, xvi. 2. He
was blindly and obftinately zealous : I think he did
not enter into the merits of the caufe, or inquire
into facts with that attention which fincerity would
have put him upon. You think that his fincerity
and zeal were the very things that made him a chofen inftrument ; he himfelf fpeaks of them as the
very things that made him peculiarly unworthy of
that honour, 1 Cor. xv. 9. ; and he tells us, that
he was fet forth as a pattern of the Lord's long-fuf-
fering and mercy, that the very chief of finners
might be encouraged, 1 Tim. i. 15. 16. Had he
been fincerely defirous to know whether Jefus was
the Meffiah, there was enough in his character,
doctrines, miracles, and the prophecies concerning
him, to have cleared up the point ; but he took it
for granted he was right in his opinion, and hurried blindly on, and was (as he faid himfelf) exceedingly mad againft them. Such a kind of fincerity is common enough.   People believe themfelves right, and therefore treat others with fcorn
or rage ; appeal to the fcriptures, but firft lay down
their own pre-conceived fentiments for truths, and
then examine what fcriptures they can find to countenance them. Surely a perfon's thinking himfelf
right, will not give a fanction to all that he does
under that perfuafion.

Ignorance and obftinacy are in themfelves finful,
and no plea of fincerity will exempt from the danger of being under their influence, If. xxvii. 11.
Luke, vi. 39. It appears to me, that though you
will not follow any man implicitly, you are defirous
of difcovering your miftakes, fuppofing you are
miftaken in any point of importance. You read and
examine the word of God, not to find arms wherewith

with to defend your fentiments at all events, but to
know whether they are defenfible or not. You
pray for God's light and teaching, and in this fearch
you are willing to rifk what men are commonly
much afraid of hazarding—character, intereft, preferment, favour, &c. A fincerity of this kind I too
feldom meet with ; when I do, I account it a token
for good, and am ready to fay, " No man can do
" this, except God be with him." However, fincerity is not converfion ; but I believe it is always a
forerunner of it.

I would not be uncharitable and cenforious, hafty
and peremptory in judging my fellow-creatures.
But if I acknowledge the word of God, I cannot
avoid forming my judgement upon it. It is true, I
cannot look into people's hearts; but hearts and
principles are delineated to my hand in the fcripture. I read that no murderer has eternal life in
him ; I read likewife, " If any man love not the
" Lord Jefus Chrift, let him be anathema;" and
therefore I conclude, that there are *fpeculative errors*, as heinous in their guilt, as deftructive in their
effects as murder ; and that the moft moral regular man, as to focial life, if he loves not the Lord
Jefus Chrift, is in the fight of God, the Judge of
all, as difpleafing as a murderer. It has pleafed
God, for the peace and fupport of fociety, to put
a black mark upon thofe fins which affect the peace
and welfare of our neighbour, fuch as adultery
and murder. But undoubtedly the fins committed
immediately againft himfelf muft be more heinous
than any which offend our fellow-creatures. The
fecond commandment, Matth. xxii. 39. is like the
firft ; but it depends upon it, and is therefore in-
ferior to it.—Men ordinarily judge otherwife. To
live regardlefs of God and the gofpel, is looked
upon as a peccadillo, in comparifon with offences
againft fociety. But fooner or later it will appear

G 3   otherwife

otherwife to all. A parcel of robbers may pique
themfelves upon the juftice, honour, and truth they
obferve towards one another ; but becaufe they fet
up a petty intereft, which is inconfiftent with the
public good, they are defervedly accounted vil-
lains, and treated as fuch, notwithftanding their
petty morality among themfelves. Now, fuch a
company of robbers bears a much greater proportion to a whole nation, than a nation, or all the
nations of the earth, bears to the great God. Our
dependence upon him is abfolute, our obligations
to him infinite. In vain fhall men plead their
moral difcharge of relative duties to each other, if
they fail in the unfpeakable greater relation under
which they ftand to God : and therefore, when I
fee people living without God in the world, as all
do till they are converted, I cannot but judge them
in a dangerous ftate ;— not becaufe I take pleafure
in cenfuring, or think myfelf authorifed to pafs fentence upon my fellow-creature, but becaufe the fcripture decides exprefsly on the cafe, and I am bound
to take my fentiments from thence.

The jailor was certainly a Chriftian when bapti-
fed, as you obferve. He trembled ; he cried out,
" What muft I do to be faved ?" Paul did not bid
him amend his life, but believe in the Lord Jefus.
He believed, and rejoiced. But the Lord bleffed
the Apoftle's words, to produce in him that faving
faith, which filled him with joy and peace. It was,
as I obferved before, fomething more than an affent to the propofition, that Jefus is the Chrift ; a
refting in him for forgivenefs and acceptance, and
a cleaving to him in love. No other faith will
purify the heart, work by love, and overcome the
world.

I need not have pleaded want of leifure as an
excufe for a fhort letter, for I have written a long
one. I feel myfelf much interefted in your concerns ;

cerns; — and your unexpected frank application to
me (though you well know the light in which I
appear to fome people) I confider as a providential call, which binds me to your fervice. I hope
our correfpondence will be productive of happy
effects, and that we fhall both one day rejoice
in it.

    I am, &c.

L E T T E R   IV.

My dear Friend,   *September 6.* 1775.

I Begin to fear I fhall fall under a fufpicion of
  unkindnefs and forgetfulnefs towards you, —
and therefore I am willing to write a line by way of
prevention, though I have not leifure to attempt
any thing like an anfwer to the letter you put into
my hand the evening before I left O———; muft
therefore content myfelf with a tender of affection
and refpect, and an inquiry after your welfare.

    Your letter will give me an opportunity of faying
fomething farther when time fhall admit ; but an
endeavour to anfwer all the objections that may be
ftarted between us, in a way of reafoning, would
require a volume, and would likewife interfere with
the leading principle upon which my hope of giving you fatisfaction in due time is grounded. You
feem to expect that *I* fhould remove your difficulties ; but it is my part only to throw in a word occafionally, as a witnefs of what the Lord has been
pleafed to teach me from the fcriptures, and to
wait for the reft, till he (who alone is able) fhall be
pleafed to communicate the fame views to you : ——
For till we fee and judge by the fame medium, and

        G 4   are

are agreed in the fundamental point, that faith is
not the effect of reasoning, but a special gift of
God, which he bestows when and to whom he
pleases, it will not be possible for me to convince
you by dint of argument. I believe, as I have ob-
served before, that he has already given you a desire to know his will; and therefore I trust he will
not disappoint your search. At present I think
you want one thing, which it is not in my power
to impart; I mean such a sense of the depravity of
human nature, and the state of all mankind confidered as sinners, as may make you feel the utter
impossibility of attaining to the peace and hope of
the gospel in any other way, than by renouncing
all hope of succeeding by any endeavours of your
own, farther than by humbly waiting at the throne
of grace, for power to cast yourself, without terms
and conditions, upon him who is able to save to the
uttermost. We must feel ourselves sick, before we
can duly prize the great physician, and feel a sen-
tence of death in ourselves, before we can effectually trust in God who raiseth the dead.

I have not brought your sermons with me; for
I thought I should not have time to read them attentively, while in this hurrying place. I purpose
to consider them with care, and to give you my
thoughts with frankness, when I return. However, if they are upon the plan intimated in your
letter, I will venture to say one thing beforehand,
that they will not answer your desired end. I am
persuaded you wish to be useful—to reclaim sinners
from their evil ways, to inspire them with a love
to God, and a sincere aim to walk in obedience to
his will. May I not venture to appeal to yourself,
that you meet with little success; that the people
to whom you preach, though they perhaps give
you a patient hearing, yet remain as they were,
unchanged, and unholy? It must be so;—there is
but

but one fort of preaching which God bleffes to
thefe purpofes — that which makes all the world
guilty before God, and fets forth Jefus Chrift, (as
the brazen ferpent was propofed by Mofes), that
guilty and condemned finners, by looking to him,
and believing on his name, may be healed and faved. The moft preffing exhortations to repentance and amendment of life, unlefs, they are en-
forced in a certain way, which only God can
teach, will leave our hearers much as they find
them. When we meet, or when I have leifure to
write from home, I will trouble you with my
thoughts more at large. Till then, permit me to affure you of my fincere regard and beft wifhes, and
that I am, &c.

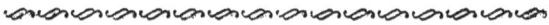

L E T T E R   V.

My Dear Friend,   *October* 21. 1775.

THE calls and engagements which I told you
engroffed and anticipated my time when I
wrote laft, have continued without any intermif-
fion hitherto, and I am ftill far behind-hand with
my bufinefs. I am willing to hope, that the cafe
has been much the fame with you, and that want
of leifure has been the only caufe of my not having
been pleafured with fo much as a note from you
fince my return from London.

I am loath, for my own fake, to charge your filence to any unwillingnefs of continuing that intercourfe which I have been, and ftill find myfelf,
defirous to improve on my part. For though we
are not agreed in our views; yet, while our preli-

G 5   minary

minary agreement, to allow mutual freedom, and
to exercife mutual candour, in expreffing our fentiments, fubfifts, we may, and I hope fhall be glad
to hear from each other. It may feem to intimate
I have a better opinion of myfelf than of you,
that while I feem confident your freedom will not
offend me, I feel now and then a fear, left mine
fhould prove difpleafing to you. But friendfhip is
a little fufpicious when exercifed with long filence,
and a plain declaration of my fentiments has more
than once put amiable and refpectable perfons to
the full trial of their patience.

I now return your fermons: I thank you for the
perufal; I fee much in them that I approve, and
nothing in them but what I formerly efpoufed.
But in a courfe of years, a confiderable alteration
has taken place in my judgement and experience. I
hope, yea, I may boldly fay, I am fure, not for
the worfe. Then I was feeking, and now through
mercy I have found, the pearl of great price. It
is both the prayer and the hope of my heart, that
a day is coming when you fhall make the fame acknowledgement. From your Letters and Sermons, I
am encouraged to addrefs you in our Lord's words,
" Thou art not far from the kingdom of God." I
am perfuaded the views you have received, will not
fuffer you to remain where you are. But fidelity
obliges me to add, " Yet one thing thou lackeft."
" That one thing" I truft the Lord will both fhew
you, and beftow upon you, in his due time. You
fpeak fomewhere of "atoning for difobedience by
repentance."— Ah! my dear Sir, when we are
brought to eftimate our difobedience, by comparing
it with fuch a fenfe of the majefty, holinefs, and
authority of God, and the fpirituality, extent, and
fanction of his holy law, as he, and he only, can
imprefs upon the heart of a finner, we fhall be
convinced that nothing but the blood of the Son of
God

God can atone for the fmalleft inftance of difobedience.

I intimated, in my letter from London, one defect of your fcheme, which will probably be the
firft to engage your notice. I am fure you have a
defire to be ufeful to the fouls of men, to be an
inftrument of reclaiming them from that courfe of
open wickednefs, or lifelefs formality, in which you
fee them enflaved; and, in a word, to prevail with
them to live foberly, righteoufly, and godly, according to the juft and comprehenfive fenfe you
have given of thofe words, in your Sermon on
Tit. ii. 11. 12. Now, inward experience, and a
pretty extenfive obfervation of what paffes abroad,
have fo perfectly convinced me there is but one
mode of preaching which the Holy Spirit owns to
the producing thefe effects, that I am not afraid
to pronounce confidently, you will not have the
defires of your heart gratified upon your prefent
plan : the people will give you a hearing, and remain juft as they are, till the Lord leads you to
fpeak to them as criminals condemned already, and
whofe firft effential ftep it is, to feek forgivenefs by
the blood of Jefus, and a change of heart and ftate
by his grace, before they can bring forth any fruit
acceptable to God.

As I have little time for writing, and little hope
of fucceeding in a way of argumentation, I have
fubftituted, inftead of a longer letter, the heads of
fome fermons I preached nine or ten years ago, on
our Lord's difcourfe with Nicodemus. However,
when I have heard that you are well, and that you
are ftill difpofed to correfpond with me, I fhall be
ready to give a more particular anfwer to the fubjects you pointed out to me in the letter you favoured me with the day before I left London. I
pray God to blefs you in all your ways, and beg
you to believe, that I am, with fincerity, &c.

G 6   LET.

L E T T E R   VI.

My Dear Friend,   *October* 28.

IT never entered my pericranium, that you expected I fhould fully and directly anfwer your
letter while I was in London; and yet you reafonably might, as you knew nothing of my engagements: but indeed it was impracticable; I could
only fend you a hafty line, as a token that I re-
membered you. I informed you, when I returned,
that I was juft going out again. Since I came home
the fecond time, I have been engroffed by things
that would admit of no delay; and at length, not
having fo much as a note from you, I thought I
would wait till I heard farther. But from firft to
laft it was my intention, and I think my promife,
to anfwer in the manner you propofed, as foon as
I could. And even now I muft beg a little longer
time.—Believe me, that as the wife and good providence of God brought us together, without any
expectation of mine, I will do all in my power to
preferve the connection, and particularly by giving
my thoughts on fuch queftions as you propofe.
And though to confider your queftions in the
manner you wifh, and to point out the agreement
of detached texts (as they occur) with my views,
feems in profpect to require a volume rather than
a fheet, yet I am not difcouraged; only I beg you to
make allowances for other things, and to be affured
that *before* I had the pleafure of correfponding with
you, I had very little fpare time. Expect then the
beft fatisfaction I am able to give you, as foon as
poffible. To prepare the way, I will try hard for a
little leifure, to give you a few thoughts upon yours,
which came laft night.

You

You complain, that I have hitherto difappointed your expectations.—If you have preferved my firft papers, I believe you will find, that I apprifed you this might probably be the event, and certainly muft, unlefs it fhould pleafe God to make what I fhould write a means of giving you the fame views with myfelf. I only propofed as a witnefs, to bear a fimple teftimony to what I had feen and known. So far as you believed me fincere and unwilling to impofe upon you, I thought you might admit, there was perhaps fome weight in what I advanced, though for the prefent you could not fee things in the fame light. And if you allowed a poffibility, that my changing the fentiments which I once held in common with yourfelf might be upon fufficient grounds, you would, as I truft you do, wait upon the great Teacher for his inftruction; otherwife I did not expect to convince you, nor do I yet, only I am glad to put myfelf in his hands as an inftrument.

You quite mifunderftood what I fpoke of the light and influence of the Spirit of God. He reveals to me no new truths, but has only fhewn me the meaning of his own written word; nor is this light a particular revelation, it is common to all who are born again. And thus though you and I cannot fully agree about it, yet I almoft daily meet with perfons from the eaft, weft, north, and fouth, whom, though I never faw them before, I find we underftand each other at once. This (as you bid me be explicit) is the one thing which I think you at prefent lack. And I limited my expreffion *to one thing*, becaufe it is our Lord's expreffion, and becaufe that *one thing* includes many. As I faid before, I cannot give it you; but the Lord can: and from the defire he has raifed in your heart, I have a warm hope that he will. You place the whole ftrefs of your inquiries upon reafon: I am far
from

from difcarding reafon, when it is enlightened and
fanctified; but *fpiritual things muft be fpiritually*
difcerned, and can be received and difcerned no
other way; for to our natural reafon they are fool-
ifhnefs, 1 Cor. ii. 14. 15.; Matth. xi. 25. This certain fomething I can no more defcribe to thofe
who have not experienced it, than I could defcribe
the tafte of a pine apple to a perfon who had never
feen one. But fcriptural proofs might be adduced
in abundance, yet not fo as to give a folid conviction of it, till we actually experience it. Thus it
was with my friend—whofe cafe I fent you. When
God gave him the key (as he expreffed it) then the
fcriptures were unlocked. His wifhing himfelf a
Deift fome time before, was not from any libertine
exceptions he made to the precepts of the gofpel,
but from the perplexing embarraffments he had
found, by endeavouring to underftand the doctrines,
by dint of reafon, though reafon in him was as
ftrong and penetrating as in moft men I ever met
with. Upon your prefent plan, how can I hope
to fatisfy you, though even St Paul afferts it, that
the carnal mind is enmity againft God? You will
readily agree with me to the propofition as it ftands
in St Paul's words, but I think will not fo readily
affent to what I have no more doubt than of my
own exiftence, is the fenfe of it, That the heart
of man, of any man, every man, however apparently amiable in his outward conduct, however
benevolent to his fellow-creatures, however abundant and zealous in his devotions, is by nature enmity againft God; not indeed againft the idea he
himfelf forms of God, but againft the character
which God has revealed of himfelf in the fcripture.
Man is an enemy to the juftice, fovereignty, and
law of God, and to the alone method of falvation
he has appointed in the gofpel by faith only; by
fuch a faith, as it is no more in his power to contribute

bute to the production of in himfelf, than he can
contribute to raifing the dead, or making a world.
Whatever is of the flefh is flefh, and can rife no
higher than its principle; but the Lord could convince you of this by a glance of thought.

But I muft break off, for want both of room and
time. Let me remind you of our agreement, to
ufe and to allow the greateft freedom, and not to
be offended with what is meant well on either fide.
Something in your laft letter made me apprehen-
five you were a little difpleafed with me. He that
knows my heart, knows that I wifh you well as my
own foul.

The expreffion, of atoning for difobedience by
repentance, was in one of your fermons. I confidered it as *unguarded;* but on my view of things,
it were in a manner impoffible I could ufe *that expreffion,* though perhaps too often unguarded myfelf.

I am, &c.

L E T T E R   VII.

My dear Friend,   *November* 17. 1775,

AT length I take up your favour of Auguft 14,
with defign to give a more explicit anfwer.
My delaying hitherto has been unavoidable; I am
forry to have your patience put to fo long a trial,
and fhould be more forry, but that I confider, that
in my former papers, fermons, Omicron's letters, &c. you already poffefs the whole (in fubftance) of what I have to offer. My prefent part
is but *aĉtum agere,* to repeat what I have elfewhere expreffed, only with fome variety and en-
largement,

largement.—You yourfelf well ftate the fituation of
our debate, when you fay, "Nor in truth do you
offer any arguments to convince me, *nor does it
feem very confiftent on your grounds fo to do.* And
if this important change is to be brought about by
the intervention of fome extraordinary impulfe of
the Holy Spirit, and cannot be brought about
without it; I do not fee any thing farther that I
have to do, than to keep my mind as much un-
biaffed as I can, and to wait and pray for it." I
think my letter from London was to the purport
of thefe your own words, though you feemed dif-
fatisfied with it.—While we fee through a different
medium, it will be eafy for you to anfwer every
text I might adduce in fupport of my fentiments,
as you have thofe I have already brought, "That
you underftand them otherwife." In order to fupport my fenfe of one text, I fhould perhaps quote
and argue from twenty more, and ftill "You
would underftand them otherwife." The life of
man, yea of Methufelah, would hardly fuffice to
prove, objeét, and defend, all that might be alledged
on both fides in this way; and at laft we fhould
leave off as we began, more fully confirmed in our
own opinions, unlefs the Lord, by his Holy Spirit,
fhould be pleafed to fhew the perfon who maintained the wrong fide of the argument where his
miftake lay. However, I mean to take fome notice of your queries as they offer themfelves.

The firft which occurs is complicated.—The
fubftance I think is, whether fuch belief and aims
as you poffefs, will ftand you in no ftead unlefs
you likewife believe grace irrefiftible, predeftination
abfolute, faith in fupernatural impulfes, &c.? You
may have obferved, I have feveral times waved
fpeaking about predeftination or eleétion, not that
I am afhamed of the doétrine; becaufe if it be indeed abfurd, fhocking, and unjuft, the blame will

                                         not

not defervedly fall upon me, for I did not invent
it, but upon the fcriptures, where, I am fure, it is
laid down in as plain terms, as that God created
the heavens and the earth. I own I cannot but
wonder, that perfons profeffing any reverence for
the Bible fhould fo openly and ftrongly declare
their abhorrence of what the Bible fo exprefsly
teaches ; namely, that there is a difcrimination of
perfons by the grace and good pleafure of God,
where by nature there is no difference; and that
all things refpecting the falvation of thefe perfons
is infallibly fecured by a divine predeftination.

I do not offer this as a rational doctrine, (though
it be highly fo to me), but it is fcriptural, or elfe
the fcripture is a mere nofe of wax, and without
a determinate meaning. What ingenuity is needful to interpret many paffages in a fenfe more favourable to our natural prejudices againft God's
fovereignty ! Matth. xi. 25. 26. and xiii. 10.—17.
Mark, xiii. 20. 22. John, xvii. *paffim.* John, x. 26.
Rom. viii. 28.—30. and ix. 13.—24. and xi. 7.
Eph. i. 4. 5. 1 Pet. i. 2. Were I fond of difputing,
as I am not, I think I could put a clofe reafoner
hard to it, to maintain the truth of fcripture prophecies, or the belief of a particular providence,
unlefs he would admit a divine predeftination of
caufes and events as the ground of his arguments.
However, as I faid, I have chofen to wave the
point ; becaufe, however true and neceffary in itfelf, the knowledge and comprehenfion of it is not
neceffary to the being of a true Chriftian, though
I can hardly conceive he can be an eftablifhed confiftent believer without it. This doctrine is not the
turning point between you and me ; the nature of
juftification, and the method of a finner's acceptance with God, are of much more immediate importance ; and therefore, if I am to fpeak plainly,
I muft fay, that I look upon your prefent fentiments,

ments, attainments, and advances, as you defcribe
them, to conftitute that kind of gain the apoftle
fpeaks of, and concerning which I hope you will
one day be of his mind, and be glad to account it
all lofs, that you may *win Chrift*, and *be found in
him*, " not having your own righteoufnefs, which
" is of the law, but the righteoufnefs which is of
" God by faith," Phil. iii. 4. 7.—10. For, as you
tell me, you never remember a time when you
were not confcious before God of great unworthinefs, and intervals of earneft endeavours to ferve
him, though not with the fame fuccefs, yet fomething in the fame way as at prefent: this is but
faying in other words, you never remember a time
when old things paffed away, and all things became new ; and yet the apoftle infifts much upon
this, 2 Cor. iv. 6. and v. 17. The convictions of
natural confcience, and thofe which are wrought
in the heart by the Holy Spirit, are different not
only in degree but in kind ; the light of a glow-
worm and of the fun do not more effentially differ.
The former are partial and fuperficial, leave us in
poffeffion of a fuppofed power of our own, are pacified by fome appearances of an outward change,
and make us no further fenfible of the neceffity of
a Saviour, than to make our doings and duties
(if I may fo exprefs myfelf) full weight, which perhaps might otherwife be a little deficient when
brought to the balances of the fanctuary. But
truly fpiritual convictions give us far other views
of fin ; they lead us to a deep and awful confideration of the *root*, our total abfolute depravity, and
our utter apoftacy from God, by which we are incapable of doing good, as a dead man is of performing the functions of life. They lead us to the
rule and *ftandard*, the ftrict, holy, inflexible law
of God, which reaches to the thoughts and intents
of the heart ; requires perfect, univerfal, perfeve-
ring

ring obedience; denounces a curfe upon every fai-
lure, Gal. iii. 10.; and affords neither place or
ftrength for repentance. Thus they fweep away
every hope and refuge we had before, and fix upon
us a fenfe of guilt and condemnation, from which
there is no relief, till we can look to Jefus, as the
wounded Ifraelites did to the brazen ferpent; which
was not to give efficacy to medicines and plafters
of their own application, but to heal them completely of itfelf by looking at it. John, iii. 14. 15.
and vi. 40. Ifaiah, xliii. 22.

You wifh me to explain my diftinction between
faith and rational affent; and though I know no
two things in the world more clearly diftinct in
themfelves, or more exprefsly diftinguifhed in fcripture, yet I fear I may not eafily make it appear to
you. You allow faith, in your fenfe, to be the gift
of God; but in my fenfe, it is likewife wrought by
the operation of God, Col. ii. 12. το υπερβαλλον
μεγεθος της δυναμεως αυτου—κατα την ενεργειαν του
κρατους της ισχυος αυτου; * that fame energy of the
power of his ftrength, by which the dead body of
Jefus was raifed from the dead: Can thefe ftrong
expreffions intend no more than a rational affent,
fuch as we give to a propofition in Euclid? I believe fallen reafon is, of itfelf, utterly incapable
even of affenting to the great truths of revelation;
it may affent to the terms in which they are propofed, but it muft put its own interpretation upon
them, or it would defpife them. The natural man
can neither receive or difcern the things of God:
and if any one would be wife, the apoftle's firft
advice to him is, Let him become a fool, that he
may be wife; for the wifdom of the world is fool-
ifhnefs with God.

* Ephef. i. 19.

Indeed

Indeed when the heart is changed, and the mind enlightened, then reafon is fanctified, and if I may fo fay, baptized, renounces its curious difquifitions, and is content humbly to tread in the path of revelation. This is one difference, affent may be the act of our natural reafon; faith is the effect of immediate almighty power. Another difference is, faith is always efficacious, " it worketh by love;" whereas affent is often given where it has little or no influence upon the conduct. Thus, for inftance, every one will affent to this truth, all men are mortal. Yet the greateft part of mankind, though they readily affent to the propofition, and it would be highly irrational to do otherwife, yet live as they might do if the reverfe were true. But they who have divine faith, feel as well as fay they are pilgrims and fojourners upon earth. Again, faith gives peace of confcience, accefs to God, and a fure evidence and fubfiftence of things not feen, Rom. v. 1. 2. Heb. xi. 1.; whereas a calm difpaffionate reafoner may be compelled to affent to the external arguments in favour of Chriftianity, and yet remain a total ftranger to that communion with God, that fpirit of adoption, that foretafte of glory, which is the privilege and portion of believers. So likewife faith overcomes the world, which rational affent will not do. Witnefs the lives and tempers of thoufands, who yet would be affronted if their affent to the gofpel fhould be queftioned. To fum up all in a word, " He that believes fhall be faved." But furely many who give a rational affent to the gofpel, live and die in thofe fins which exclude from the kingdom of God, Gal. v. 19.—21. Faith is the effect of a principle of new life implanted in the foul, that was before dead in trefpaffes and fins; and it qualifies not only for obeying the Saviour's precepts, but chiefly and primarily for receiving from

and

and rejoicing in his fulnefs, admiring his love, his work, his perfon, his glory, his advocacy. It makes Chrift precious, enthrones him in the heart, prefents him as the moft delightful objeƈt to our meditations ; as our wifdom, righteoufnefs, fanctification, and ftrength ; our root, head, life, fhepherd, and hufband. Thefe are all fcriptural expreffions and images, fetting forth, fo far as words can declare, what Jefus is in himfelf and to his believing people. But how cold is the comment which rational affent puts upon very many paffages, wherein the Apoftle Paul endeavours (but in vain) to exprefs the fulnefs of his heart upon this fubjeƈt. A moft valued friend of mine, a clergyman now living, had for many years given a rational affent to the gofpel. He laboured with much earneftnefs upon your plan, was very exemplary in his whole conduƈt, preached almoft inceffantly, (two or three times every day in the week for years), having a parifh in the remote parts of *Yorkfhire*, of great extent, and containing five or fix different hamlets at fome diftance from each other. He fucceeded likewife with his people, fo far as to break them off from outward irregularities ; and was mentioned in a letter to the Society for propagating the Gofpel (which I have feen in print) as the moft perfeƈt example of a parifh-prieft which this nation, or perhaps this age, has produced. Thus he went on for many years, teaching his people what he knew, for he could teach them no more. He lived in fuch retirement and recefs, that he was unacquainted with the perfons and principles of any who are now branded as enthufiafts and methodifts. One day reading Ephef. iii. in his Greek Teftament, his thoughts were ftopped by the word ανεξιχνιαστον in verfe 8. He was ftruck, and led to think with himfelf to this purpofe : " The apoftle, when fpeaking of the love and riches of Chrift, ufes remarkable

able expreffions ; he fpeaks of heights, depths, and
lengths, and breadths, and unfearchables, where I
feem to find every thing plain, eafy, and rational.
He finds myfteries where I can perceive none. Surely, though I ufe the words gofpel, faith, and grace
with him, my ideas of them muft be different from
his." This led him to a clofe examination of all
his epiftles, and, by the bleffing of God, brought
on a total change in his views and preaching. He
no longer fet his people to keep a law of faith, to
truft in their finceity and endeavours, upon fome
general hope that Chrift would help them out where
they came fhort ; but he preached Chrift himfelf,
as the end of the law for righteoufnefs to every
one that believeth. He felt himfelf, and laboured to convince others, that there is no hope for a
finner, but merely in the blood of Jefus, and no
poffibility of his doing any works acceptable to God,
till he himfelf be firft made accepted in the beloved. Nor did he labour in vain. Now his preaching effected not only an outward reformation, but
a real change of heart in very many of his hearers.
The word was received, as Paul expreffes it, not
with a rational affent only, but with demonftration
and power, in the Holy Ghoft, and in much affurance ; and their endeavours to obferve the gofpel-
precepts were abundantly more extenfive, uniform,
and fuccefsful, when they were brought to fay with
the apoftle, " I am crucified with Chrift : never-
" thelefs I live, yet not I, but Chrift liveth in me ;
" and the life I live in the flefh, I live by faith in
" the Son of God."

Such a change of views and fentiments I pray
God my friend may experience. Thefe things may
appear uncouth to you at prefent, as they have
done to many, who now blefs God for fhewing
them what their reafon could never have taught
them. My divinity is unfafhionable enough at
                                              prefent,

prefent, but it was not fo always; you will find few books written from the æra of the Reformation till a little before Laud's time, that fet forth any other. There were few pulpits till after the Reftoration from which any other was heard. A lamentable change has indeed fince taken place; but God has not left himfelf without witneffes. You think, though I difclaim infallibility, I arrogate too much in fpeaking with fo much certainty. I am fallible indeed; but I am fure of the main points of doctrine I hold. I am not in the leaft doubt, whether falvation be of faith or of works; whether faith be of our own power or of God's operation; whether Chrift's obedience, or our own, be the juft ground of our hope; whether a man can truly call Jefus Lord but by the teaching of the Holy Ghoft. I have no more hefitation about thefe points than I fhould have were I afked, Whether it was God or man who created the heavens and the earth? Befides, as I have more than once obferved, your fentiments were once my own; fo that I, who have travelled both roads, may have perhaps fome ftronger reafons to determine me which is the right, than you can have who have only travelled one.

Your two fheets may lead me to write as many quires, if I do not check myfelf. I now come to the two queries you propofe, the folution of which you think will clearly mark the difference of our fentiments. The fubftance of them is, 1*ft*, Whether I think any finner ever perifhed in his fins (to whom the gofpel has been preached) becaufe God refufed to fupply him with fuch a proportion of his affiftance as was abfolutely neceffary to his believing and repenting, or without his having previoufly rejected the incitements of his Holy Spirit? A full anfwer to this would require a fheet. But briefly, I believe that all mankind, being corrupt and guilty

'ty before God, he might, without impeachment to his juſtice, have left them all to periſh, as we are aſſured he did the fallen angels. But he has pleaſed to ſhew mercy, and mercy muſt be free. If the ſinner has any claim to it, ſo far it is juſtice, not mercy. HE, who is to be our judge, aſſures us, that *few* find the gate that leadeth to life; while many throng the road to deſtruction. Your queſtion ſeems to imply, that you think God either did make ſalvation equally *open to all*, or that it would have been more becoming his goodneſs to have done ſo.

But he is the potter, we are the clay: his ways and thoughts are above ours, as the heavens are higher than the earth. The Judge of all the earth *will* do right. He has appointed a day, when he will manifeſt, to the conviction of *all*, that *He has done right.* Till then, I hold it beſt to take things upon his word, and not too harſhly determine what it becomes Jehovah to do. Inſtead of ſaying what *I* think, let it ſuffice to remind you of what St Paul thought, Rom. ix. 15.—21. But farther, I ſay, that unleſs mercy were afforded to thoſe who are ſaved, in a way peculiar to themſelves, and which is not afforded to thoſe who periſh, I believe no one ſoul could be ſaved. For I believe fallen man, univerſally conſidered *as* ſuch, is as incapable of doing the leaſt thing towards his ſalvation, till prevented by the grace of God, (as our article ſpeaks), as a dead body is of reſtoring itſelf to life. Whatever difference takes place between men in this reſpect is *of Grace*, that is of God, undeſerved. Yea, his firſt approaches to our hearts are undeſired too; for till he ſeeks us, we cannot, we will not ſeek him, Pſalm cx. 3. It is in the day of his power, and not before, his people are made willing. But I believe where the goſpel is preached, they who do periſh, do wilfully reſiſt the
light,

light, and chufe and cleave to darknefs, and ftifle
the convictions which the truths of God, *when his
true gofpel is indeed preached,* will, in one degree or
other, force upon their minds. The cares of this
world, the deceitfulnefs of riches, the love of other
things, the violence of finful appetites, their prejudices, pride, and felf-righteoufnefs, either prevent the reception, or choke the growth of the
good feed: thus their own fin and obftinacy is the
proper caufe of their deftruction; they *will* not
come to Chrift that they may have life. At the
fame time, it is true that they cannot, unlefs they are
fupernaturally drawn of God, John, v. 40. vi. 44.
They will not, and they cannot come. Both are
equally true, and they are confiftent. For a man's
cannot is not a natural but a moral inability: not
an impoffibility in the nature of things, as it is for
me to walk upon the water, or to fly in the air;
but fuch an inability, as inftead of extenuating, does
exceedingly enhance and aggravate his guilt. He is
fo blinded by Satan, fo alienated from God by nature and wicked works, fo given up to fin, fo averfe
from that way of falvation, which is contrary to his
pride and natural wifdom, that he will not embrace
it or feek after it; and therefore he cannot, till the
grace of God powerfully enlightens his mind, and
overcomes his obftacles.—But this brings me to
your fecond query.

II. Do I think that God, in the ordinary courfe
of his providence, grants this affiftance in an irrefiftible manner, or effects faith and converfion without the finner's own hearty confent and concurrence? I rather chofe to term grace *invincible* than
irrefiftible: For it is too often refifted even by thofe
who believe; but becaufe it is invincible, it triumphs
over all refiftance when he is pleafed to beftow it.
For the reft, I believe no finner is converted without his own hearty will and concurrence. But he
VOL. II   H   is

is not willing till he is made fo. Why does he at all refufe? Becaufe he is infenfible of his ftate; becaufe he knows not the evil of fin, the ftrictnefs of the law, the majefty of God whom he has offended, nor the total apoftacy of his heart; becaufe he is blind to eternity, and ignorant of the excellency of Chrift; becaufe he is comparatively whole, and fees not his need of this great phyfician; becaufe he relies upon his own wifdom, power, and fuppofed righteoufnefs. Now in this ftate of things, when God comes with a purpofe of mercy, he begins by convincing the perfon of fin, judgement, and righteoufnefs, caufes him to feel and know that he is a loft, condemned, helplefs creature, and then difcovers to him the neceffity, fufficiency, and willingnefs of Chrift to fave them that are ready to perifh, without money or price, without doings or defervings.—Then he fees faith to be very different from a rational affent, finds that nothing but the power of God can produce a well-grounded hope in the heart of a convinced finner; therefore looks to Jefus, who is the author and finifher of faith, to enable him to believe. For this he waits in what we call the means of grace; he prays, he reads the word, he thirfts for God, as the hart pants for the water-brooks; and though perhaps for a while he is diftreffed with many doubts and fears, he is encouraged to wait on, becaufe Jefus has faid, "Him "that cometh unto me, I will in no wife caft out." The obftinacy of the will remains while the underftanding is dark, and ceafes when that is enlightened. Suppofe a man walking in the dark, where there are pits and precipices of which he is not aware: *You* are fenfible of his danger, and call after him; but he thinks he knows better than you, refufes your advice, and is perhaps angry with you for your importunity. He fees no danger, therefore will not be perfuaded there is any; but if you

go

go with a light, get before him, and fhew him
plainly, that if he takes another ftep he falls beyond the power of recovery,—then he will ftop of
his own accord, blame himfelf for not minding
you before, and be ready to comply with your farther directions. In either cafe man's will acts with
equal freedom; the difference of his conduct arifes
from conviction. Something like this is the cafe
of our fpiritual concerns. Sinners are called and
warned by the word; but they are wife in their
own eyes, and take but little notice till the Lord
gives them light, which he is not bound to give to
any, and therefore cannot be bound to give to *all.*
They who have it have reafon to be thankful, and
fubfcribe to the apoftle's words : " By grace are ye
" faved, through faith; and that not of yourfelves,
" it is the gift of God."

I have not yet half done with the firft fheet;
fhall confider the reft at leifure, but fend this as a
fpecimen of my willingnefs to clear my fentiments
to you as far as I can. Unlefs it fhould pleafe
God to make what I offer fatisfactory, I well know
beforehand what objections and anfwers will occur to you; for thefe points have been often de-
bated; and after a courfe of twenty-feven years,
in which religion has been the chief object of my
thoughts and enquiries, I am not entirely a ftranger
to what can be offered on either fide. What I
write, I write fimply and in love ; befeeching him,
who alone can fet a feal to his own truth, to guide
you and blefs you. This letter has been more than
a week in hand; I have been called from it I fuppofe ten times, frequently in the middle of a period
or a line. My leifure, which before was fmall, is
now reduced almoft to a nothing. But I am defirous
to keep up my correfpondence with you, becaufe I
feel an affectionate intereft in you, and becaufe it
pleafed God to put it into your heart to apply to

H 2 me.

me. You cannot think how your firſt letter ſtruck
me: it was ſo unexpected, and ſeemed ſo impro-
bable that you ſhould open your mind to me, I
immediately conceived a hope that it would prove
for good. Nor am I yet diſcouraged.

When you have leiſure and inclination, write; I
ſhall always be glad to hear from you,. and I will
proceed in anſwering what I have already by me,
as faſt as I can.—But I have many letters now waiting for anſwers, which muſt be attended to.

I recommend you to the bleſſing and care of the
great Shepherd; and remain, &c.

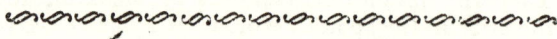

LETTER   VIII.

My dear Friend,   *December* 8. 1775.

ARE you willing I ſhould ſtill call you ſo, or
are you quite weary of me? Your ſilence makes
me ſuſpect the latter. However, it is my part to
fulfil my promiſe, and then leave the event to God.
As I have but an imperfect remembrance of what
I have already written, I may be liable to ſome re-
petitions. I cannot ſtay to comment upon every
line in your letter, but I proceed to notice ſuch
paſſages as ſeem moſt to affect the ſubject in debate.
When you ſpeak of the ſcripture's maintaining one
conſiſtent ſenſe, which, if the word of God, it
certainly muſt do, you ſay you read and underſtand it in this one conſiſtent ſenſe; nay, you cannot remember the time when you did not. It is
otherwiſe with me, and with multitudes; we remember when it was a ſealed book, and we are ſure
it would have been ſo ſtill, had not the Holy
Spirit opened our underſtandings. But when you
                                          add,

add, though I pretend not to underſtand the
whole, yet what I do underſtand appears perfectly
conſiſtent: I know not how far this exception may
extend, for perhaps the reaſon why you allow you
do not underſtand ſome parts, is becauſe you cannot make them conſiſtent with the ſenſe you put
upon other parts. You quote my words, " That
when we are conſcious of our depravity, reaſoning
ſtands us in no ſtead." Undoubtedly reaſon always
will ſtand rational creatures in ſome ſtead ; but my
meaning is, that when we are deeply convinced of
ſin, all our former reaſonings upon the ways of
God, while we made *our* conceptions the ſtandard
by which we judge what is befitting him to do, as
if we were altogether ſuch an one as ourſelves —
all thoſe cobweb reaſonings are ſwept away, and we
ſubmit to his αυτος εφη without *reaſoning*, though
not without *reaſon*. For we have the ſtrongeſt
reaſon imaginable to acknowledge ourſelves vile
and loſt, without righteouſneſs and ſtrength, when
we actually feel ourſelves to be ſo.—You ſpeak of
the goſpel terms of juſtification.—This term is *faith.*
Mark, xvi. 16. Acts, xiii. 39. The goſpel pro-
pounds, admits no other term. But this *faith,* as
I endeavoured to ſhew in my former letter, is very
different from rational aſſent. You ſpeak likewiſe
of the law of *faith ;* by which, if you mean what
ſome call the remedial law, which we are to obey
as well as we can, and ſuch obedience, together
with our faith, will entitle us to acceptance with
God, I am perſuaded the ſcripture ſpeaks of no
ſuch thing. Grace and works of any kind, in the
point of acceptance with God, are mentioned by
the apoſtle not only as oppoſites or contraries, but
as abſolutely contradictory to each other, like fire
and water, light and darkneſs ; ſo that the affirma-
tion of one is the denial of the other. Rom. iv. 5.
and xi. 6. God juſtifies freely, juſtifies the ungod-

H 3   ly,

ly, and him that worketh not. Though juſtifying
faith be indeed an active principle, it worketh by *love*,
yet not for acceptance. Thoſe whom the apoſtle
exhorts " to work out their own ſalvation with
" *fear* and *trembling*," he conſiders as juſtified already ; for he conſiders them as believers, in whom
he ſuppoſed God had already begun a good work ;
and if ſo, was confident he would accompliſh it.
Phil. i. 6. To them, the conſideration, that God
(who dwells in the hearts of believers) wrought in
them to will and to do, was a powerful motive and
encouragement to them to work ; that is, to give
all diligence in his appointed means ; as a right
ſenſe of the ſin that dwelleth in us, and the ſnares
and temptations around us, will teach us ſtill to
work with fear and trembling. You ſuppoſe a difference between Chriſtians (ſo called) who are
devoted to God in baptiſm, and thoſe who in the
firſt ages were converted from abominable ſuperſti-
tions and idolatrous vices.—It is true, in Chriſtian
countries we do not worſhip Heathen divinities *eo
nomine*. And this is the principal difference I can
find. Neither reaſon or obſervation will allow me
to think, that human nature is a whit better now
than it was in the apoſtle's time. I know no kinds
or degrees of wickedneſs which prevailed among
Heathens, which are not prevalent among nominal
Chriſtians, who have perhaps been baptiſed in their
infancy ; and therefore, as the ſtreams in the life
are equally worldly, ſenſual, deviliſh, I doubt not
but the fountain in the heart is equally polluted
and poiſonous ; and that it is as true, as in the
days of Chriſt and his apoſtles, that unleſs a man
be born again, he cannot ſee the kingdom of God.
You ſent me a ſermon upon the new birth, or regeneration, and you have ſeveral of mine on the
ſame ſubject. I wiſh you to compare them with
each other, and with the ſcripture ; and I pray
God

God to fhew you wherein the difference confifts, and on which fide the truth lies.

When you defire me to reconcile God's being the author of fin with his juftice, you fhew that you mifunderftand the whole ftrain of my fentiments; for I am perfuaded you would not mifreprefent them. It is eafy to charge harfh confequences, which I neither allow, nor indeed do they follow from my fentiments. God cannot be the author of fin in that fenfe you would fix upon me; but is it poffible that upon your plan you find no difficulty in what the fcripture teaches us upon this fubject? I conceive, that thofe who were concerned in the death of Chrift were very great finners; and that in nailing him to the crofs they committed atrocious wickednefs: Yet, if the apoftle may be believed, all this was according to the determinate council and foreknowledge of God, Acts, ii. 23.; and they did no more than what his hand and purpofe had determined fhould be done, chap. iv. 28. And you will obferve, that this wicked act (wicked with refpect to the perpetrators) was not only permitted, but fore-ordained in the ftrongeft and moft abfolute fenfe of the word: The glory of God and the falvation of men depended upon its being done, and juft in that manner, and with all thofe circumftances which actually took place; and yet Judas and the reft acted freely, and their wickednefs was properly their own. Now, my friend, the arguments which fatisfy you, that the fcripture does not reprefent God as the author of this fin in this appointment, will plead for me at the fame time; and when you think you eafily overcome me by afking, " Can God be the author of fin?" your imputation falls as directly upon the word of God himfelf. God is no more the author of fin, than the fun is the caufe of ice; but it is in the nature of water to congeal into ice when the fun's

influence

influence is fufpended to a certain degree. So
there is fin enough in the hearts of men to make
the earth the very image of hell, and to prove that
men are no better than incarnate devils, were he
to fufpend his influence and reftraint. Sometimes,
and in fome inftances, he is pleafed to fufpend it
confiderably; and fo far as *he* does, human nature
quickly appears in its true colours. Objections of
this kind have been repeated and refuted before
either you or I were born; and the apoftle evidently
fuppofes they would be urged againft his doctrine,
when he obviates the queftion, Why doth he yet
find fault? who hath refifted his will? To which
he gives no other anfwer than by referring it to
God's fovereignty, and the power which a potter
has over the clay. I think I have in a former letter made fome reply to the charge of pofitivenefs
in my own opinion. I acknowledge that I am fallible; yet I muft again lay claim to a certainty about
the way of falvation. I am as fure of fome things
as of my own exiftence: I fhould be fo if there was
no human creature upon earth but myfelf. However, my fentiments are confirmed by the fuffrages
of thoufands who have lived before me, of many
with whom I have perfonally converfed in different
places and circumftances, unknown to each other;
yet all have received the fame views, becaufe taught
by the fame Spirit. And I have likewife been
greatly confirmed by the teftimony of many with
whom I have converfed in their dying hours. I
have feen them rejoicing in the profpect of death,
free from fears, breathing the air of immortality;
heartily difclaiming their duties and performances;
acknowledging that their beft actions were attended
with evil fufficient to condemn them; renouncing
every fhadow of hope, but what they derived from
the blood of Chrift, as the fole caufe of their acceptance; yet triumphing in him over every enemy
and

and fear, and as fure of heaven as if they were already there. And fuch were the apoftle's hopes, wholly founded on knowing whom he had believed, and his perfuafion of his ability to keep that which he had committed unto him. This is faith, a renouncing of every thing we are apt to call our own, and relying wholly upon the blood, righteoufnefs, and interceffion of Jefus. However, I cannot communicate this my certainty to you; I only tell you there is fuch a thing, in hopes, if you do not think I wilfully lie both to God and man, you will be earneft to feek it from him, who beftowed it on me, and who will beftow it upon all who will fincerely apply to him, and patiently wait upon him for it.

I cannot but wonder, that while you profefs to believe the depravity of human nature, you fhould fpeak of good qualities inherent in it. The word of God defcribes it as *evil, only evil,* and that *continually.* That there are fuch qualities as Stoics and infidels call virtue, I allow. God has not left man deftitute of fuch difpofitions as are neceffary to the peace of fociety; but I deny there is any moral goodnefs in them, unlefs they are founded in a fupreme love to God, have his glory for their aim, and are produced by faith in Jefus Chrift. A man may give all his goods to feed the poor, and his body to be burned, in zeal for the truth, and yet be a mere nothing, a tinkling cymbal, in the fight of him who feeth not as man feeth, but judgeth the heart. Many infidels and avowed enemies to the grace and gofpel of Chrift, have made a fair fhew of what the world call virtue; but Chriftian *virtue* is *grace,* the effect of a new nature and new life; and works thus wrought in God are as different from the faint partial imitations of them which fallen nature is capable of producing, as a living man is from a ftatue. A ftatue may exprefs the features and li-

H 5 　　　　　neaments

neaments of the perfon whom it reprefents, but there is no life.

Your comment on the feventh to the Romans, latter part, contradicts my feelings. You are either of a different make and nature from me, or elfe you are not rightly apprifed of your own ftate, if you do not find the Apoftle's complaints very fuitable to yourfelf. I believe it applicable to the moft holy Chriftian upon earth. But controverfies of this kind are worn thread-bare. When you fpeak of the fpiritual part of a natural man, it founds to me like the living part of a dead man, or the feeing part of a blind man. Paul tells me, that the natural man (whatever his fpiritual part may be) can neither receive or difcern the things of God. What the Apoftle fpeaks of himfelf, Rom. vii. is no more, when rightly underftood, than what he affirms of all who are partakers of a fpiritual life, or who are true believers, Gal. v. 17. The carnal natural mind is enmity againft God, not fubject to the law of God, neither indeed can be.—When you fubjoin, " Till it be fet at liberty from the law of fin," you do not comment upon the text, but make an addition of your own, which the text will by no means bear. The carnal mind is enmity. An enemy may be reconciled ; but enmity itfelf is incurable. This carnal mind, natural man, old man, flefh, for the expreffions are all equivalent, and denote and include the heart of man as he is by nature, may be *crucified, muft* be *mortified,* but cannot be *fanctified. All* that is *good* or *gracious* is the effect of a *new creation,* a *fupernatural principle,* wrought in the heart by the gofpel of Chrift, and the agency of his Spirit ; and till that is effected, the το υψηλον, the higheft attainment, the fineft qualifications in man, however they may exalt him in his own eyes, or recommend him to the notice of his fellow-worms, are but abomination in the fight of God, Luke,

xvi.

xvi. 15. The gofpel is calculated and defigned to
ftain the pride of human glory. It is provided, not
for the wife and the righteous, for thofe who think
they have good difpofitions and good works to plead,
but for the guilty, the helplefs, the wretched, for
thofe who are ready to perifh; it fills the hungry
with good things, but it fends the rich empty away.
See Rev. iii. 17. 18.

You afk, If man can do nothing without an extraordinary impulfe from on high, is he to fit ftill
and carelefs ? By no means.—I am far from faying man can do nothing, though I believe he
cannot open his own eyes, or give himfelf faith.—
I wifh every man to abftain carefully from finful
company, and finful actions, to read the Bible, to
pray to God for his heavenly teaching. For this
waiting upon God he has a moral ability; and if he
perfevere thus in feeking, the promife is fure, that
he fhall not feek in vain. But I would not have
him miftake the means for the end; think himfelf
good becaufe he is preferved from grofs vices and
follies; or truft to his religious courfe of duties for
acceptance; nor be fatisfied till Chrift be revealed
in him, formed within him, dwell in his heart by
faith, and till he can fay upon good grounds, " I
" am crucified with Chrift : neverthelefs I live; yet
" not I, but Chrift liveth in me." I need not tell
you thefe are fcriptural expreffions; I am perfuaded, if they were not, they would be exploded by
many as unintelligible jargon. True faith, my dear
Sir, unites the foul to Chrift, and thereby gives accefs to God, and fills it with a peace paffing underftanding, a hope, a joy unfpeakable and full of
glory; teaches us that we are weak in ourfelves,
but enables us to be ftrong in the Lord, and in the
power of his might. To thofe who thus believe,
Chrift is precious, their beloved; they hear and
know his voice; the very found of his name glad-

H 6   dens

dens their hearts, and *he manifests himself* to *them*
as *he does not* to the *world.* Thus the scriptures
speak, thus the first Christians experienced; and
this is precisely the language which in our days is
despised as enthusiasm and folly. For it is now as
it was then, though *these things* are *revealed* to
babes, and they are as sure of them as that they see
the noon-day sun, they are hidden from the wise and
prudent, till the Lord makes them willing to renounce
their own wisdom, and to become fools, that they
may be truly wise, 1 Cor. i. 18. 19.; iii. 8.; viii. 2.
Attention to the education of children is an un-
doubted duty; and it is a mercy when it so far suc-
ceeds as to preserve them from gross wickedness;
but it will not change the heart. They who receive
Christ are born, not of blood, nor of the will of
the flesh, nor of the will of man, but of God; John,
i. 13.

If a man professes to love the Lord Jesus, I am
willing to believe him, if he does not give me proof
to the contrary; but I am sure, at the same time,
no one can love him in the scriptural sense who does
not know the need and the worth of a Saviour;
in other words, who is not brought, as a ruined
helpless sinner, to live upon him for wisdom, righteousness, sanctification, and redemption. They
who love him thus will speak highly of him, and
acknowledge that he is their all in all. And they
who thus love him, and speak of him, will get little
thanks for their pains in such a world as this:——
" All that live godly in Christ Jesus must suffer
" persecution; the world that hated him, will hate
" them." And though it is possible by his grace
to put to silence, in some measure, the ignorance
of foolish men; and though his providence can
protect his people, so that not a hair of their
heads can be hurt without his permission; yet the
world will *shew their teeth,* if they are not *suffer-*
ed

ed to *bite.* The Apoftles were accounted bablers, ως περικαθαρματα του κοσμου και παντων περιψημα. I need not point out to you the force of thefe ex- preffions. We are no better than the apoftles ; nor have we reafon to expect much better treatment, fo far as we walk in their fteps. On the other hand, there is a fober decent way of fpeaking of God, and goodnefs, and benevolence, and fobriety, which the world will bear well enough ;—nay, we may fay a little about Jefus Chrift, as ready to make up the deficiencies of our honeft and good endea- vours, and this will not difpleafe them. But if we preach him as the only foundation, lay open the horrid evils of the human heart, tell our hearers that they are dead in trefpaffes and fins, and have no better ground of hope in themfelves than the vileft malefactors, in order to exalt the glory of Jefus, as faving thofe who are faved wholly and freely for his own name's fake ; if we tell the *vir- tuous* and *decent,* as well as the *profligate,* that un- lefs they are *born again,* and made *partakers* of *li- ving faith,* and *count all things lofs* for *the excel- lency of the knowledge of Chrift,* they cannot be fa- ved ; this the world cannot bear. We fhall be call- ed knaves or fools, uncharitable bigots, and twenty hard names. If you have met with nothing like this, I wifh it may lead you to fufpect whether you have yet received the right key to the doctrines of Chrift ; for, depend upon it, the offence of the crofs is not ceafed.

I am grieved and furprifed that you feem to take little notice of any thing in the account of my de- ceafed friend, but his wifhing himfelf to be a Deift, and his having play-books about him in his illnefs. As to the plays, they were *Shakefpeare's,* which, as a man of tafte, it is no great wonder he fhould fometimes look in. Your remark on the other point fhews that you are not much acquainted with the

the exercifes of the human mind under certain
circumftances. I believe I obferved formerly, that
it was not a libertine wifh. Had you known him,
you would have known one of the moft amiable and
unblemifhed characters. Few were more beloved
and admired for an uniform courfe of integrity, moderation, and benevolence; but he was difcouraged.
He ftudied the Bible, believed it in general to be
the word of God; but his wifdom, his ftrong turn
for reafoning, ftood fo in his way, that he could
get no folid comfort from it. He felt the vanity
of the fchemes propofed by many men admired in
the world as teachers of divinity; and he felt the
vanity likewife of his own. He was alfo a minifter, and had a fincere defign of doing good. He
wifhed to reform the profligate, and comfort the
afflicted by his preaching; but as he was not acquainted with that one kind of preaching which
God owns to the edification of the hearers, he found
he could do neither. A fenfe of difappointments
of this kind diftreffed him. Finding in himfelf
none of that peace which the fcripture fpeaks of,
and none of the influence he hoped for, attending
his miniftry, he was led fometimes to queftion the
truth of the fcripture. We have a fpiritual enemy
always near, to prefs upon a mind in this defpond-
ing fituation : nor am I furprifed that ne fhould
then wifh himfelf a Deift; fince, if there were
any hope for a finner but by faith in the blood of
Jefus, he had as much of his own goodnefs to depend upon as moft I have known. As for the reft,
if you could fee nothing admirable and wonderful
in the clearnefs, the dignity, the fpirituality of his
expreffions, after the Lord revealed the gofpel to
him, I can only fay, I am forry for it. This I
know, that fome perfons of fenfe, tafte, learning,
and reafon, and far enough from *my fentiments*, have
been greatly ftruck with them. You fay, a death-bed
                                        repentance

repentance is what you would be forry to give any
hope of.   My dear friend, it is well for poor finners
that God's thoughts and ways are as much above
mens, as the heavens are higher than the earth.
We agreed to communicate our fentiments freely,
and promifed not to be offended with each other's
freedom, if we could help it.   I am afraid of offend-
ing you by a thought juft now upon my mind, and
yet I dare not in confcience fupprefs it: I muft
therefore venture to fay, that I hope they who depend upon fuch a repentance as your fcheme points
out, will repent of their repentance itfelf upon their
deathbed at leaft, if not fooner.   You and I, perhaps, fhould have encouraged the fair-fpoken young
man, who faid he had kept all the commandments
from his youth, and rather have left the thief upon
the crofs to perifh like a villain, as he lived.   But
Jefus thought differently.   I do not encourage finners to defer their repentance to their deathbeds—
I prefs the neceffity of a repentance this moment.
But then I take care to tell them, that repentance
is the gift of God; that Jefus is exalted to beftow
it; and that all their endeavours that way, unlefs
they feek to him for grace, will be vain as wafhing
a Blackmoor, and tranfient as wafhing a fwine,
which will foon return to the mire again.   I know
the evil heart will abufe the grace of God; the A-
poftle knew this likewife, Rom. iii. 8. and vi. 3.   But
this did not tempt him to fupprefs the glorious grace
of the gofpel, the power of Jefus to fave to the uttermoft, and his merciful promife, that whofoever
cometh unto him, he will in no wife caft out.   The
repentance of a natural heart, proceeding wholly
from fear, like that of fome malefactors, who are
forry, not that they have committed robbery or
murder, but that they muft be hanged for it; this
undoubtedly is nothing worth, whether in time
of health, or in a dying hour.   But that μετανοια,
that

that gracious change of heart, views, and difpofitions, which always takes place when Jefus is made
known to the foul as having died that the finner
might live, and been wounded that he might be
healed ; this, at whatever period God is pleafed
to afford and effect it by his Spirit, brings a fure
and everlafting falvation with it.

Still I find I have not done : you afk my expofition of the parables of the talents and pounds ; but
at prefent I can write no more. I have only juft
time to tell you, that when I begged your acceptance of Omicron, nothing was farther from my
expectation than a correfpondence with you. The
frank and kind manner in which you wrote prefently won upon my heart. In the courfe of our
letters upon Subfcription, I obferved an integrity
and difintereftednefs in you, which endeared you
to me ftill more. Since that our debates have taken a much more interefting turn ; I have confidered it as a call, and an opportunity put in my
hand, by the efpecial providence of him who ruleth
over all. I have embraced the occafion to lay before you fimply, and rather in a way of teftimony
than argumentation, what (in the main) I am fure
is truth. I have done enough to difcharge my confcience, but fhall never think I do enough to anfwer
the affection I bear you. I have done enough likewife to make you weary of my correfpondence, unlefs it fhould pleafe God to fix the fubject deeply
upon your mind, and make you attentive to the
poffibility and vaft importance of a miftake in matters of everlafting concernment. I pray that the
good Spirit of God may guide you into all truths.
He only is the effectual teacher. I ftill retain a
chearful hope, that fome things you cannot at prefent receive will hereafter be the joy and comfort
of your heart : but I know it cannot be till the
Lord's own time. I cannot promife to give fuch

long

long anfwers as your letters require, to clear up
every text that may be propofed, and to anfwer
every objection that may be ftarted; yet I fhall be
glad to change a letter now and then.   At prefent
it remains with you, whether our correfpondence
continues or not, as this is the third letter I have
written fince I heard from you, and therefore muft
be the laft till I do.   I fhould think what remains
might be better fettled *viva voce*; for which purpofe I fhall be glad to fee you, or ready to wait on
you when leifure will permit, and when I know it
will be agreeable: but if (as life and all its affairs
are precarious) we fhould never meet in this world,
I pray God we may meet at the right hand of Jefus,
in the great day, when he fhall come to gather up
his jewels, and to judge the world.   There is an
endlefs diverfity of opinions in matters of religion;
which of them are right and fafe, and will lead to
eternal glory, *Dies ifte indicabit.*   I am ftill in a
manner loft amidft more engagements than I have
time to comply with; but I feel and know that I
am, &c.

E L E-

ELEVEN

LETTERS

TO

MR B——, &c.

LETTER I.

My dearest Sir,　　　　　*September* 28. 1774.

I See the necessity of having, if possible, my principles at my fingers ends, that I may apply them as occasions arise every hour. Certainly if my ability was equal to my inclination, I would remove your tumor with a word or a touch; I would exempt you instantly and constantly from every inconvenience and pain: but you are in the hands of one who could do all this and more, and who loves you infinitely better than I can do, and yet he is pleased to permit you to suffer. What is the plain inference? Certainly, that at the present juncture, he to whom all the concatenations and consequences of events are present in one view, sees it better for you to have this tumor than to be without it; for I have no more idea of a tumor rising (or any other incidental trial befalling you) without a cause, without a need be, without a designed advantage to result from it, than I have of a mountain or pyramid rising up of its own accord in the middle of Salisbury Plain. The promise is express, and literally true, that all things, universally and without exception, shall work together for good to them that love God. But they work *together*;— the smallest as well as the greatest events have their place and use,—like the several stones in the arch of a bridge, where no one would singly be useful, but every one in its place is necessary to the structure and support of the arch;—or rather, like the movement of a watch, where, though there is an evident subordination of parts, and some pieces

have

have a greater comparative importance than others, yet the fmalleft pieces have their place and ufe, and are fo far equally important, that the whole defign of the machine would be obftructed for want of them. Some difpenfations and turns of Divine Providence may be compared to the main fpring or capital wheels, which have a more vifible, fenfible, and determining influence upon the whole tenor of our lives; but the more ordinary occurences of every day are at leaft pins and pivots, adjufted, timed, and fuited with equal accuracy, by the hand of the fame great artift who planned and executes the whole; and we are fometimes furprifed to fee how much more depends and turns upon them than we were aware of. Then we admire his fkill, and fay he has done all things well. Indeed, with refpect to his works of providence, as well as of creation, he well deferves the title of *Maximus in minimis.* Such thoughts as thefe, when I am enabled to realife them, in fome meafure reconcile me to what he allots for myfelf or my friends, and convince me of the propriety of that expoftulation, which fpeaks the language of love as well as authority, " Be ftill, and know that I am God." I fympathife with you in your trial, and pray and truft that your fhepherd will be your phyfician; will fuperintend and blefs the ufe of means; will give you in his good time health and cure, and at all times reveal unto you abundance of peace. His promifes and power are neceffary for our prefervation in the fmoother fcenes he has allotted for us, and they are likewife fufficient for the rougheft. We are always equally in danger in ourfelves, and always equally fafe under the fhadow of his wings. No ftorms, affaults, fieges, or peftilences, can hurt us till we have filled up his appointed meafure of fervice; and when our work is done, and he has ripened us for glory, it is no great matter

by

by what means he is pleafed to call us home to himfelf.

I have only room to prefent our joint and fin-
cereft refpects. The Lord blefs you all.

I am, &c.

L E T T E R   II.

My deareft Sir,   *October* 15. 1774.

I Think the greatnefs of trials is to be eftimated,
rather by the impreffion they make upon our
fpirits, than by their outward appearance. The
fmalleft will be too heavy for us if we are left to
grapple with it in our own ftrength, or rather
weaknefs ; and if the Lord is pleafed to put forth
his power in us, he can make the heavieft light. A
lively impreffion of his love, or of his fufferings for
us, or of the glories within the vail, accompanied
with a due fenfe of the mifery from which we are
redeemed ; thefe thoughts will enable us to be not
only fubmiffive, but even joyful in tribulations.
When faith is in exercife, though the flefh will have
its feelings, the fpirit will triumph over them. But
it is needful we fhould know that we have no fufficiency in ourfelves, and in order to know it we
muft feel it ; and therefore the Lord fometimes
withdraws his fenfible influence, and then the buz-
zing of a fly will be an overmatch for our patience :
at other times he will fhew us what he can do in
us and for us ; then we can adopt the apoftle's
words, and fay, I can do or fuffer all things through
Chrift ftrengthening me. He has faid, My grace
is fufficient for thee. It is obfervable, that the children of God feldom difappoint our expectations
                                                    under

under great trials; if they ſhew a wrongneſs of
ſpirit, it is uſually in ſuch little incidents that we
are ready to wonder at them. For which, two rea-
ſons may be principally aſſigned. When great trials
are in view, we run ſimply and immediately to our
all-ſufficient friend, feel our dependence, and cry
in good earneſt for help; but if the occaſion ſeems
ſmall, we are too apt ſecretly to lean to our own
wiſdom and ſtrength, as if in ſuch ſlight matters we
could make ſhift without him. Therefore in theſe
we often fail. Again, the Lord deals with us as we
ſometimes ſee mothers with their children.—When
a child begins to walk, he is often very ſelf-impor-
ant; he thinks he needs no help, and can hardly
bear to be ſupported by the finger of another. Now
in ſuch a caſe, if there is no danger of harm from
a fall, as if he is on a plain carpet, the mother will
let him alone to try how he *can* walk. He is pleaſed at firſt, but preſently down he comes; and a
few experiments of this kind convince him he is not
ſo ſtrong and able as he thought, and make him
willing to be led. But was he upon the brink of a
river or a precipice, from whence a fall might be
fatal, the tender mother would not truſt him to
himſelf, no not for a moment. I have not room
to make the application, nor is it needful. It requires the ſame grace to bear with a right ſpirit a
croſs word, as a croſs injury; or the breaking of a
china-plate, as the death of an only ſon.

  I am, &c.

LET-

L E T T E R   III.

My dear Sir,   *November* 23. 1774.

I Hope to be informed in due time, that the
Lord has given you full health and cure. He
has preferved me hitherto from the hands of fur-
geons; but I feel as if my flefh would prove, as you
fay, a very coward, were it needful to fubmit to a
painful operation. Yet I obferve, when fuch operations are neceffary, if people are fatisfied of a
furgeon's fkill and prudence, they will not only
yield to be cut at his pleafure, without pretending
to direct him where, or how long he fhall make
the incifion, but will thank and pay him for putting them to pain, becaufe they believe it for their
advantage I wifh I could be more like them in
my concerns. My body, as I faid, is, through
mercy, free from confiderable ailments, but I have
a foul that requires furgeon's work continually;—
there is fome tumor to be difcuffed or laid open,
fome diflocation to be reduced, fome fracture to be
healed almoft daily It is my great mercy, that one
who is infallible in fkill, who exercifes inceffant
care and boundlefs compaffion towards all his pa-
tients, has undertaken my cafe; and complicated as
it is, I dare not doubt his making a perfect cure.
Yet, alas! I too often difcover fuch impatience,
diftruft, and complaining, when under his hand, am
fo apt to find fault with the *inftruments* he is pleafed to make ufe of, fo ready to think the falutary
wounds he makes unneceffary, or too large; in a
word, I fhew fuch a promptnefs to controul, were
I able, or to direct his operations, that, were not
his patience beyond expreffion, he would before
now have given me up. I am perfuaded, no money

would induce Mr —— to attend upon a patient who fhould act towards him as I have towards my beft phyfician. Sometimes I indulge a hope that I am growing wifer, and think furely, after fuch innumerable proofs as I have had, that he does all things well, I fhall now be fatisfied to leave myfelf quietly and without referve to his difpofal. A thoufand fuch furrenders I have made, and a thoufand times I have interpretatively retracted them. Yet ftill he is gracious. O, how fhall I praife him at laft!

I thank you for your letter; I never receive one from you without pleafure, and I believe, feldom without profit, at leaft for the time. I believe with you, that there is much of the proper and defigned efficacy of the gofpel myftery which I have not yet experienced—And I fuppofe, they who are advanced far beyond me in the divine life, judge the fame of their utmoft prefent attainments. Yet I have no idea of any *permanent* ftate in this life, that fhall make my experience ceafe to be a ftate of warfare and humiliation. At my firft fetting out, indeed, I thought to be better, and to feel myfelf better from year to year; I expected by degrees to attain every thing which I *then* comprifed *in my idea* of a faint. I thought my grain of grace, by much diligence and careful improvement, would in time amount to a pound, that pound in a farther fpace of time to a talent, and then I hoped to increafe from one talent to many; fo that fuppofing the Lord fhould fpare me a competent number of years, I pleafed myfelf with the thought of dying rich.—But alas! thefe my golden expectations have been like South-Sea dreams; I have lived hitherto a poor finner, and I believe I fhall die one. Have I then gained nothing by waiting upon the Lord? Yes, I have gained that, which I once would rather have been without, fuch accumulated proofs

of

of the deceitfulnefs and defperate wickednefs of
my heart, as I hope, by the Lord's bleffing, has in
fome meafure taught me to know what I mean,
when I fay, Behold I am vile! And in connection
with this, I have gained fuch experience of the
wifdom, power, and compaffion of my Redeemer,
the need, the worth of his blood, righteoufnefs,
attention, and interceffion—the glory that he dif-
plays, in pardoning iniquity and fin, and paffing by
the tranfgreffion of the remnant of his heritage,
that my foul cannot but cry out, Who is a God like
unto thee!—Thus, if I have any meaner thoughts
of myfelf, Ezek. xvi. 63. and any higher thoughts
of him than I had twenty years ago, I have reafon
to be thankful; every grain of this experience is
worth mountains of gold. And if, by his mercy, I
fhall yet fink more in my own efteem, and he will
be pleafed to rife ftill more glorious to my eyes,
and more precious to my heart; I expect it will be
much in the fame way.—I was afhamed when I
began to feek him, I am more afhamed now; and
I expect to be moft of all afhamed when he fhall
appear to deftroy my laft enemy. But O! I may
rejoice in him, to think that he will not be afhamed of me.

  I am, &c.

LETTER   IV.

My dear Sir,   *May* 19. 1775.

I Hope you will find the Lord prefent at all times,
  and in all places. When it is fo, we are at
home, every where; when it is otherwife, *home* is
a prifon, and *abroad* a wildernefs. I know what I

ought to defire, and what I do defire. I point him
out to others as the all in all; I efteem him as fuch
in my own judgement; but alas! my experience
abounds with complaints. He is my fun; but
clouds, and fometimes walls, intercept him from my
view. He is my ftrength; yet I am prone to lean
upon reeds. He is my friend; but on my part there
is fuch coldnefs and ingratitude, as no other friend
could bear. But ftill he is gracious, and fhames
me with his repeated multiplied goodnefs. O for a
warmer heart, a more fimple dependence, a more
active zeal, a more fenfible deliverance from the
effects of this body of fin and death! He helps me
in my endeavours to keep the vineyards of others;
but alas! my own does not feem to flourifh as fome
do around me. However, though I cannot fay I
labour more abundantly than they all, I have reafon to fay with thankfulnefs, by the grace of God,
I am what I am. My poor ftory would foon be
much worfe, did not he fupport, reftrain, and
watch over me every minute. Let me intreat your
praifes and prayers, on the behalf of me and mine;
and may the Lord blefs you and yours with an increafe in every good.

I am, &c.

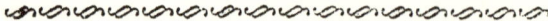

LETTER V.

My dear Sir,   *September 2. 1776.*

THE young woman I fpoke of is ftill living,
and not much weaker than when I left her.
The Lord was pleafed to relieve her on Tuefday
evening, and fhe was comfortable the remainder of
the week. But yefterday her conflicts returned, and
          fhe

fhe was in great diftrefs. The enemy, who always
fights againft the peace of the Lord's children, finds
great advantage againft them when their fpirits are
weakened and worn down by long illnefs, and is
often permitted to affault them. The reafons are
hidden from us, but they are doubtlefs worthy of
his wifdom and love, and they terminate in victory
to the praife of his glorious grace, which is more
fignally manifefted by his leading them fafely
through fire and water, than if their path was always fmooth. He is fovereign in his difpenfations,
and appoints fome of his people to trials and exercifes, to which others, perhaps, are ftrangers all their
days. Believers are foldiers : all foldiers by their
profeffion are engaged to fight, if called upon ; but
who fhall be called to fuftain the hotteft fervice,
and be moft frequently expofed upon the field
of battle, depends upon the will of the general or
king. Some of our foldiers are now upon hard
fervice in America, while others are ftationed round
the palace, fee the King's face daily, and have no
dangers or hardfhips to encounter. Thefe, however, are as liable to a call as the others ; but, if
not called upon, they may enjoy with thankfulnefs
the more eafy poft affigned them. Thus, the Captain of our Salvation allots to his foldiers fuch
ftations as he thinks proper. He has a right to
employ whom he will, and where he will. Some
are comparatively at eafe ; they are not expofed
to the fierceft onfets, but live near his prefence :
others are, to appearance, preffed above meafure,
beyond ftrength, fo that they defpair even of life ;
yet they are fupported, and in the end made more
than conquerors through him who hath loved them.
Long obfervation convinces me, that the temptations which fome endure, are not chaftifements
brought upon them by unfaithfulnefs, or for any
thing remarkably wrong in their fpirit or walk ; I

often

often rather confider that in *his* warfare, as in
worldly wars, the poft of danger and difficulty is
the poft of honour, and as fuch affigned to thofe
whom he has favoured with a peculiar meafure of
his grace. This young woman, in particular, was
always from her firft awakening remarkably humble
and fpiritual, and poffeffed of a broken and contrite
fpirit. I never faw her in a wrong fpirit, or heard
her fpeak an unadvifed word. Yet I believe it is
impoffible to exprefs the agonies fhe has endured.
The effect of them is vifible. Her animal frame was'
unable to fuftain the burden. I believe they were
the immediate caufe of that illnefs which is now
bringing her down to the grave. I doubt not
but thefe cafes depend, in a great meafure, upon
conftitution ; but then the temperament of our
bodies depends upon his pleafure ; for if the very
hairs of our head are numbered, it is impoffible that
thofe circumftances of our frame, which, by the
near connection between body and foul, have a
powerful influence upon the ftate of our minds,
can efcape his notice. He could cure fuch bodily
diforders as affect the peace of his people in a
moment ; yet he does not, though he loves them.
There muft be, therefore, wife reafons why he
does not; and though we know them not now,
we fhall know them hereafter. Poffibly fome fuffer for the inftruction of the reft, that we may
learn to be more thankful to him for the peace we
enjoy, and to be more humbly dependent upon him
for the continuance of it. The Lord's way is in
the deep, and his path in the great waters, untrace-
able by our feeble reafonings ; but faith brings in a
good report. We need not doubt but he does all
things well, and in due time we fhall fee it. In
the mean while he checks our vain inquiries, and
calls upon us to be ftill, and know that he is God.

    I brought home with me a thankful fenfe of the
kindnefs

kindnefs and friendfhip I am favoured with from you and all yours. I account this connection one of the great comforts of my life ; and I hope it has been, and will be, not only pleafant but profitable to me. Though I am but an unapt fcholar, I hope I am not unwilling to learn ; and the Lord, in his merciful providence, appoints me many teachers. There is little praife due to us, if we either communicate or receive benefit in our intercourfe with our fellow-difciples. In both we are but inftruments under the influence of a higher hand. Were Chriftians to meet together without their Lord, they would either trifle or quarrel their time away. But as he has faid, where two or three are met, there am I in the midft of them, we may well be glad of opportunities of coming together. And though, for my own part, I am fo poor an improver of fuch feafons, that the recollection of them, when paft, is generally accompanied with fhame and regret ; yet he is gracious and merciful, and feldom leaves me to complain that they were wholly in vain.

I am, &c.

LETTER   VI.

My dear Sir,   *July 22. 1777.*

- -

THE complaints you make of what paffes *within,* encourage me under what I feel myfelf. Indeed, if thofe whom I have reafon to believe are more fpiritual and humble than I am, did not give fome teftimony that they find their hearts made of the fame materials as mine is, I fhould be fometimes

I 4   hard

hard put to it to believe that I have any part or lot
in the matter, or any real knowledge of the life of
faith.   But this concurrent teftimony of many witneffes, confirms me in what I think the fcripture
plainly teaches, that the foil of human nature,
though many fpots are certainly better weeded,
planted, and manured than others, is every where
the fame, univerfally bad ; fo bad that it cannot be
worfe, and of itfelf is only capable of producing
noxious weeds, and nourifhing venomous creatures.
We often fee, the effects of culture, fkill, and ex-
pence will make a garden where all was defert before.
When Jefus the good hufbandman inclofes a foil,
and feparates it from the wafte of the world, to make
it a refidence for himfelf a change prefently takes
place ; it is planted and watered from above, and
vifited with beams infinitely more chearing and
fertilizing than thofe of the material fun.—But its
natural propenfity to bring forth weeds ftill continues, and one half of his difpenfations may be
compared to a company of weeders, whom he fends
forth into his garden to pluck up all which he has
not planted with his own hand, and which, if left
to grow, would quickly overpower and overtop the
reft.   But, alas! the ground is fo impregnated with
evil feeds, and they fhoot in fuch quick fucceffion,
that if this weeding work were not conftantly repeated, all former labour would be loft.   *Hinc illæ
lachrymæ.*   Hence arifes the neceffity of daily croffes
and difappointments, daily changes of frame, and
fuch multiplied convictions, that we are nothing
and can do nothing of ourfelves; all are needful
and barely fufficient to prevent our hearts from
being over-run with pride, felf-dependence, and
fecurity.
     Yours, &c.

L E T T E R   VII.

My dear Sir,   *November* 6. 1777.

YOU fay you are more difpofed to cry *miferere*
than *hallelujah.* — Why not both together ?
When the treble is praife, and heart-humiliation
for the bafe, the melody is pleafant, and the harmony good. However, if not both together, we
muft have them alternately; not all finging, not all
fighing, but an interchange and balance, that we
may be neither lifted too high, nor caft down too
low, which would be the cafe if we were very comfortable or very forrowful for a long continuance.
But though we change, the Saviour changes not.
All our concerns are in his hands, and therefore
fafe. His path is in the deep waters, his thoughts
and methods of conduct are as high above ours, as
the heavens are high above the earth; and he often
takes a courfe for accomplifhing his purpofes directly contrary to what our narrow views would
prefcribe. He wounds in order to heal, kills that
he may make alive, cafts down when he defigns to
raife, brings a death upon our feelings, wifhes, and
profpects, when he is about to give us the defire of
our hearts. Thefe things he does to *prove* us; but
he himfelf knows, and has determined beforehand,
what he will do. The proof indeed ufually turns
out to our fhame. Impatience and unbelief fhew
their heads, and prompt us to fuppofe this and the
other thing, yea perhaps all things are againft us,
to queftion whether he be with us and for us, or
not. But it iffues likewife in the praife of his goodnefs, when we find that, maugre all our unkind
complaints and fufpicions, he is ftill working won-
I 5   derfully

derfully for us, caufing light to fhine out of darknefs, and doing us good in defiance of ourfelves.
    I am, &c.

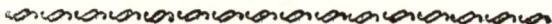

LETTER VIII.

To Mr B—— jun.

Dear Sir,   *Auguft* 24. 1774.

THE lownefs of your voice, and a blameable
    abfence of mind on my part, prevented me
from underftanding what you faid when you took
your leave of me ; nor did I juft at that inftant recollect that you were fo foon going away. I could
not otherwife have parted with you, without a particular expreffion of my warmeft wifhes for your
welfare, and commending you with an emotion,
which my heart always feels for you, to our God,
and the word of his grace. Permit me therefore
by writing to affure you, fo far as I can anfwer for
myfelf, that the requeft you were pleafed to make
for my remembrance will not be forgotten by me.
    You are going abroad ; you will carry with you,
I doubt not, the beft advice, ftrengthened by the
authority and affection of parents, whom you
greatly love and greatly reverence. This may feem
to make any thing a ftranger can offer unneceffary,
if not impertinent ; yet, confiding in your candour,
and in your good opinion of my intention, I fhall
venture to let my pen run on a little longer. Not
only my wifhes, but my hopes are ftrong in your
behalf. Perhaps there is hardly a young man in
the kingdom, born to a fortune, who is fetting out
in life upon equal advantages with yourfelf. How
                                              many

many at your years, who have been brought up in affluence, are unprincipled, uninftructed, and have already entered upon a courfe of diffipation and folly, in which it is impoffible they themfelves can find fatisfaction, and which, (unlefs they are reclaimed from it by an Almighty arm) will infallibly preclude them from ufefulnefs or efteem ! whereas your early years have been fuccefsfully employed in the purfuit of knowledge, and your education formed under the moft animating and endearing influence; and the Lord has furnifhed you with every natural ability of body and mind, which may qualify you to ferve him in that fituation of life which his providence has allotted you.

What may I not then further hope from thefe beginnings, efpecially as it is eafy to obferve, that he has given you an amiable and promifing difpofition of fpirit, and has not only preferved you from being hurried down the ftream of a giddy world, but enabled you to account the tender reftraint under which you have been educated, not a yoke, but a privilege.

I fympathife with you at what you will feel when you are firft feparated from your happy family. But the Lord God, who is the fun and fhield of thofe who fear him, will be always near you ! His favour is the one thing needful, which no outward advantages can compenfate the want of; and the right knowledge of him is the one thing needful, which no human teaching can communicate.

Were I more intimate with you, I could have afked the queftion, and perhaps received the fatiffaction to know, that you have already begun to confider him in this light; that you feel a vanity in fcience, an emptinefs in creatures, and find that you have defires, which only *He* who gave them can fatisfy. I truft it either is, or will be thus. As to learning, though it is ufeful when we know how to make a right use of it, yet considered as in our own power, and to those who trust to it, without seeking a superior guidance, it is usually the source of perplexity, strife, scepticism, and infidelity. It is indeed like a sword in a madman's hands, which gives him the more opportunity of hurting himself and others. As to what the world calls pleasure, there is so little in it, that even the philosophers of old, or many of them, though they had little of value to substitute in its room, could despise it. You will perhaps meet with some, who will talk another language, who will pretend to be too wise to submit to the Bible, and too happy in worldly things, to expect or desire any happiness beside; but I trust you have seen enough to enable you to treat such persons with the pity, and such pretensions with the contempt they deserve.

Should we set our concerns with an *eternal world* aside for a moment, it would be easy to demonstrate that religion is necessary, in order to make the most of this life, and to enjoy temporal good with the highest relish. In such a world as this, where we are every moment liable to so many unforeseen and unavoidable contingencies, a man without religion may be compared to a ship in a storm, without either rudder, anchor, or pilot. But then, the religion which *only* deserves the name, must come from above; it must be suited to the state and wants of a sinner, it must be capable of comforting the heart, it must take away the sting and dread of death, and fix our confidence upon one who is always able to help us. Such is the religion of Jesus, such are its effects, and such are the criteria whereby we are to judge of the various forms and schemes under which it is proposed to us. But I forbear; I am only reminding you of what you know, and what you have known to be verified by *living* and *dying* examples. This happiness, my dear Sir, is open

to

to you, to all who feek. He is enthroned in heaven, but prayer will bring him down to the heart.
Indeed he is always beforehand with us ; and if we
feel one defire towards him, we may accept it as a
token that he gave it us to encourage us to afk for
more.

   May he be your guide and guard, be with you at
all times, and in all places, and bring you back to
your father's houfe in peace. Should I live to fee
that day, you have few friends whofe congratulations would be warmer or more fincere than mine ;
and if when you are fettled and at leifure, you will
afford me a letter, it will be both a pleafure and a
favour to, dear Sir,

   Yours, &c.

LETTER   IX.

To Mifs M—— B——.

My dear Mifs M——,   *November* 11. 1775.

O UR late vifit to —— was very pleafant to my-
    felf ; if any thing that paffed was of fervice to
you, we know to whom the thanks are due ; for
we can neither communicate or receive any thing
but fo far as he is pleafed to enable us. One reafon why he often difappoints us is, that we may
learn to depend on him alone. We are prone, as
you obferve, to reft too much upon fenfible comforts, yet they are very defirable ; only as to the
meafure and feafons, it is well to be fubmiffive to
his will, to be thankful for them when we have
them, and humbly waiting for them when we have
them not. They are not, however, the proper
                                    ground

ground of our hope; a good hope fprings from
fuch a fenfe of our wants, and fuch a perfuafion of
his power and grace, as engages the heart to venture, upon the warrant of his promifes, to truft in
him for falvation. In a fenfe, we are often hin-
dering him by our impatience and unbelief; but
ftrictly fpeaking, when he really begins the good
work, and gives us a defire which will be fatisfied
with nothing fhort of himfelf, *he will not be hindered from carrying it on*; for he has faid, I will
work, and none fhall let it. Ah! had it depended
upon myfelf, upon my wifdom or faithfulnefs, I
fhould have hindered him to purpofe, and ruined
myfelf long ago. How often have I grieved and
refifted his Spirit! but hereby I have learned more
of his patience and tendernefs than I could otherwife have known. He knows our frame, and what
effects our evil nature, fomented by the artifices of
Satan, will have; he fees us from firft to laft. A
thoufand evils arife in our hearts, a thoufand
wrongneffes in our conduct, which, as they do a-
rife, are new to ourfelves, and perhaps at fometimes
we were ready to think we were incapable of fuch
things; but none of them are new to him, to whom
paft, prefent, and future, are the fame. The fore-
fight of them did not prevent his calling us by his
grace.—Though he knew we were vile, and fhould
prove ungrateful and unfaithful, yet he would be
found of us; he would knock at the door of our
hearts, and gain himfelf an entrance. Nor fhall
they prevent his accomplifhing his gracious purpofe. It is our part to be abafed before him, and
quietly to hope and wait for his falvation in the ufe
of his appointed means. The power, fuccefs, and
bleffing, are wholly from himfelf. To make us
more fenfible of this, he often withdraws from our
perceptions: and as, in the abfence of the fun, the
wild beafts of the foreft roam abroad; fo, when Jefus

fus hides himfelf, we prefently perceive what is in
our hearts, and what a poor fhift we can make
without him ; when he returns, his light chafes
the evils away, and we are well again. However,
they are not dead when moft controuled by his prefence.

It is your great and fingular mercy, my dear
Mifs, that he has taught you to feek him fo early
in life. You are entered in the way of falvation,
but you muft not expect all at once. The work
of grace is compared to the corn and to a building;
the growth of the one, and the carrying forward of
the other, are gradual. In a building, for inftance,
if it be large, there is much to be done in preparing
and laying the foundation, before the walls appear
above ground; much is doing within, when the
work does not feem perhaps to advance without ;
and when it is confiderably forward, yet being in-
cumbered with fcaffolds and rubbifh, a bye-ftander
fees it at a great difadvantage, and can form but
an imperfect judgement of it. But all this while
the architect himfelf, even from the laying of the
firft ftone, conceives of it according to the plan
and defign he has formed ; he prepares and adjufts
the materials, difpofing each in its proper time and
place, and views it in idea as already finifhed. In
due feafon it is completed, but not in a day. The
top-ftone is fixed, and then the fcaffolds and rubbifh being removed, it appears to others as he intended it fhould be. Men indeed often plan what,
for want of fkill or ability, or from unforefeen difappointments, they are unable to execute. But nothing can difappoint the heavenly Builder ; nor will
he ever be reproached with forfaking the work of
his own hands, or beginning that which he could
not or would not accomplifh, Phil. i. 6. Let us
therefore be thankful for beginnings, and patiently
wait the event. His enemies ftrive to retard the
work,

work, as they did when the Jews, by his order, fet about rebuilding the temple. Yet it was finifhed in defiance of them all.

Believe me to be, &c.

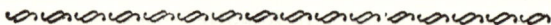

LETTER X.

My dear Mifs M——,   *April* 29. 1776.

I Thank you for your laft; and I rejoice in the Lord's goodnefs to you. To be drawn by love, exempted from thofe diftreffing terrors and temptations which fome are befet with; to be favoured with the ordinances and means of grace, and connected with thofe, and with thofe only, who are difpofed and qualified to affift and encourage you in feeking the Saviour; thefe are peculiar privileges, which all concur in your cafe : he loves you, he deals gently with you, he provides well for you, and accompanies every outward privilege with his fpecial bleffing; and I truft he will lead you on from ftrength to ftrength, and fhew you ftill greater things than you have yet feen. They whom he teaches are always increafing in knowledge, both of themfelves and of him. The heart is deep, and, like Ezekiel's vifion, prefents fo many chambers of imagery, one within another, that it requires time to get a confiderable acquaintance with it, and we fhall never know it thoroughly. It is now more than twenty-eight years fince the Lord began to open mine to my own view; and from that time to this, almoft every day has difcovered to me fomething which till then was unobferved; and the farther I go, the more I feem convinced that I have entered but a little way. A perfon that travels in

fome

fome parts of Derbyfhire may eafily be fatisfied that
the country is cavernous ; but how large, how deep,
how numerous the caverns may be, which are hidden from us by the furface of the ground, and what
is contained in them, are queftions which our nicefl
inquirers cannot fully anfwer. Thus I judge of
my heart, that it is very deep and dark, and full of
evil ; but as to particulars, I know not one of a
thoufand.

And if our own hearts are beyond our comprehenfion, how much more incomprehenfible is the
heart of Jefus ! If fin abounds in us, grace and love
fuperabound in him : his ways and thoughts are
higher than ours, as the heavens are higher than
the earth ; his love has a height, and depth, and
length, and breadth, that paffeth all knowledge;
and his riches of grace are unfearchable riches,
Ephef. iii. 8. 18. 19.   All that we have received, or
can receive from him, or know of him in this life,
compared with what he *is* in himfelf, or what he
has for us, is but as the drop of a bucket compared
with the ocean, or a fingle ray of light in refpect
of the fun.   The waters of the fanctuary flow to
us at firft almoft upon a level, ankle deep, fo gracioufly does the Lord condefcend to our weaknefs;
but they rife as we advance, and conftrain us to cry
out with the Apoftle, O the depth !   We find before us, as Dr Watts beautifully expreffes it,

> *A fea of love and grace unknown,*
> *Without a bottom or a fhore.*

O the excellency of the knowledge of Chrift !   It
will be growing upon us through time, yea, I believe through eternity.   What an aftonifhing and
what a chearing thought, that this high and lofty
One fhould unite himfelf to our nature, that fo, in
a way worthy of his adorable perfections, he might

by

by his Spirit unite us to himfelf! Could fuch a thought have arifen in our hearts, without the warrant of his word, (but it is a thought which no created mind was capable of conceiving till he revealed it), it would have been prefumption and blafphemy; but now he has made it known, it is the foundation of our hope, and an inexhauftible fpring of life and joy Well may we fay, Lord, what is man, that thou fhouldft thus vifit him!

 I am, &c.

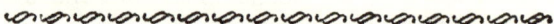

L E T T E R   XI.

My dear Mifs M——,   *September* 3. 1776.

WE faw no danger upon the road homeward; but my judgement tells me we are always upon the brink of danger, though we fee it not; and that, without the immediate protection and care of him who preferveth the ftars in their courfes, there could be no travelling fafely a few miles, nor even fitting in fafety by the fire-fide. But with him we are fafe in all places and circumftances, till our race is done, and his gracious purpofes concerning us, in the prefent life, are completely anfwered;—then he will call us home, that we may fee his face, and be with him for ever, and then it will not much fignify what meffenger he fhall be pleafed to fend for us.

 While he took care of us abroad, he watched over our concerns at home likewife; fo that we found all well upon our return, and met with nothing to grieve us. Many go out and return home no more, and many find diftreffing things have happened in their abfence; but we have to fet up

our

our Ebenezer, and to fay, Hitherto he has helped
us.   Affift me to praife him.   The Lord is leading
you in the good old way, in which you may perceive the footfteps of his flock who have gone before you.   They had in their day the fame difficulties, fears, and complaints as we have, and through
mercy we partake of the fame confolation which
fupported and refrefhed them; and the promifes
which they trufted and found faithful, are equally
fure to us.   It is ftill true, that they who believe
fhall never be confounded.   If left to ourfelves, we
fhould have built upon fand; but he has provided
and revealed a fure foundation, removed our natural prejudices againft it; and now, though rains,
and floods, and ftorms affault our building, it cannot fall, for it is founded upon a rock.   The fufpicions and fears which arife in an awakened mind
proceed, in a good meafure, from remaining unbelief; but not wholly fo, for there is a jealoufy
and diffidence of ourfelves, a warinefs, owing to a
fenfe of the deceitfulnefs of our hearts, which is a
grace, and a gift of the Lord.   Some people who
have much zeal, but are deftitute of this jealous
fear, may be compared to a fhip that fpreads a great
deal of fail, but is not properly ballafted, and is
therefore in danger of being overfet whenever a
ftorm comes.   A fincere perfon has many reafons
for diftrufting his own judgement; is fenfible of
the vaft importance of the cafe, and afraid of too
haftily concluding in his own favour, and therefore
not eafily fatisfied.   However, this fear, though
ufeful, efpecially to young beginners, is not comfortable; and they who fimply wait upon Jefus, are
gradually freed from it, in proportion as their knowledge of him, and their experience of his goodnefs,
increafes.   He has a time for fettling and eftablifh-
ing them in himfelf, and his time is beft.   We are
hafty, and would be fatisfied at once, but his word
is,

is, Tarry thou the Lord's leifure. The work of
grace is not like Jonah's gourd, which fprang up
and flourifhed in a night, and as quickly withered,
but rather like the oak, which, from a little acorn
and a tender plant, advances with an almoft imperceptible growth from year to year, till it becomes
a broad, fpreading, and deep-rooted tree, and then
it ftands for ages   The Chriftian oak fhall grow
and flourifh for ever. When I fee any foon after
they appear to be awakened, making a fpeedy profeffion of great joy, before they have a due acquaintance with their own hearts, I am in pain for
them. I am not forry to hear them afterwards
complain that their joys are gone, and they are almoft at their wits end; for without fome fuch
check, to make them feel their weaknefs and dependence, I feldom find them turn out well; either
their fervour infenfibly abates, till they become
quite cold, and fink into the world again, (of which
I have feen many inftances), or, if they do not give
up all, their walk is uneven, and their fpirit has not
that favour of brokennefs and true humility which
is a chief ornament of our holy profeffion. It they
do not feel the plague of their hearts at firft, they
find it out afterwards, and too often manifeft it to
others.   Therefore, though I know the Spirit of
the Lord is free, and will not be confined to our
rules, and there may be excepted cafes; yet, in general, I believe the old proverb, " Soft and fair
" goes far," will hold good in Chriftian experience.
Let us be thankful for the beginnings of grace, and
wait upon our Saviour patiently for the increafe.
And as we have chofen him for our phyfician, let
us commit ourfelves to his management, and not
prefcribe to him what he fhall prefcribe for us. He
knows us, and he loves us better than we do ourfelves, and will do all things well.

　　You fay, " It never came with power and life to
　　　　　　　　　　　　　　　　　　　　my

my foul, that he died for me." If you mean, you
never had any extraordinary fudden manifeftation,
fomething like a vifion or a voice from heaven,
confirming it to you, I can fay the fame. But I
know he died for finners; I know I am a finner:
I know he invites them that are ready to perifh; I
am fuch a one: I know, upon his own invitation,
I have committed myfelf to him; and I know, by
the effects, that he has been with me hitherto, o-
therwife I fhould have been an apoftate long ago;
and therefore I know that he died for me; for had
he been pleafed to kill me, (as he juftly might have
done), he would not have fhewn me fuch things as
thefe.

> *If I muft perifh, would the Lord*
> *Have taught my heart to love his word?*
> *Would he have giv'n me eyes to fee*
> *My danger and my remedy?*
> *Reveal'd his name, and bid me pray,*
> *Had he refolv'd to fay me nay?*

I know that I am a child, becaufe he teaches me
to fay, Abba, Father. I know that I am *his*, becaufe he has enabled me to chufe him for *mine*.
For fuch a choice and defire could never have taken
place in my heart, if he had not placed it there
himfelf. By nature I was too blind to know him,
too proud to truft him, too obftinate to ferve him,
too bafe-minded to love him. The enmity I was
filled with againft his government, righteoufnefs,
and grace, was too ftrong to be fubdued by any
power but his own. The love I bear him is but
a faint and feeble fpark, but it is an emanation
from himfelf: He kindled it, and he keeps it alive;
and becaufe it is his work, I truft many waters
fhall not quench it.

I have only room to affure you, that I am, &c.

FOUR

FOUR

LETTERS

TO THE

Rev. Mr R——.

LETTER I.

My dear Sir,   *April* 15. 1776.

I often rejoice on your behalf. Your call out of the world was a fingular comfortable inftance of the power of grace. And when I confider the difficulties and fnares of your fituation, and that you have been kept in the middle path, preferved from undue compliances on the one hand, and unneceffary fingularities on the other, I cannot doubt but the Lord has hitherto helped and guided you. Indeed you have need of his guidance. At your years, and with your expectations in life, your health firm, and your natural fpirits lively, you are expofed to many fnares: Yet if the Lord keeps you fenfible of your danger, and dependent upon him, you will walk fafely. Your fecurity, fuccefs, and comfort, depend upon him; and in the way of means, chiefly upon your being preferved in an humble fenfe of your own weaknefs. It is written, " Fear not, I am with thee." It is written again, " Bleffed is the man who feareth al- " ways." There is a perfect harmony in thofe feemingly different texts. May the wifdom that cometh from above, teach you and me to keep them both united in our view. If the Lord be with us, we have no caufe of fear. His eye is upon us, his arm over us, his ear open to our prayer; his grace fufficient, his promife unchangeable. Under his protection, though the path of duty fhould lie through fire and water, we may chearfully and

VOL. II.   K   confidently

confidently purfue it. On the other hand, our
hearts are fo deceitful, fallible, and frail; our fpiritual enemies fo fubtle, watchful, and powerful;
and they derive fo many advantages from the occafions of every day, in which we are unavoidably
and unexpectedly concerned; there is fo much
combuftible within, and fo many temptations arifing from without, capable of fetting all in a flame;
that we cannot be too jealous of ourfelves and our
circumftances. The Duke of Devonfhire's motto
(if I miftake not) well fuits the Chriftian, *Cavendo
tutus.* When we can fay in the Pfalmift's fpirit,
Hold thou me up, we may warrantably draw his conclufion, *and I fhall be fafe;* but the moment we
lean to our own underftanding, we are in immi-
nent danger of falling. The enemy who wars againft
our fouls, is a confummate mafter in his way, fertile
in ftratagems, and equally fkilful in carrying on
his affaults by fap or by a ftorm. He ftudies us,
if I may fo fay, all round, to difcover our weak
fides; and he is a very Proteus for changing his
appearances, and can appear as a fly ferpent, a
roaring lion, or an angel of light, as beft fuits his
purpofe. It is a great mercy to be in fome meafure
acquainted with his devices, and aware of them.
They who wait humbly upon the Lord, and confult carefully at his word and throne of grace, are
made wifer than their enemy, and enabled to efcape
and withftand his wiles. I know you will not expect me to apologize for putting you in mind of
thefe things, though you know them. I have a
double warrant; the love I bear you, and the
Lord's command, Heb. iii. 13. Ufe the like freedom with me, I need it, and hope to be thankful
for it, and accept it as one of the beft proofs of
friendfhip.

The Lord blefs and keep you. Pray for us, and
believe me to be, fincerely yours.

LET-

L E T T E R   II.

My dear Sir,   *July* 13. 1776.

THE Lord, who mercifully called you out of
a ſtate of thoughtleſs diſſipation, and has hitherto been with you, will I truſt ſweeten all your
trials, and cauſe his light to ſhine upon your paths.
It ſeems probable, that if you pay a juſt regard to
your father's negative, which I really think he has
a right to expect from you, and at the ſame time
make a ſteady and conſcientious uſe of that negative, which he generouſly allows you to put upon
his propoſals, to which I think you have an equal
right; I ſay, while things remain in this ſituation,
and you continue to think differently, it ſeems
probable, that the hour of your exchanging a ſingle
for the marriage ſtate, is yet at ſome diſtance. But
let not this grieve you.   The Lord is all-ſufficient.
A lively ſenſe of his love, a deep impreſſion of
eternity, a heart filled with zeal for his cauſe, and
a thirſt for the good of ſouls, will I hope enable
you to make a chearful ſacrifice of whatever has
no neceſſary connection with your peace and his
ſervice   And you may reſt aſſured, that whenever
he, who loves you better than you do yourſelf, ſees
it beſt for you upon the whole to change your
condition, he will bring it about, he will point out
the perſon, prepare the means, and ſecure the ſucceſs, by his providence, and the power he has over
every heart.   And you ſhall ſee that all previous
difficulties were either gracious preventions which
he threw in the way, to prevent your taking a
wrong ſtep, or temporary bars, which, by his re-
moving them afterwards, ſhould give you opportunity of more clearly perceiving his care and inter-

K 2   poſition

pofition in your favour. In the mean time remember your high calling.—You are a minifter and ambaffador of Chrift; you are intrufted with the moft honourable and important employment that can engage and animate the heart of man. Ταῦτα μελετα. ἐν τυτοις ἰσθι, ἐπιμενε αὐτοῖς. *

Filled and fired with a conftraining fenfe of the love of Jefus, and the worth of fouls, impreffed with an ardour to carry war into Satan's kingdom, to ftorm his ftrongholds, and refcue his captives; you will have little leifure to think of any thing elfe. How does the love of glory ftimulate the foldier, make him forget and forego a thoufand perfonal tenderneffes, and prompt him to crofs oceans, to traverfe deferts, to fcale mountains, and plunge into the greateft hardfhips and the thickeft dangers! They do it for a corruptible crown, a puff of breath, an empty fame; their higheft profpect is the applaufe and favour of their prince. We likewife are foldiers, we have a prince and captain who deferves our all. They who know him, and have hearts to conceive of his excellence, and to feel their obligations to him, cannot indeed feek their own glory, but his glory is dearer to them than a thoufand lives. They owe him their fouls, for he redeemed them with blood, his own blood; and by his grace he fubdued and pardoned them when they were rebels, and in arms againft him. Therefore they are not their own, they would not be their own. When his ftandard is raifed, when his enemies are in motion, when his people are to be refcued; they go forth clothed with his panoply, they fight under his eye, they are fure of his fupport, and he fhews them the conqueror's crown. O when they think of that ευ δυλε αγαθε, † with which he has promifed to welcome them home,

* 1 Tim. iv. 15.   † Well done, good fervant.

when

when the campaign is over, hard things feem eafy, and bitter things fweet; they count nothing, not even their own lives dear, fo that they may finifh their courfe with joy. May the Lord make us thus minded; give us a hearty concern for *his* bufinefs, and he has engaged to take care of *ours;* and nothing that can conduce to our real comfort and ufefulnefs fhall be with-held.

Believe me to be fincerely yours.

L E T T E R   III.

My dear Friend,   *December* 21. 1776.

YOur letter brought me tidings of joy, and then furnifhed me with materials for a bonfire upon the occafion. It was an act of paffive obedience to burn it, but I did obey. I congratulate you upon the happy iffue to which the Lord has brought your affairs. I fee that his good Spirit and good providence have been and are with you. I doubt not but your union with Mifs —— will be a mutual bleffing, and, on your part, heightened by being connected with fuch a family. I could enlarge upon this head, if *my* letter likewife was to be burnt as foon as you have read it. I look upon the friendfhip the Lord has given me there, as one of my prime privileges; and I hope I fhall always be thankful that it proved a means of introducing you into it.

I congratulate you likewife upon your acceffion to ——, not becaufe it is a good living, in a genteel neighbourhood, and a fine country; but becaufe I believe the Lord fends you there for fulfilling the defires he has given you, of being ufeful

K 3   to

to fouls. Church preferment, in any other view,
is dreadful; and I would as foon congratulate a
man upon feeing a millftone tied about his neck,
to fink him into the depths of the fea, as upon his
obtaining what is called a good living, except I
thought him determined to fpend and be fpent in
the caufe of the gofpel. A parifh is an awful millftone indeed, to thofe who fee nothing valuable
in the flock but the fleece: But the Lord has impreffed your heart with a fenfe of the glory and
importance of his truth, and the worth of fouls;
and animated your zeal by the moft powerful motive, the knowledge of his conftraining love. Your
cafe is extraordinary. Perhaps, when you review
in your mind the circle of your former gay acquaintance, you may fay with Job's fervant, " I
" only am efcaped alive :"—The reft are either removed into an eternal ftate, or are ftill hurrying
down the ftream of diffipation, and living without
God in the world. Yet there was a time when
there feemed no more probability on your fide than
on theirs, that you fhould obtain mercy, and be
called to the honour of preaching the glorious gofpel. You are fetting out with every poffible advantage.—In early life, with a chearful flow of fpirits, affluent circumftances, and now, to crown all,
the Lord gives you the very choice of your heart
in a partner; one who, befides deferving and meeting your affection, will, I am perfuaded, be a real
helpmeet to you in your fpiritual walk. How much
is here to be thankful for !

I truft the Lord has given you, and will maintain
in you a right fpirit, fo as not to reft in his gifts,
but to hold them in connection with the love and
favour of the giver. It is a low time with us, when
the greateft affemblage of earthly bleffings can feem
to fatisfy us without a real communion with him.
His grace is fufficient for you; but undoubtedly
                                                    fuch

such a scene of prosperity as seems to lie before
you, is full of snares, and calls for a double effort
of watchfulness and prayer. Your situation will
fix many eyes upon you, and Satan will doubtless
watch you, and examine every corner of the hedge
around you, to see if he can find a gap by which
to enter. We have but few rich gospel ministers;
but it is too evident that he has found a way to
damp the zeal and hurt the spirits of some of those
few, who for a time acted nobly, and seemed' to
walk out of the reach of the allurements of the
world. I am not jealous of you; I feel a comfortable persuasion, that the Lord has taken a fast
hold of your heart, and given you a fast hold of
his almighty arm: Yet I believe you will not be
displeased with me for dropping a hint of this kind,
and at this time.

You have heard of the trial with which the Lord
has been pleased to visit us; it still continues,
though considerably alleviated. It is tempered with
many mercies, and I hope he disposes us in a measure to submission. I trust it will be for good. My
dear friend, you are now coming into my school,
where you will learn, as occasions offer, to feel
more in the person of another than in your own.
But be not discouraged; the Lord only afflicts for
our good. It is necessary that our sharpest trials
should sometimes spring from our dearest comforts,
else we should be in danger of forgetting ourselves,
and setting up our rest here. In such a world, and
with such hearts as we have, we shall often need
something to prevent our cleaving to the dust,
to quicken us to prayer, and to make us feel that
our dependence for one hour's peace is upon the
Lord alone. I am ready to think I have known
as much of the good and happiness which this
world can afford, as most people who live in it.
I never saw the person with whom I wished to ex-

K 4   change

change in temporals. And for many years paſt I have thought my trials have been light and few, compared with what many, or moſt of the Lord's people have endured. And yet, though in the main poſſeſſed of my own wiſhes, when I look back upon the twenty-ſeven years paſt, I am ready to ſtyle them, with Jacob, few and evil ; and to give the ſum total of their contents in Solomon's words —all is vanity. If I take theſe years to pieces, I ſee a great part of them was filled up with ſins, ſorrows, and inquietudes. The pleaſures too are gone, and have no more real exiſtence than the baſeleſs fabric of a dream. The ſhadows of the evening will ſoon begin to come over us; and if our lives are prolonged, a thouſand pains and infirmities, from which the Lord has in a remarkable meaſure exempted us hitherto, will probably overtake us; and at laſt we muſt feel the parting pang. *Sic tranſit gloria mundi.* Sin has ſo envenomed the ſoil of this earth, that the amaranth will not grow upon it. But we are haſting to a better world, and bright unclouded ſkies, where our ſun will go down no more, and all tears ſhall be wiped from our eyes.

    I am, &c.

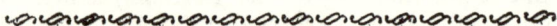

LETTER IV.

My dear Friend,   *Sept.* 27. 1777.

MR —— called on us Thurſday evening, and from that hour my thoughts, when awake, have ſeldom been abſent from ————. Few people are better qualified to feel for *you*, yourſelf and the family excepted ; perhaps there is no perſon living more nearly intereſted in what concerns

                                      Mrs

Mrs ——— than myfelf. I could not, therefore, at
fuch a time as this refrain from writing ; and glad
fhould I be, if the Lord may help me to drop a
fuitable word, and accompany it with a blefling to
you in the reading.

I am glad to be affured (though I expected no
lefs) that Mrs ——— happily feels herfelf fafe in
the Lord's hand, and under the care of the Good
Shepherd and Saviour, to whom fhe has often committed herfelf ; and finds him faithful to his promife, giving her ftrength in her foul according to
her day, and enabling her quietly to fubmit to his
holy, wife, and gracious will. And it is my prayer,
that he may ftrengthen you likewife, and reveal his
own all-fufficiency fo clearly and powerfully to your
heart, that you may not be afraid of any event,
but chearfully rely upon him, to be all that to you,
in every circumftance and change, which his promife warrants you to expect.

I am willing to hope, that this is but a fhort feafon of anxiety, appointed for the exercife of your
faith and patience, and to give you, in his good
time, a fignal proof of his power and goodnefs in
anfwering prayer. He fometimes brings us into
fuch a fituation that the help of creatures is utterly
unavailing, that we may afterwards be more clearly
fenfible of his interpofition. Then we experimentally learn the vanity of all things here below, and
are brought to a more immediate and abfolute dependence upon himfelf. We have need of having
thefe leffons frequently inculcated upon us ; but
when his end is anfwered, how often, after he has
caufed grief, does he fhew his great compaffions,
and fave us from our fears by an outftretched arm,
and fuch a feafonable and almoft unexpected relief,
as conftrains us to cry out, What has God
wrought ? and who is a God like unto thee ? Such,
I hope, will be the iffue of your prefent trial, and

that he who gave her to you at firft, will reftore
her to you again. I fee you in the furnace; but
the Lord is fitting by it as a refiner of filver, to
moderate the fire, and manage the procefs, fo that
you fhall lofe nothing but drofs, and be brought
forth refined as gold, to praife his name. Apparent difficulties, however great, are nothing to him.
If he fpeaks it is done; for to God the Lord belong
the iffues from death. Should his pleafure be otherwife, and fhould he call your dear partner to a ftate
of glory before you, ftill I know he is able to fupport you. What he does, however painful to the
flefh, muft be right, becaufe he does it. Having
bought us with his blood, and faved our fouls from
hell, he has every kind of right to difpofe of us
and ours as he pleafes; and this we are fure of, he
will not lay fo much upon us as he freely endured for us; and he can make us amends for all we
fuffer, and for all we lofe, by the light of his countenance. A few years will fet all to rights; and
they who love him and are beloved by him, though
they may fuffer as others, fhall not forrow as
others; for the Lord will be with them here, and
he will foon have them with him: there all tears
fhall be wiped from their eyes.

Perhaps I know as well how to calculate the
pain of fuch a feparation, as any one who has not
actually experienced it. Many a time the defire of
my eyes has been threatened, many a time my heart
has been brought low; but from what I have
known at fuch feafons, I have reafon to hope, that
had it been his pleafure to bring upon me the thing
that I feared, his everlafting arm would have upheld me from finking under the ftroke. As minifters, we are called to comfort the Lord's afflicted
people, and to tell them the knowledge of his love
is a cordial able to keep the foul alive under the
fharpeft trials. We muft not wonder that he fometimes.

times puts us in a way of fhewing, that we do not
deal in unfelt truths, but that we find ourfelves
that folid confolation in the gofpel, which we encourage others to expect from it. You have now
fuch an occafion of glorifying the Lord; I pray he
may enable you to improve it, and that all around
you may fee that he is with you, and that his good
word is the fupport and anchor of your foul. Then
I am fure, if it upon the whole is beft for you, he
will give you the defire of your heart, and you
fhall yet live to praife him together.

  I am, &c.

A

LETTER

TO THE

REV. MR O———.

L E T T E R.

Dear Sir,   April 3. 1759.

YOU fee I have prevented you in your promife of writing firft; and having found a
pretext for troubling Mr ———— , I was willing
to venture upon you without any, unlefs you will
let me plead a defire of fhewing you, how welcome
your correfpondence would be to me. I know
not if my heart was ever more united to any perfon, in fo fhort a fpace of time, than to you, and
what engaged me fo much was, the fpirit of meeknefs and of love (that peculiar and inimitable mark
of true Chriftianity) which I obferved in you I
mean it not to your praife. May all the praife be to
him, from whom every good and perfect gift cometh,
who alone maketh the beft to differ from the worft:
but I think I may well mention, to your encouragement, that all who converfed with you, greatly
regret your fpeedy departure ; and I am perfuaded,
the fame temper, the fame candour, will make you
acceptable, honourable, and ufeful, where-ever you
go. Bleffed are the poor in fpirit, the meek, the
merciful, and the peace-makers, they fhall obtain
the mercy they want, and poffefs the peace they
love. They fhall inherit the earth. The earth, finful
and miferable as it is, fhall be worthy to be called
an inheritance to them, for they fhall enjoy a comparative heaven in it. They fhall be called the
children of God, though dignified with no title
among men. Alas ! how much are thefe things
overlooked, even by many who, I would hope,
are

are real believers. Methinks a very different spirit from that of the church of Laodicea, is to be seen amongst us, though perhaps it is not easy to say which is the best of the two. That was neither cold nor hot, this (*mirabile dictu*) is both cold and hot at once, and both to the extreme. Hot, hasty, and arbitrary, in those few things where mediocrity is a virtue ; but cool and remiss in those great points, where the application of the whole heart, and soul, and mind, and strength, is so absolutely necessary, and so positively enjoined. Surely there is too much room for this observation, and I perhaps stand self-condemned in making it.

I hope you will take opportunity to improve your interest in Mr —— by letter. He expressed much satisfaction in the hour he spent with you before you sailed, and a great regard for you ; therefore would, I doubt not, give you a fair hearing ; and the phrase *litera scripta manet* is true in more senses than one. He makes such large concessions sometimes, that I am apt to think he is conscious of the weakness of his own argument, and then he is as soon angry with himself for complying so far, and flies off to the other extreme. Yet for the most part when he speaks plain, and is not restrained by complaisance for particular persons, he appears not only a stranger to experimental religion, but averse to the notion, and generally inclined to treat it with levity. His obstacles are very many and very great; his reputation as a learned man, his years, his regular life, and perhaps above all, his performances in print, especially his last book, are so many barriers that must be broke through before conviction can reach him. But the grace of God can do all this and more ; and indeed when I think of the many truly valuable parts of his character, and the indefatigable pains he has taken in his researches after truth, I am willing to hope,

hope, that the Lord will at length teach him the true wifdom, and enable him (however hard it may feem) to give up his own attainments, and fit down like a little child at the feet of Jefus.

I hope to hear foon and often from you. I number my Chriftian correfpondents among my principal bleffings, a few judicious pious friends, to whom, when I can get leifure to write, I fend my heart by turns. I can truft them with my inmoft fentiments, and can write with no more difguife than I think. I fhall rejoice to add you to the number, if you can agree to take me as I am, (as I think you will), and fuffer me to commit my whole felf to paper, without refpect to names, parties, and fentiments. I endeavour to obferve my Lord's commands, to call no man mafter upon earth; yet I defire to own and honour the image of God where-ever I find it. I dare not fay I have no bigotry, for I know not myfelf; and remember to my fhame, that formerly, when I ignorantly profeffed myfelf free from it, I was indeed over-run with it; but this I can fay, I allow it not; I ftrive and pray againft it; and thus far, by the grace of God, I have attained, that I find my heart as much united to many who differ from me in fome points, as to any who agree with me in all. I fet no value upon any doctrinal truth, farther than it has a tendency to promote practical holinefs. If others fhould think thofe things hinderances which I judge to be helps in this refpect, I am content they fhould go on in their own way, according to the light God has given them, provided they will agree with me ἐν τῷ Ἐπάναγκες. If it fhould be afked, Which are the neceffary things? I anfwer, Thofe in which the fpiritual worfhippers of all ages and countries have been agreed Thofe on the contrary are mere fubordinate matters, in
which

which the beft men, thofe who have been the moft
eminent for faith, prayer, humility, and nearnefs
to God, always have been, and ftill are, divided in
their judgements. Upon this plan, I fhould think it
no hard matter to draw up a form of found words,
(whether dignified with the name of a creed or no,
I care not), to which true believers of all forts and
fizes would unanimoufly fubfcribe. Suppofe it ran
fomething in the following manner : I believe that
fin is the moft hateful thing in the world : that I
and all men are by nature in a ftate of wrath and
depravity, utterly unable to fuftain the penalty, or
to fulfil the commands of God's holy law; and
that we have no fufficiency of ourfelves to think a
good thought. I believe that Jefus Chrift is the
chief among ten thoufands; that he came into the
world to fave the chief of finners, by making a
propitiation for fin by his death, by paying a perfect obedience to the law in our behalf; and that
he is now exalted on high, to give repentance and
remiffion of fins to all that believe; and that he
ever liveth to make interceffion for us. I believe
that the Holy Spirit, (the gift of God through
Jefus Chrift), is the fure and only guide into all
truth, and the common privilege of all believers;
and under his influence, I believe the holy fcriptures are able to make us wife unto falvation, and
to furnifh us thoroughly for every good work. I
believe that love to God, and to man for God's
fake, is the effence of religion, and the fulfilling of
the law ; that without holinefs no man fhall fee the
Lord ; that thofe who, by a patient courfe in well-
doing, feek glory, honour, and immortality, fhall
receive eternal life; and I believe that this reward
is not of debt but of grace, even to the praife and
glory of that grace, whereby he has made us accepted in the Beloved. Amen.

I pretend not to accuracy in this hafty draught ; they are only outlines, which if you pleafe to re-touch, and fill up at your leifure, I hope you will favour me with a fight of it. I fear I have tired you. Shall only add my prayers, that the Lord may be with you, and crown your labours of love with fuccefs, that you may hereafter fhine among thofe who have been inftrumental in turning many to righteoufnefs.

I am, &c.

SEVEN

SEVEN

LETTERS

TO THE

REVEREND Mr P——.

LETTER I.

Dear Sir,

THE account which I received by Mr C——, and by the letter which he brought from you, of your welfare and the welfare of your people, was very pleafing, though indeed no more than I expected. I believed, from the firft of your going to S——, that you would like the people, and I believed the Lord had given you that frame of fpirit which he has promifed to blefs. What reafon have we to praife him for the knowledge of his gofpel, and for the honour of being called to preach it to others ! and likewife that he has been pleafed to caft your lot and mine amongft a people who value it, and to crown our poor labours with fome meafure of acceptance and ufefulnefs. How little did we think, in the unawakened part of our life, to what it was his good pleafure to referve us !

The Lord is pleafed, in a meafure, to fhew me the fuitablenefs and neceffity of an humble dependent frame of heart, a ceafing from felf, and a reliance upon him in the due ufe of appointed means; I am far from having attained, but I hope I am preffing, at leaft feeking after it. I wifh to fpeak the word fimply and experimentally, and to be fo engaged with the importance of the fubject, the worth of fouls, and the thought that I am fpeaking in the name and prefence of the moft high God, as that I might, if poffible, forget every thing elfe. This would be an attainment indeed ! More good might be expected from a broken difcourfe, delivered in fuch a frame, than from the moft advantageous

tageous difplay of knowledge and gifts without it.
Not that I would undervalue propriety and perti-
nence of expreffion : it is our duty to ftudy to find
out acceptable words, and to endeavour to appear as
workmen that need not be afhamed ; but thofe who
have moft ability in this way, have need of a double
guard of grace and wifdom, left they be tempted to
truft in it, or to value themfelves upon it. They
that truft in the Lord fhall never be moved; and
they that abafe themfelves before him, he will exalt.
I am well perfuaded that your conduct and views
have been agreeable to thefe fentiments ; and therefore the Lord has fupported, encouraged, and owned
you; and I truft he will ftill blefs you, and make
you a bleffing to many. He that walketh humbly
walketh furely.

Believe me to be, &c.

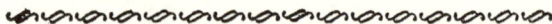

LETTER   II.

My dear Sir,   *Aug.* 14. 1770.

YOur letter did me good when I received it,
at leaft gave me much pleafure; and I think
it has given me a lift while I have been juft now
reading it. I know not that I ever had thofe awful
views of fin which you fpeak of; and though I believe I fhould be better for them, I dare not ferioufly
wifh for them. There is a petition which I have
heard in public prayer, Lord, fhew us the evil of
our hearts. To this petition I cannot venture to
fet my Amen, at leaft not without a qualification,
Shew me enough of thyfelf to balance the view,
and then fhew me what thou pleafeft I think I
have a very clear and ftrong conviction in my *judge-*
ment

ment, that I am vile and worthlefs, that my heart
is full of evil, only evil, and that continually.   I
know fomething of it too experimentally; and therefore, judging of the whole by the fample, though
I am not fuitably affected with what I do fee, I
tremble at the thought of feeing more.   A man
may look with fome pleafure upon the fea in a ftorm,
provided he ftands fafe upon the land himfelf; but
to be *upon* the fea in a ftorm, is quite another thing.
And yet furely the coldnefs, worldlinefs, pride, and
twenty other evils under which I groan, owe much
of their ftrength to the want of that feeling fenfe
of my own abominations with which you have
been favoured:—I fay favoured; for I doubt not but
the Lord gave it you in mercy, and that it has
proved and will prove a mercy to you, to make
you more humble, fpiritual, and dependent, as
well as to increafe your ability for preaching the
gofpel of his grace.   Upon thefe accounts, I can
affure you, that upon a firft reading, and till I
ftopped a moment to count the coft, I was ready
to envy you all that you had felt.   I often feem to
know what the fcripture teaches both of fin and
grace, as if I knew them not; fo faint and languid
are my perceptions, I often feem to think and talk
of fin without any forrow, and of grace without
any joy.

I have had fome people awakened by dreams, as
you had by ftreamers; but for ought I know, we
are no lefs inftrumental to the good of thefe, than
to any other perfon, upon whom when we look,
our hearts are ready to exult and fay, See what the
Lord has done by me.   I do not think that, ftrictly
fpeaking, all the ftreamers of the north are able
to awaken a dead foul.   I fuppofe people may be
terrified by them, and made thoughtful, but awakened only by the *word*.   The ftreamers either fent
them to hear the gofpel, or roufed them to attend to

it; but it was the knowledge of the truth brought
home to the heart, that did the bufinefs. Perhaps the
ftreamers reminded them of what they had heard
from you before. Two perfons here, who lived
like Heathens, and never came to church, were
alarmed by fome terrifying dreams, and came out
to hearing forthwith. There the Lord was pleafed
to meet with them. One of them died triumphing;
the other, I hope, will do fo when her time comes.
Whatever means, inftruments, or occafions he is
pleafed to employ, the work is all his own; and I
truft you and I are made willing to give him all
the glory, and to fink into the duft at the thought
that he fhould ever permit us to take his holy name
upon our polluted lips.

I am, &c.

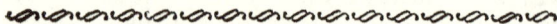

L E T T E R   III.

My dear Sir,   *June* 13. 1772.

YOU fay that your experience agrees with mine.
It muft be fo, becaufe our hearts are alike.
The heart is deceitful and defperately wicked, deftitute of good, and prone to evil. This is the
character of mankind univerfally, and thofe who
are made partakers of grace are renewed but in part;
the evil nature ftill cleaves to them, and the root of
fin, though mortified, is far from being dead.—
While the caufe remains it will have effects, and
while we are burdened with the body of this death,
we muft groan under it. But we need not be fwallowed up with overmuch forrow, fince we have in
Jefus, a Saviour, a Righteoufnefs, an Advocate, a
Shepherd. "He knows our frame, and remembers
"that

" that we are but duſt." If ſin abounds in us, grace
abounds much more in him; nor would he ſuffer
ſin to remain in his people, if he did not know
how to over-rule it, and make it an occaſion of
endearing his love and grace ſo much the more to
their ſouls. The Lord forbid that we ſhould plead
his goodneſs as an encouragement to ſloth and indifference. Humiliation, godly ſorrow, and ſelf-
abaſement become us; but at the ſame time we
may rejoice in the Lord. Though ſin remains, it
ſhall not have dominion over us; though it wars
in us, it ſhall not prevail againſt us. We have a
mercy-ſeat ſprinkled with blood, we have an advocate with the Father, we are called to this warfare,
and we fight under the eye of the Captain of our
Salvation, who is always near to renew our ſtrength,
to heal our wounds, and to cover our heads in the
heat of battle. As miniſters, we preach to thoſe
who have like paſſions and infirmities with ourſelves, and by our own feelings, fears, and changes,
we learn to ſpeak a word in ſeaſon to them that
are weary, to warn thoſe who ſtand, and to ſtretch
out a hand of compaſſion towards them that are
fallen; and to commend it to others, from our own
experience, as a faithful ſaying, "that Jeſus came
" to ſave the chief of ſinners." Beſides, if the Lord
is pleaſed to give us ſome liberty, acceptance, and
ſucceſs in preaching the goſpel, we ſhould be in
great danger of running mad with ſpiritual pride, if
the Lord did not permit us to feel the depravity and
vileneſs of our hearts, and thereby keep us from forgetting *what we are in ourſelves.*

With regard to your young people, you muſt
expect to meet with ſome diſappointment. Perhaps
not every one of whom you have conceived hopes
will ſtand, and ſome who do belong to the Lord are
permitted to make ſad miſtakes for their future
humiliation. It is our part to watch, warn, and

admonifh, and we ought likewife to be concerned
for thofe flips and mifcarriages which we cannot
prevent. A minifter, if faithful, and of a right fpirit, can have no greater joy than to fee his people
walking honourably and fteadily in the truth; and
hardly any thing will give him more fenfible grief,
than to fee any of them taken in Satan's wiles. Yet
ftill the gofpel brings relief here. He is wifer than we
are, and knows how to make thofe things fubfervient to promote his work, which we ought to guard
againft as evils and hindrances. We are to ufe the
means—He is to rule the whole. If the faults of
fome are made warnings to others, and prove in
the end occafions of illuftrating the riches of Divine grace, this fhould reconcile us to what we
cannot help, though fuch confiderations fhould not
flacken our diligence in founding an alarm, and reminding our hearers of their continual danger.

    I am, &c.

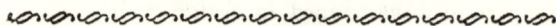

LETTER IV.

Dear Sir,   *Jan.* 26. 1775.

I Lately read a fermon of Mr Baxter's (in the fifth
  volume of the Morning Exercifes) on Matth.
v. 16. My mind is fomething impreffed with the
fubject, and with his manner of treating it. Some
of Mr Baxter's fentiments in divinity are rather
cloudy, and he fometimes upon that account met
with but poor quarter from the ftaunch Calvinifts
of his day. But by what I have read of him, where
he is quiet, and not ruffled by controverfy, he appears to me, notwithftanding fome miftakes, to have
been one of the greateft men of his age, and perhaps in fervour, fpirituality, and fuccefs, more than
                   equal,

equal, both as a minifter and a Chriftian, to fome
twenty taken together, of thofe who affect to undervalue him in this prefent day.   There is a fpirit
in fome paffages of his Saint's Reft, his Dying
Thoughts, and other of his practical treatifes, compared with which, many modern compofitions,
though well written and well meant, appear to me
to a great difadvantage.   But I was fpeaking of his
fermon.   He points out the way at which we fhould
aim to let our light fhine in the world, for the glory of God, and the conviction and edification of
men.   I have mentioned where it is to be found,
that, if you have the Morning Exercifes, or they
fhould come in your way, you may look at it.   I
think you would like it.   The perufal fuggefted to
me fome inftruction, and much reproof.   Alas !
my friend, are we not too often chargeable with a
fad, fhameful felfifhnefs and narrownefs of fpirit,
far, very far different from that activity, enlarge-
ment, and generofity of foul, which fuch a gofpel
as we have received might be expected to produce ?
For myfelf, I muft plead guilty.   It feems as if my
heart was always awake, and keenly fenfible to my
own concernments, while thofe of my Lord and
Mafter affect me much lefs forcibly, at leaft only by
intervals.   Were a ftranger to judge of me by what
I fometimes fay in the pulpit, he might think that,
like the angels, I had but two things in view, to do
the will of God, and to behold his face.   But, alas !
would he not be almoft as much miftaken, as if,
feeing Mr G—— in the character of a tragedy-he-
ro, he fhould fuppofe him to be the very perfon
whom he only reprefents.   I hope Satan will never
be able to perfuade me that I am a *mere hypocrite*
and *ftage-player*; but fure I am, that there is fo
much hypocrify in me, fo many littlenefles and felf-
feekings infinuating into my plan of conduct, that
I have humbling caufe to account myfelf unworthy

and

and unprofitable, and to fay, " Enter not into judge-
" ment with thy fervant, 'O Lord." I have fome tolerable idea of what a Chriftian ought to be, and it
is, I hope, what I defire to be. A Chriftian fhould
be conformable to Chrift in his fpirit and in his
practice; that is, he fhould be fpiritually minded,
dead to the world, filled with zeal for the glory of
God, the fpread of the gofpel, and the good of fouls.
He fhould be humble, patient, meek, chearful,
thankful under all events and changes. He fhould
account it the bufinefs and honour of his life, to
imitate him, who pleafed not himfelf, who went
about doing good, and has expreffed to us the very
feelings of his heart, in that divine aphorifm, which
furpaffes all the fine admired fayings of the philofophers, as much as the fun outfhines a candle, " It
" is more bleffed to give than to receive." The
whole deportment of a Chriftian fhould fhew that
the knowledge of Jefus, which he has received
from the gofpel, affords him all he could expect
from it;—a balm for every grief, an amends for
every lofs, a motive for every duty, a reftraint from
every evil, a pattern for every thing which he is
called to do or fuffer, and a principle fufficient to
conftitute the actions of every day, even in common
life, acts of religion. He fhould (as the children
of this world are wife to do in their generation)
make every occurrence through which he paffes
fubfervient and fubordinate to his main defign.
Gold is the worldly man's god, and his worfhip
and fervice are uniform and confiftent, not by fits
and ftarts, but from morning to night, from the beginning to the end of the year, he is the fame man.
He will not flip an opportunity of adding to his pelf
to-day, becaufe he may have another to-morrow,
but he heartily and eagerly embraces both ; and fo
far as he carries his point, though his perfeverance may expofe him to the ridicule or reproach
of

of his neighbours, he thinks himfelf well paid, and
fays,

> *Populus me fibilat ; at mihi plaudo*
> *Ipfe domi, fimul nummos contemplor in arca.*

I am, &c.

LETTER   V.

Dear Sir,   *Jan.*—1776.

I May learn (only I am a fad dunce) by fmall and
common incidents, as well as by fome more ftriking and important turns in life, that it is not in
man that walketh to direct his fteps. It is not for
me to fay, To-day or to-morrow I will do this or
that. I cannot write a letter to a friend without
leave or without help, for neither opportunity or
ability are at my own difpofal. It is not needful
that the Lord fhould raife a mountain in my way,
to ftop my purpofe; if he only withdraw a certain
kind of imperceptible fupport, which in general I
have, and ufe without duly confidering whofe it
is; then, in a moment, I feel myfelf unftrung and
difabled, like a fhip that has loft her mafts, and
cannot proceed till he is pleafed to refit me and
renew my ftrength. My pride and propenfity to
felf-dependence render frequent changes of this
kind neceffary to me, or I fhould foon forget what
I am, and facrifice to my own drag. Therefore,
upon the whole, I am fatisfied, and fee it beft that
I fhould be abfolutely poor and pennylefs in myfelf, and forced to depend upon the Lord for the
fmalleft things as well as the greateft. And if, by

his

his blessing, my experience should at length tally
with my judgement in this point, that without him
I can do nothing; then I know I shall find it easy,
through him, to do all things; for the door of his
mercy is always open, and it is but ask and have.
But, alas! a secret persuasion (though contrary to
repeated convictions) that I have something at
home, too often prevents me going to him for it,
and then no wonder I am disappointed. The life
of faith seems so simple and easy in theory, that I
can point it out to others in few words; but in
practice it is very difficult, and my advances are so
slow that I hardly dare say I get forward at all.
It is a great thing indeed to have the spirit of a
little child, so as to be habitually afraid of taking a
single step without leading.

I have heard of you more than once since I heard
from you, and am glad to know the Lord is still
with you: I trust he has not withdrawn wholly
from us. We have much call for thankfulness,
and much for humiliation. Some have been removed, some are evidently ripening for glory, and
now and then we have a new enquirer.—But the
progress of wickedness amongst the unconverted
here is awful. Convictions repeatedly stifled in
many, have issued in a hardness and boldness in
sinning, which, I believe, is seldom found but in
those places where the light of the gospel has been
long resisted and abused. If my eyes suitably affected my heart, I should weep day and night upon this account; but, alas! I am too indifferent.
I feel a woeful defect in my zeal for God and
compassion for souls; and when Satan and conscience charge me with cowardice, treachery, and
stupidity, I know not what to reply. I am generally carried through my public work with some
liberty; and because I am not put to shame before
the people, I seem content and satisfied. I wish to
be

be more thankful for what the Lord is pleafed to do amongft us, but, at the fame time, to be more earneft with him for a farther out-pouring of his Spirit. Affift me herein with your prayers.

As to my own private experience, the enemy is not fuffered to touch the foundation of my faith and hope; thus far I have peace:—But my conflicts and exercifes, with the effects of indwelling fin, are very diftreffing. I cannot doubt of my ftate and acceptance; and yet it feems no one can have more caufe for doubts and fears than myfelf, if fuch doubtings were at all encouraged by the gofpel; but I fee they are not; I fee that what I want and hope for, the Lord promifes to do for his own name's fake, and with a *non obftante* to all my vilenefs and perverfenefs; and I cannot queftion but he has given me (for how elfe could I have it) a thirft for that communion with him in love and conformity to his image, of which, as yet, I have experienced but very faint and imperfect beginnings. But if he has begun, I venture, upon his word, that he will not forfake the work of his own hands.

On public affairs I fay but little.—Many are cenfuring men and meafures; but I would lay all the blame upon fin. It appears plain to me that the Lord has a controverfy with us; and therefore I fear what we have yet feen is but the beginning of forrows. I am ready to dread the event of this fummer; but I remember the Lord reigns. He has his own glory and the good of his church in view, and will not be difappointed. He knows how likewife to take care of thofe who fear him. I wifh there was more fighing and mourning amongft profeffors, for the fins of the nation and the churches. But I muft conclude, and am, &c.

LETTER VI.

Dear Sir,

NO very confiderable alteration has taken place fince I wrote, except the death of Mrs L——, who was removed to a better world in September laft. The latter part of her courfe was very painful; but the Lord made her more than conqueror, and fhe had good caufe to apply the apoftle's words, 2 Tim. iv. 7. 8. She repeated that paffage in her laft illnefs, and chofe it for her funeral text. She was a Chriftian indeed. Her faith was great, and fo were her trials. Now fhe is above them all, now fhe is before the throne. The good Lord help us to be followers of thofe who through faith and patience have attained to the hope fet before them.

The number of profeffors ftill increafes with us, and a greater number of perfons affords a greater variety of cafes, and gives greater fcope to obferve the workings of the heart and Satan. For feven years I had to fay, that I had not feen a perfon of whom I had conceived a good hope go back. but I have met with a few difappointments fince. However, upon the whole, I truft the Lord is ftill with us. The enemy tries to difturb and defile us, and if the Lord did not keep the city, the poor watchman would wake in vain. But the eye that never flumbereth nor fleepeth has been upon us for good; and though we have caufe of humiliation and complaint, we have likewife much caufe of thankfulnefs. My health is ftill preferved; and I hope that the Lord does not fuffer my defires of perfonal communion with him, and of ufefulnefs in the miniftry, to decline. He fupplies me with frefh

strength

ftrength and matter in my public work: I hear now and then of one brought to enquire the way; and his prefence is at times made known to many in the ordinances.

To combine zeal with prudence is indeed difficult. There is often too much felf in our zeal, and too much of the fear of man in our prudence. However, what we cannot *attain* by any fkill or refolution of our own, we may hope in meafure to *receive* from him who giveth liberally to thofe who feek him, and defire to ferve him. Prudence is a word much abufed; but there is a heavenly wifdom, which the Lord has promifed to give to thofe who humbly wait upon him for it. It does not confift in forming a bundle of rules and maxims, but in a fpiritual tafte and difcernment, derived from an experimental knowledge of the truth, and of the heart of man, as defcribed in the word of God; and its exercife confifts much in a fimple dependence upon the Lord, to guide and prompt us in every action. We feldom act wrong, when we truly depend upon him, and can ceafe from leaning to our own underftanding. When the heart is thus in a right tune and frame, and his word dwells richly in us, there is a kind of immediate perception of what is proper for us to do in prefent circumftances, without much painful inquiry; a light fhines before us upon the path of duty; and if he permits us in fuch a fpirit to make fome miftakes, he will likewife teach us to profit by them; and our reflections upon what was wrong one day, will make us to act more wifely the next. At the beft, we muft always expect to meet with new proofs of our own weaknefs and infufficiency; otherwife, how fhould we be kept humble, or know how to prize the liberty he allows us of coming to the throne of grace, for frefh forgivenefs and direction every day? But if he enables us to walk before him with a fingle eye, he will gracioufly accept our defire of ferving him better if we could, and his blefling will make our feeble endeavours in fome degree fuccefsful, at the fame time that we fee defects and evils attending our beft fervices, fufficient to make us afhamed of them.

I am, &c.

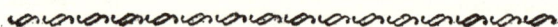

LETTER VII.

Dear Sir, *January* 11. 1777.

WE all need, and at the feafons the Lord fees beft we all receive chaftifement. I hope you likewife have reafon to praife him, for fupporting, fanctifying, and delivering mercy. The coward flefh prefently fhrinks under the rod, but faith need not fear it, for it is in the hand of one who loves us better than we do ourfelves, and who knows our frame that we are but duft, and therefore will not fuffer us to be overdone and overwhelmed.

I feel as a friend fhould feel for Mr B——; were I able, I would foon fend him health. If the Lord, who is able to remove his illnefs in a minute, permits it to continue, we may be fure upon the whole it will be better for him. It is, however, very lawful to pray that his health may be reftored, and his ufefulnefs prolonged. I beg you to give my love to him, and tell him that my heart bears him an affectionate remembrance ; and I know the God whom he ferves will make every difpenfation fupportable and profitable to him.

If, as you obferve, the Song of Solomon defcribes the experience of his church, it fhews the
dark

dark as well as the bright fide. No one part of it is the experience of every individual at any particular time. Some are in his banqueting-house, others upon their beds. Some fit under his banner, fupported by his arm; while others have a faint perception of him at a diftance, with many a hill and mountain between. In one thing, however, they all agree, that he is the leading object of their defires, and that they have had fuch a difcovery of his perfon, work, and love, as makes him precious to their hearts. Their judgement of him is always the fame, but their fenfibility varies. The love they bear him, though rooted and grounded in their hearts, is not always equally in exercife, nor can it be fo. We are like trees, which, though alive, cannot put forth their leaves and fruit without the influence of the fun. They are alive in winter as well as in fummer; but how different is their appearance in thefe different feafons! Were we always alike, could we always believe, love, and rejoice, we fhould think the power inherent and our own; but it is more for the Lord's glory, and more fuited to form us to a temper becoming the gofpel, that we fhould be made deeply fenfible of our own inability and dependence, than that we fhould be always in a lively frame. I am perfuaded a broken and a contrite fpirit, a conviction of our vilenefs and nothingnefs, connected with a cordial acceptance of Jefus as revealed in the gofpel, is the higheft attainment we can reach in this life. Senfible comforts are defirable, and we muft be fadly declined when they do not appear fo to us; but I believe there may be a real exercife of faith and growth in grace, when our fenfible feelings are faint and low. A foul may be in as thriving a ftate when thirfting, feeking, and mourning after the Lord, as when actually rejoicing in him, as much in earneft when fighting in the valley, as when finging

ing upon the mount; nay, dark feafons afford the fureft and ftrongeft manifeftations of the power of faith. To hold faft the word of promife, to maintain a hatred of fin, to go on ftedfaftly in the path of duty, in defiance both of the frowns and the fmiles of the world, when we have but little comfort, is a more certain evidence of grace, than a thoufand things which we may do or forbear when our fpirits are warm and lively. I have feen many who have been upon the whole but uneven walkers, though at times they have feemed to enjoy, at leaft have talked of great comforts. I have feen others, for the moft part, complain of much darknefs and coldnefs, who have been remarkably humble, tender, and exemplary in their fpirit and conduct. Surely were I to chufe my lot, it fhould be with the latter.

I am, &c.

THREE

THREE
LETTERS
TO
Mrs G————.

LETTER I.

Madam,   *June* 20. 1776.

IT would be both unkind and ungrateful in me, to avail myself of any plea of bufinefs, for delaying the acknowledgement I owe you for your acceptable favour from ——, which though dated the 6th inftant, I did not receive till the 10th.

Could I have known in time that you was at Mr ——, I fhould have endeavoured to have called upon you while there; and very glad fhould I have been to have feen you with us. But they who fear the Lord may be fure, that whatever is not practicable is not neceffary. He could have over-ruled every difficulty in your way, had he feen it expedient; but he is pleafed to fhew you, that you depend not upon men, but upon himfelf; and that, notwithftanding your connections may exclude you from fome advantages in point of outward means, he who has begun a good work in you, is able to carry it on, in defiance of all feeming hindrances, and make all things (even thofe which have the moft unfavourable appearances) work together for your good.

A fure effect of his grace, is a defire and longing for gofpel-ordinances; and when they are afforded, they cannot be neglected without lofs. But the Lord fees many fouls who are dear to him, and whom he is training up in a growing meetnefs for his kingdom, who are by his providence fo fituated, that it is not in their power to attend upon gofpel-preaching; and perhaps they have feldom either Chriftian minifter or Chriftian friend to affift or

comfort

comfort them. Such a fituation is a ftate of trial ;
but Jefus is all-fufficient, and he is always near.
They cannot be debarred from his word of grace,
which is every where at hand, nor from his throne
of grace ; for they who feel their need of him, and
whofe hearts are drawn towards him, are always at
the foot of it. Every room in the houfe, yea every
fpot they ftand on, fields, lanes, and hedge-rows, all
is holy ground to them ; for the Lord is there. The
chief difference between us, and the difciples when
our Saviour was upon earth, is in this : They then
walked by fight, and we are called to walk by faith.
They could fee him with their bodily eyes, we cannot ; but he faid before he left them, " It is expe-
" dient for you that I go away." How could this be,
unlefs that fpiritual communion which he promifed to maintain with his people after his afcen-
fion, were preferable to that intercourfe he allowed
them whilft he was vifibly with them ? But we are
fure it is preferable, and they who had tried both
were well fatisfied he had made good his promife ;
fo that though they had known him after the flefh,
they were content not to know him fo any more.
Yes, Madam, though we cannot fee him, he fees us,
he is nearer to us than we are to ourfelves. In a
natural ftate, we have very dark, and indeed difhonourable thoughts of God ; we conceive of him as
at a diftance. But when the heart is awakened, we
begin to make Jacob's reflection, " Surely the Lord
" is in this place, and I knew it not." And when
we receive faith, we begin to know that this ever-
prefent God is in Chrift ; that the government of
heaven and earth, the difpenfations of the kingdom
of nature, providence, and grace, are in the hands
of Jefus ; that it is he with whom we have to do, who
once fuffered agony and death for our redemption,
and whofe compaffion and tendernefs are the fame,
now he reigns over all bleffed for ever, as when he

converfed

converfed amongft men in the days of his humiliation.　Thus God is made known to us by the gofpel, in the endearing views of a Saviour, a Shepherd,
a Hufband, a Friend ; and a way of accefs is opened
for us through the veil, that is, the human nature
of our Redeemer, to enter, with humble confidence,
into the holieft of all, and to repofe all our cares and
concerns upon the ftrength of that everlafting arm
which upholds heaven and earth, and upon that infinite love which fubmitted to the fhame, pain, and
death of the crofs, to redeem finners from wrath and
mifery.

Though there is a height, a breadth, a length,
and a depth, in this myftery of redeeming love, exceeding the comprehenfion of all finite minds ; yet
the great and leading principles which are neceffary
for the fupport and comfort of our fouls, may be
fummed up in a very few words.　Such a fummary
we are favoured with in Titus, ii. 11.—14. where
the whole of falvation, all that is needful to be
known, experienced, practifed, and hoped for, is
comprifed within the compafs of four verfes.　If
many books, much ftudy, and great difcernment,
were neceffary in order to be happy, what muft the
poor and fimple do ?　Yet for them efpecially is the
gofpel defigned ; and few but fuch as thefe attain
the knowledge and comfort of it.　The Bible is a
fealed book till the heart be awakened, and then he
that runs may read.　The propofitions are few ; I
am a finner, therefore I need a Saviour, one who
is able and willing to fave to the uttermoft : fuch a
one is Jefus ; he is all that I want, wifdom, righteoufnefs, fanctification, and redemption.　But will
he receive me ?　Can I anfwer a previous queftion ?
Am I willing to receive him ?　If fo, and if his
word may be taken, if he meant what he faid, and
promifed no more than he can perform, I may be
fure of a welcome : he knew long before, the doubts,

fears,

fears, and fufpicions, which would arife in my mind when I fhould come to know what I am, what I have done, and what I have deferved; and therefore he declared, before he left the earth, " Him that " cometh to me, I will in no wife caft out." I have no money or price in my hand, no worthinefs to recommend me; and I need none, for he faveth freely for his own name's fake. I have only to be thankful for what he has already fhewn me, and to wait upon him for more. It is my part to commit myfelf to him as the phyfician of fin-fick fouls, not to prefcribe to him how he fhall treat me.— To begin, carry on, and perfect the cure, is his part.

The doubts and fears you fpeak of, are, in a greater or lefs degree, the common experience of all the Lord's people, at leaft for a time; whilft any unbelief remains in the heart, and Satan is permitted to tempt, we fhall feel thefe things. In themfelves they are groundlefs and evil; yet the Lord permits and over-rules them for good. They tend to make us know more of the plague of our own hearts, and feel more fenfibly the need of a Saviour, and make his reft (when we attain it) doubly fweet and fure. And they likewife qualify us for pitying and comforting others. Fear not; only believe, wait, and pray. Expect not all at once. A Chriftian is not of hafty growth, like a mufhroom, but rather like the oak, the progrefs of which is hardly perceptible, but in time becomes a great deep-rooted tree. If my writings have been ufeful to you, may the Lord have the praife. To adminifter any comfort to his children is the greateft honour and pleafure I can receive in this life. I cannot promife to be a very punctual correfpondent, having many engagements; but I hope to do all in my power to fhew myfelf, Madam,

      Yours, &c.

                                    LET-

L E T T E R   II.

Madam,   *Auguſt* 20. 1776.

THough in general I think myſelf tolerably punctual when I can anſwer a letter in ſix or ſeven
weeks after the receipt, yet I feel ſome pain for
not having acknowledged yours ſooner. A caſe
like that which you have favoured me with an account of, deſerved an immediate attention, and
when I read it, I propoſed writing within a poſt
or two, and I can hardly allow any plea of buſineſs to be ſufficient excuſe for delaying it ſo long;
but our times are in the Lord's hands: May he
now enable me to ſend you what may prove a word
in ſeaſon.

Your exerciſes have been by no means ſingular,
though they may appear ſo to yourſelf; becauſe, in
your retired ſituation, you have not (as you obſerve)
had much opportunity of knowing the experience
of other Chriſtians; nor has the guilt with which
your mind has been ſo greatly burdened been properly your own. It was a temptation forced upon
you by the enemy, and he ſhall anſwer for it. Undoubtedly it is a mournful proof of the depravity of
our nature, that there is that within us which renders us ſo eaſily ſuſceptive of his ſuggeſtions; a proof
of our extreme weakneſs, that after the cleareſt and
moſt ſatisfying evidences of the truth, we are not
able to hold faſt our confidence, if the Lord permits Satan to ſift and ſhake us. But I can aſſure you
theſe changes are not uncommon. I have known
perſons, who, after walking with God comfortably
in the main for forty years, have been at their wits
end from ſuch aſſaults as you mention, and been
brought to doubt, not only of the reality of their
own hopes, but of the very ground and foundation
upon

upon which their hopes were built. Had you remained, as it feems you once were, attached to the
vanities of a gay and diffipated life, or could you
have been content with a form of godlinefs, deftitute of the power, it is probable you would have
remained a ftranger to thefe troubles. Satan would
have employed his arts in a different and lefs perceptible way, to have foothed you into a falfe peace,
and prevented any thought or fufpicion of danger
from arifing in your mind. But when he could no
longer detain you in his bondage, or feduce you
back again into the world, then of courfe he would
change his method, and declare open war againft
you. A fpecimen of his power and malice you
have experienced; and the Lord whom you loved,
becaufe he firft loved you, permitted it, not to gratify Satan, but for your benefit—to humble and
prove you, to fhew you what is in your heart, and
to do you good in the iffue. Thefe things, for the
prefent, are not joyous but grievous; yet ·in the
end they yield the peaceable fruits of righteoufnefs.
In the mean time his eye is upon you; he has appointed bounds both to the degree and the duration
of the trial; and he does and will afford you fuch
fupports, that you fhall not be tried beyond what
you are enabled to bear. I doubt not but your
conflicts and forrows will in due time terminate in
praife and victory, and be fanctified to your fuller
eftablifhment in the truth.

I greatly rejoice in the Lord's goodnefs to your
dying parent. How wifely timed, and how exactly
fuited was that affecting difpenfation, to break the
force of thofe fuggeftions with which the enemy
was aiming to overwhelm your fpirit! He could
not ftand againft fuch an illuftrious demonftrative
atteftation, that the doctrines you had embraced
were not cunningly devifed fables. He could proceed no farther in that way; but he is fruitful in
reiources.

refources. His next attempt of courfe was to fix guilt upon your confcience, as if you had yourfelf formed and willingly entertained thofe thoughts, which, indeed, you fuffered with extreme reluctance and pain. Here likewife I find he fucceeded for a time; but he who broke the former fnare, will deliver you from this likewife.

The dark and difhonourable thoughts of God, which I hinted at as belonging to a natural ftate, are very different from the thoughts of your heart concerning him. You do not conceive of him as a hard mafter, or think you could be more happy in the breach than in the obfervance of his precepts. You do not prefer the world to his favour, or think you can pleafe him, and make amends for your· fins by an obedience of your own. Thefe, and fuch as thefe, are the thoughts of the natural heart—the very reverfe of yours. One thought, however, I confefs you have indulged, which is no lefs difhonourable to the Lord than uncomfortable to yourfelf. You fay, "I dare not believe that God will not impute to me as fin, the admiffion of thoughts which my foul ever abhorred, and to which my will never confented." Nay, you fear left they fhould not only be imputed, but unpardonable. But how can this be poffible! Indeed I will not call it your *thought*, it is your *temptation*. You tell me you have children. Then you will eafily feel a plain illuftration, which juft now occurs to me.—Let me fuppofe a cafe which has fometimes happened ; a child, three or four years of age we will fay, while playing incautioufly at a little diftance from home, fhould be fuddenly feized and carried away by a gipfey. Poor thing! how terrified, how diftreffed muft it be! Methinks I hear its cries. The fight and violence of the ftranger, the recollection of its dear parents, the lofs of its pleafing home, the dread and uncertainty of what is yet to befall it—Is it

not

not a wonder that it does not die in agonies? But
see, help is at hand! the gipsey is pursued, and
the child recovered. Now, my dear Madam, permit me to ask you, if this were your child, how
would you receive it? Perhaps, when the first trans-
ports of your joy for its safety would permit you,
you might gently chide it for leaving your door—
But would you disinherit it? Would you disown it?
Would you deliver it up again to the gipsey with
your own hands, because it had suffered a violence
which it could not withstand, *which it abhorred, and
to which its will never consented?* And yet what is
the tenderness of a mother, of ten thousand mothers, to that which our compassionate Saviour bears
to every poor soul that has been enabled to flee to
him for salvation! Let us be far from charging that
to him, of which we think we are utterly incapable
ourselves. Take courage, Madam; resist the devil
and he will flee from you. If he were to tempt
you to any thing criminal, you would start at the
thought, and renounce it with abhorrence. Do
the same when he tempts you to question the Lord's
compassion and goodness. But there he imposes
upon us with a shew of humility, and persuades us
that we do well to oppose our unworthiness as a
sufficient exception to the many express promises
of the word. It is said, the blood of Jesus clean-
seth from all sin; that all manner of sin shall be
forgiven for his sake; that whoever cometh he
will in no wise cast out; and that he is able to save
to the uttermost. Believe his word, and Satan
shall be found a liar. If the child had deliberately
gone away with the gipsey, had preferred that
wretched way of life, had refused to return, tho'
frequently and tenderly invited home; perhaps a
parent's love might, in time, be too weak to plead
for the pardon of such continued obstinacy. But,
indeed, in this manner we have all dealt with the
Lord;

Lord; and yet whenever we are willing to return, he is willing to receive us with open arms, and without an upbraiding word, Luke, xv. 20.—22. Though our fins have been deep-dyed like fcarlet and crimfon, enormous as mountains, and count-lefs as the fands, the fum total is, but *fin has a-bounded;* but where fin hath abounded, grace has much more abounded. After all, I know the Lord keeps the key of comfort in his own hands, yet he has commanded us to attempt comforting one an-other. I fhould rejoice to be his inftrument of ad-miniftering comfort to you. I fhall hope to hear from you foon; and that you will then be able to inform me he has reftored to you the joys of his falvation. But if not yet, wait for him, and you fhall not wait in vain.

I am, &c.

LETTER   III.

My dear Madam,   *June* —— 1777.

TEmptations may be compared to the wind, which, when it has ceafed raging from one point, after a fhort calm, frequently renews its violence from another quarter. The Lord fikenced Satan's former affaults againft you, but he is per-mitted to try you again in another way. Be of good courage, Madam, wait upon the Lord, and the prefent ftorm fhall likewife fubfide in good time. You have an infallible pilot, and are em-barked in a bottom againft which the winds and waves cannot prevail You may be toffed about, and think yourfelf in apparent jeopardy, but fink you fhall not, except the promifes and faithfulnefs

of God can fail. Upon an attentive confideration
of your complaint, it feems to me to amount only
to this, that though the Lord has done great things
for you, he has not yet brought you to a ftate of
independence on himfelf, nor releafed you from
that impoffibility which all his people feel, of doing
any thing without him. And is this indeed a matter of complaint? Is it not every way better, more
for his glory, and more fuited to keep us mindful
of our obligations to him, and in the event more
for our fafety, that we fhould be reduced to a
happy neceffity of receiving daily out of his fulnefs,
(as the Ifraelites received the manna), than to be
fet up with fomething of a ftock of wifdom, power,
and goodnefs of our own? Adam was thus furnifhed at the beginning with ftrength to ftand; yet
mutability being effential to a creature, he quickly
fell and loft all. We who are by nature finners, are
not left to fo hazardous an experiment. He has
himfelf engaged to keep us, and treafured up all
fulnefs of grace for our fupport, in a head who
cannot fail. Our gracious Saviour will communicate all needful fupplies to his members, yet in
fuch a manner that they fhall feel their need and
weaknefs, and have nothing to boaft of from firft
to laft but his wifdom, compaffion, and care. We
are in no worfe circumftances than the Apoftle
Paul, who, though eminent and exemplary in the
Chriftian life, found and freely confeffed that he
had no fufficiency in himfelf to think a good
thought. Nor did he wifh it otherwife; he even
gloried in his infirmities, that the power of Chrift
might reft upon him. Unbelief, and a thoufand
evils, are ftill in our hearts: though their reign and
dominion is at an end, they are not flain or eradicated; their effects will be felt more or lefs fenfibly, as the Lord is pleafed more or lefs to afford
er abate his gracious influence. When they are
kept

kept down we are no better in ourfelves, for they are not kept down by us; but we are very prone to think better of ourfelves at fuch a time, and therefore he is pleafed to permit us at feafons to feel a difference, that we may never forget how weak and how vile we are. We cannot abfolutely conquer thefe evils, but it becomes us to be humbled for them; and we are to fight, and ftrive, and pray againft them. Our great duty is to be at his footftool, and to cry to him who has promifed to perform all things for us. Why are we called foldiers, but becaufe we are called to a warfare? And how could we fight, if there were no enemies to refift? The Lord's foldiers are not merely for fhew, to make an empty parade in a uniform, and to brandifh their arms when none but friends and fpeftators are around them. No, we muft ftand upon the field of battle; we muft face the fiery darts; we muft wreftle (which is the clofeft and moft arduous kind of fighting) with our foes; nor can we well expeft wholly to efcape wounds: but the leaves of the tree of life are provided for their healing. The Captain of our Salvation is at hand, and leads us on with an affurance, which might make even a coward bold,—that in the end we fhall be more than conquerors through him who has loved us.

I am ready to think, that fome of the fentiments in your letters are not properly yours, fuch as you yourfelf have derived from the fcriptures, but rather borrowed from authors or preachers, whofe judgement your humility has led you to prefer to your own. At leaft, I am fure the fcripture does not authorife the conclufion which diftreffes you, that if you were a child of God you fhould not feel fuch changes and oppofitions. Were I to define a Chriftian, or rather to defcribe him at large, I know no text I would chufe fooner, as a ground

M 2 for

for the fubject, than Gal. v. 17. A Chriftian has
noble aims, which diftinguifh him from the bulk
of mankind. His leading principles, motives, and
defires, are all fupernatural and divine. Could he
do as he would, there is not a fpirit before the
throne fhould excel him in holinefs, love, and obedience. He would tread in the very footfteps of
his Saviour, fill up every moment in his fervice,
and employ every breath in his praife. This he
would do, but alas! he cannot. Againft this defire of the fpirit, there is a contrary defire and
working of a corrupt nature, which meets him at
every turn. He has a beautiful copy fet before
him; he is enamoured with it, and though he does
not expect to equal it, he writes carefully after it,
and longs to attain to the neareft poffible imitation.
But indwelling fin and Satan continually jog his
hand, and fpoil his ftrokes. You cannot, Madam,
form a right judgement of yourfelf, except you
make due allowance for thofe things which are not
peculiar to yourfelf, but common to all who have
fpiritual perception, and are indeed the infeparable
appendages of this mortal ftate. If it were not fo,
why fhould the moft fpiritual and gracious people
be fo ready to confefs themfelves vile and worthlefs? One eminent branch of our holinefs, is a fenfe
of fhame and humiliation for thofe evils which are
only known to ourfelves, and to him who fearches
our hearts, joined with an acquiefcence in Jefus,
who is appointed of God, wifdom, righteoufnefs,
fanctification, and redemption. I will venture to
affure you, that though you will poffefs a more
ftable peace, in proportion as the Lord enables
you to live more fimply upon the blood, righteoufnefs, and grace of the Mediator, you will never
grow into a better opinion of yourfelf than you
have at prefent. The nearer you are brought to
him, the quicker fenfe you will have of your continual

tinual need of him, and thereby your admiration
of his power, love, and compaſſion, will increaſe
likewiſe from year to year.

I would obſerve farther, that our ſpiritual exerciſes are not a little influenced by our conſtitutional
temperament. As you are only an ideal correſpon-
dent, I can but conjecture about you upon this
head. If your frame is delicate, and your nervous
ſyſtem very ſenſible and tender, I ſhould probably
aſcribe ſome of your apprehenſions to this cauſe.
It is an abſtruſe ſubject, and I will not enter into
it ; but according to the obſervations I have made,
perſons of this habit ſeem to live more upon the
confines of the inviſible world, if I may ſo ſpeak,
and to be more ſuſceptive of impreſſions from it,
than others. That complaint, which for want of
a better name we call lowneſs of ſpirits, may probably afford the enemy ſome peculiar advantages
and occaſions of diſtreſſing you. The mind then
perceives objects as through a tinctured medium,
which gives them a dark and diſcouraging appearance ; and I believe Satan has more influence and
addreſs than we are aware of in managing the glaſs.
And when this is not the caſe at all times, it may
be ſo occaſionally, from ſickneſs or other circumſtances. You tell me that you have lately been ill,
which, together with your preſent ſituation, and
the proſpect of your approaching hour, may probably have ſuch an effect as I have hinted. You
may be charging yourſelf with guilt, for what
ſprings from indiſpoſition, in which you are merely
paſſive, and which may be no more properly ſinful,
than the head-ach, or any of the thouſand natural
ſhocks the fleſh is heir to. The enemy can take no
advantage but what the Lord permits him ; and he
will permit him none but what he deſigns to over-
rule for your greater advantage in the end. He delights in your proſperity ; and you ſhould not be in

　　　　　heavineſs

heavinefs for an hour, were there not a need-be for it. Notwithftanding your fears, I have a good hope, that he who you fay has helped you in fix troubles, will appear for you in the feventh, that you will not die, but live, and declare the works of the Lord, and come forth to teftify to his praife, that he has turned your mourning into joy.

    I am, &c.

TWO

TWO
LETTERS
TO
MISS F——.

LETTER I.

Dear Madam,   *October* 3. 1778.

YOU would have me tell you what are the best
means to be used by a young person, to prevent the world, with all its opening and ensnaring
scenes, from drawing the heart aside from God. It
is an important question; but I apprehend your own
heart will tell you, that you are already possessed of
all the information concerning it which you can well
expect from me. I could only attempt to answer it
from the Bible, which lies open to you likewise.
If your heart is like mine, it must confess, that
when it turns aside from God, it is seldom through
ignorance of the proper means or motives which
should have kept us near him, but rather from an
evil principle within, which prevails against our better judgement, and renders us unfaithful to light
already received.

I could offer you rules, cautions, and advices in
abundance; for I find it comparatively easy to
preach to others. But if you should farther ask
me, How you shall effectually reduce them to practice? I feel that I am so deficient, and so much at
a loss in this matter *myself*, that I know not well
what to say to *you*. Yet something must be said.

In the first place, then, I would observe, that
though it be our bounden duty, and the highest
privilege we can propose to ourselves, to have our
hearts kept close to the Lord; yet we must not expect it absolutely or perfectly, much less all at once:
we shall keep close to him, in proportion as we are

M 5.   solidly

folidly convinced of the infinite difparity between
him and the things which would prefume to ftand
in competition with him, and the folly, as well as
ingratitude, of departing from him. But thefe points
are only to be learned by experience, and by fmart-
ing under a feries of painful difappointments in our
expectations from creatures. Our judgements may
be quickly fatisfied that his favour is better than life,
while yet it is in the power of a mere trifle to turn
us afide. The Lord permits us to feel our weaknefs, that we may be fenfible of it; for though we
are ready in words to confefs that we are weak, we
do not fo properly know it, till that fecret, though
unallowed dependence we have upon fome ftrength
in ourfelves, is brought to the trial, and fails us.
To be humble and like a little child, afraid of taking a ftep alone, and fo confcious of fnares and
dangers around us, as to cry to him continually to
hold us up that we may be fafe, is the fure, the
infallible, the only fecret of walking clofely with
him.

But how fhall we attain this humble frame of fpirit? It muft be, as I faid, from a real and fenfible
conviction of our weaknefs and vilenefs, which we
cannot learn (at leaft I have not been able to learn
it) merely from books or preachers. The providence of God concurs with his Holy Spirit in his
merciful defign of making us acquainted with ourfelves. It is indeed a great mercy to be preferved
from fuch declenfions as might fall under the notice
of our fellow-creatures; but when *they* can obferve
nothing of confequence to object to us, things may
be far from right with us in the fight of him who
judges not only actions, but the thoughts and firft
motions of the heart. And indeed could we for a
feafon fo cleave to God as to find little or nothing in
ourfelves to be afhamed of, we are fuch poor creatures, that we fhould prefently grow vain and felf-
fufficient,

fufficient, and expofe ourfelves to the greateft danger of falling.

There are, however, means to be obferved on
our part; and though you know them, I will repeat
the principal, becaufe you defire me. The firft is
Prayer; and here, above all things, we fhould pray
for humility. It may be called both the guard of
all other graces, and the foil in which they grow.
The fecond, Attention to the fcripture. Your queftion is directly anfwered in Pfalm cxix. 9. The
precepts are our rule and delight, the promifes our
ftrength and encouragement : the good recorded of
the faints is propofed for our encouragement; their
mifcarriages are as land-marks fet up to warn us of
the rocks and fhoals which lie in the way of our
paffage. The ftudy of the whole fcheme of gofpel-
falvation, refpecting the perfon, life, doctrine, death,
and glory of our Redeemer, is appointed to form
our fouls to a fpiritual and divine tafte ; and, fo far
as this prevails and grows in us, the trifles that
would draw us from the Lord, will lofe their influence, and appear, divefted of the glare with which
they ftrike the fenfes, mere vanity and nothing.
The third grand means, is, Confideration or Recollection; a careful regard to thofe temptations and fnares,
to which, from our tempers, fituations, or connections, we are more immediately expofed, and by
which we have been formerly hindered. It may be
well in the morning, ere we leave our chambers, to
forecaft, as far as we are able, the probable circumftances of the day before us. Yet the obfervance
of this, as well as of every rule that can be offered,
may dwindle into a mere form. However, I truft
the Lord, who has given you a defire to live to him,
will be your guard and teacher. There is none
teacheth like him.

I am, &c.

LETTER II.

Dear Madam, March — 1779.

OUR experiences pretty much tally; they may be drawn out into ſheets and quires, but the ſum total may be compriſed in a ſhort ſentence, " Our life is a warfare." For our encouragement, the apoſtle calls it a *good* warfare. We are engaged in a good cauſe, fight under a good captain, the victory is ſure beforehand, and the prize is a crown, a crown of life. Such conſiderations might make even a coward bold. But then we muſt be content to fight; and, conſidering the nature, number, ſituation, and ſubtilty of our enemies, we may expect ſometimes to receive a wound: but there is a medicinal tree, the leaves of which are always at hand to heal us. We cannot be too attentive to the evil which is always working in us, or to the ſtratagems which are employed againſt us; yet our attention ſhould not be wholly confined to theſe things. We are to look upwards likewiſe to him, who is our head, our life, our ſtrength. One glance of Jeſus will convey more effectual aſſiſtance than poring upon our own hearts for a month. The one is to be done, but the other ſhould upon no account be omitted. It was not by counting their wounds, but by beholding the brazen ſerpent, the Lord's inſtituted means of cure, that the Iſraelites were healed. That was an emblem for our inſtruction. One great cauſe of our frequent conflicts is, that *we* have a ſecret deſire to be rich, and it is the Lord's deſign to make us poor: *We* want to gain an ability of doing ſomething; and he ſuits his diſpenſations, to convince us that we can do nothing: *We* want a ſtock in ourſelves, and he would have

us

us abſolutely dependent upon him. So far as we are content to be weak, that his power may be magnified in us, ſo far we ſhall make our enemies know that we are ſtrong, though we ourſelves ſhall never be directly ſenſible that we are ſo ; only by comparing what we are, with the oppoſition we ſtand againſt, we may come to a comfortable concluſion, that the Lord worketh mightily in us. Pſalm xli. 11.

If our views are ſimple, and our deſires towards the Lord, it may be of uſe to conſider ſome of your faults and mine, not as the faults of you and me in particular, but as the fault of that depraved nature, which is common with us to all the Lord's people, and which made Paul groan as feelingly and as heartily as we can do. But this conſideration, though true and ſcriptural, can only be ſafely applied when the mind is ſincerely and in good earneſt devoted to the Lord. There are too many unſound and half profeſſors, who eagerly catch at it, as an excuſe for thoſe evils they are unwilling to part with. But I truſt I may ſafely recommend it to you. This evil nature, this indwelling ſin, is a living principle, an active, powerful cauſe ; and a cauſe that is active will neceſſarily produce an effect. Sin is the ſame thing in believers as in the unregenerate ; they have indeed a contrary principle of grace, which counteracts and reſiſts it, which can prevent its out-breakings, but will not ſuppreſs its riſings. As grace reſiſts ſin, ſo ſin reſiſts grace, Gal. v. 17. The proper tendency of each is mutually weakened on both ſides ; and between the two, the poor believer, however blameleſs and exemplary in the ſight of men, appears in his own view the moſt inconſiſtent character under the ſun. He can hardly think it is ſo with others ; and judging of *them* by what he *ſees*, and of *himſelf* by what he *feels*, in lowlineſs of heart,
he

he efteems others better than himfelf. This proves
him to be right; for it is the will of God concerning him, Phil. ii. 3. This is the warfare. But it
fhall not always be fo. Grace fhall prevail. The
evil nature is already enervated, and ere long it fhall
die the death. Jefus will make us more than conquerors.

  I am, &c.

TWO

TWO

LETTERS

TO

MR A—— B——.

LETTER I.

Dear Sir,   1758.

I Suppofe you will receive many congratulations on your recovery from your late dangerous ill-nefs; moft of them perhaps more fprightly and better turned, but none, I perfuade myfelf, more fincere and affectionate than mine. I beg you would prepare yourfelf by this good opinion of me, before you read further; and let the reality of my regard excufe what you may diflike in my manner of expreffing it.

When a perfon is returned from a doubtful di-ftant voyage, we are naturally led to inquire into the incidents he has met with, and the difcoveries he has made. Indulge me in a curiofity of this kind, efpecially as my affection gives me an intereft and concern in the event. You have been, my friend, upon the brink, the very edge of an eternal ftate; but God has reftored you back to the world again. Did you meet with, or have you brought back, nothing *new?* Did nothing occur to ftop or turn your ufual train of thought? Were your appre-henfions of invifible things exactly the fame in the height of your diforder, when you were cut off from the world and all its engagements, as when you were in perfect health, and in the higheft enjoy-ment of your own inclinations? If you anfwer me, " Yes, all things are juft the fame as formerly, the difference between ficknefs and health only ex-cepted;" I am at a lofs how to reply. I can only figh and wonder; *figh,* that it fhould be thus with any, that it fhould be thus with you whom I dearly
love;

love; and *wonder,* fince this unhappy cafe, ftrange
as it feems in one view, is yet fo frequent, why it
was not always thus with myfelf; for long and often it was juft fo.   Many a time, when ficknefs had
brought me, as we fay, to death's door, I was as
eafy and infenfible as the failor, who, in the height
of a ftorm, fhould prefume to fleep upon the top of
the maft, quite regardlefs that the next toffing wave
might plunge him into the raging ocean, beyond
all poffibility of relief.   But at length a day came,
which, though the moft terrible day I ever faw, I
can now look back upon with thankfulnefs and
pleafure : I fay, the time came, when in fuch a
helplefs extremity, and under the expectation of
immediate death, it pleafed God to command the
veil from my eyes, and I faw things in fome meafure as they really were.   Imagine with yourfelf
a perfon trembling upon the point of a dreadful
precipice, a powerful and inexorable enemy eager
to pufh him down, and an affemblage of all that is
horrible waiting at the bottom for his fall; even
this will give you but a faint reprefentation of the
ftate of my mind at that time.   Believe me, it was
not a whim or a dream, which changed my fentiments and conduct, but a powerful conviction which
will not admit the leaft doubt; an evidence which,
like that I have of my own exiftence, I cannot call
in queftion without contradicting all my fenfes.
And though my cafe was in fome refpects uncommon, yet fomething like it is known by one and
another every day : and I have myfelf converfed
with many, who, after a courfe of years fpent in
defending Deiftical principles, or indulging libertine
practices, when they have thought themfelves confirmed in their fchemes by the cool affent of what
they then deemed Impartial Reafon, have been, like
me, brought to glory in the crofs of Chrift, and to
live by that faith which they had before flighted and
                                                    oppofed.

oppofed. By thefe inftances I know that nothing is
too hard for the Almighty. The fame power which
humbled me, can undoubtedly bring down the
moft haughty infidel upon earth; and as I likewife
know, that, to fhew his power, he is often pleafed
to make ufe of weak inftruments, I am encouraged,
notwithftanding the apparent difficulty of fucceeding, to warn thofe over whom friendfhip or affection gives me any influence, of the evil and the danger of a courfe of life formed upon the prevailing
maxims of the world. So far as I neglect this, I
am unfaithful in my profeffions both to God and
man.

I fhall not at prefent trouble you in an argu-
mentative way. If by dint of reafoning I could
effect fome change in your notions, my arguments,
unlefs applied by a fuperior power, would ftill leave
your heart unchanged and untouched. A man may
give his affent to the gofpel, and be able to defend
it againft others, and yet not have his own fpirit
truly influenced by it. This thought I fhall leave
with you, that if your fcheme be not true to a demonftration, it muft neceffarily be falfe; for the
iffue is too important to make a doubt on the dangerous fide tolerable. If the Chriftian could poffibly be miftaken, he is ftill upon equal terms with
thofe who pronounce him to be fo; but if the Deift
be wrong, (that is, if we are in the right), the confequence to him muft be unavoidable and intolerable.
This, you will fay, is a trite argument: I own it;
but beaten as it is, it will never be worn out or anfwered.

Permit me to remind you, that the points in debate between us are already fettled in themfelves,
and that our talking cannot alter or affect the nature of things; for they will be as they are, whatever apprehenfions we may form of them : and remember likewife, that we muft all, each one for
himfelf,

himſelf, experience on which ſide the truth lies. I uſed a wrong word when I ſpoke of your *recovery*; my dear friend, look upon it only as a *reprieve*; for you carry the ſentence of death about with you ſtill; and unleſs you ſhould be cut off (which God of his mercy forbid!) by a ſudden ſtroke, you will as ſurely lie upon a deathbed, as you have been now raiſed from a bed of ſickneſs. And remember likewiſe, (how can I bear to write it!), that, ſhould you neglect my admonitions, they will notwithſtanding have an effect upon you, though not ſuch an effect as I could wiſh: they will render you more inexcuſable. I have delivered my own ſoul by faithfully warning you: but if you will not examine the matter with that ſeriouſneſs it calls for; if you will not look up to God, the former of your body, and the preſerver of your ſpirit, for direction and aſſiſtance how to pleaſe him; if you will have your reading and converſation only on one ſide of the queſtion; if you determine to let afflictions and dangers, mercies and deliverances, all paſs without reflection and improvement; if you will ſpend your life as though you thought you were ſent into the world only to eat, ſleep, and play, and, after a courſe of years, be extinguiſhed like the ſnuff of a candle,—why then, you muſt abide the conſequences. But aſſuredly, ſooner or later, God will meet you. My hearty daily prayer is, that it may be in a way of mercy, and that you may be added to the number of the trophies of his invincible grace.

I am, &c.

LETTER II.

Dear Sir,   1760.

THough I truly love you, and have no reason to
doubt of the reality of your friendſhip to me;
yet I cannot but apprehend that, notwithſtanding
our mutual regard, and my frequent attempts
to be witty (if I could) for your diverſion, there is
ſomething in moſt of my letters (which I cannot,
dare not, wholly ſuppreſs) that diſguſts and wearies
you, and makes you leſs inclined to keep up a frequent intercourſe than you would otherwiſe be.
Rather than loſe you quite, I will in general ſpare
you as much as I can; but at preſent you muſt bear
with me, and allow me full ſcope. You have given me a challenge, which I know not how to paſs
over; and ſince you ſo far juſtify my preaching, as
to condeſcend to preach (in your way) yourſelf,
permit me for this time to preach again, and to
take ſome paſſages in your letter for my text.

In the preſent debate, I will accept your compli-
ment, and ſuppoſe myſelf to be, as you ſay, a man
of ſenſe. You allow, then, that *all* the ſenſe is
not on your ſide. This indeed you cannot deny;
for whatever becomes of me, it is needleſs to tell
you, that Hale, Boyle, and other great names I
could mention, were men of as great penetration
and judgement, had as good opportunities, and
took as much pains to be informed of the truth, as
any of the advocates for infidelity can pretend to.
And you cannot, with any modeſty or confiſtence,
abſolutely determine, that they had not as good
grounds for thinking themſelves right, as you can
have for concluding they were wrong.

But declining the advantage of human authority,

I

I am content the point fhall reft between you and me.   And here I beg you to obferve, that I have one evident advantage over you in judging, namely, that I have experienced the good and evil on *both* fides, and you only on *one.*   If you were to fend me an inventory of your pleafures, how charmingly your time runs on, and how dextroufly it is divided between the coffee-houfes, play-houfe, the card-table and tavern, with intervals of balls, concerts, &c.; I could anfwer, that moft of thefe I have tried and tried again, and know the utmoft they can yield, and have feen enough of the reft, moft heartily to defpife them all.   Setting religion entirely out of the queftion, I profefs I had rather be a worm to crawl upon the ground, than to bear the name of MAN upon the poor terms of whiling away my life in an infipid round of fuch infignificant and unmanly trifles.   I will return your own expreffion,—I believe you to be a perfon of fenfe; but, alas ! how do you proftitute your talents and capacity, how far do you act below yourfelf, if you know no higher purpofe of life than thefe childifh diffipations, together with the more ferious bufinefs of rifing early and fitting up late, to amafs money, that you may be able to enlarge your expences !   I am fure while I lived in thefe things, I found them unfatisfying and empty to the laft degree; and the only advantage they afforded (miferable are they who are forced to *deem* it an advantage) was, that they often relieved me from the trouble and burden of thinking.   If you have any other pleafures than thefe, they are fuch as muft be evil and inconvenient even upon your own plan ; and therefore my friendfhip will not allow me to bring them into the account.   I am willing to hope you do not ftoop ftill lower in purfuit of fatisfaction.   Thus far we ftand upon even ground.   You know all that a life of pleafure can give, and I know it likewife.

On

On the other hand, if I fhould attempt to explain to you the fource and ftreams of *my* beft
plefures, fuch as a comfortable affurance of the
pardon of my fins, an habitual communion with
the God who made heaven and earth, a calm reliance on the Divine Providence, the chearing profpect of a better life in a better world, with the
pleafing foretaftes of heaven in my own foul;
fhould I, or could I, tell you the pleafure I often
find in reading the fcripture, in the exercife of
prayer, and in that fort of preaching and converfation which you defpife; I doubt not but you
would think as meanly of my happinefs as I do of
yours. But here lies the difference, my dear
friend; you condemn that which you have never
tried. You know no more of thefe things than a
blind man does of colours; and, notwithftanding
all your flourifhes, I defy you to be at all times able
to fatisfy yourfelf, that things may not poffibly be
as I have reprefented them.

Befides, what do I lofe upon my plan, that fhould
make me fo worthy of your pity? Have you a
quicker relifh in the prudent ufe of temporal
comforts? Do you think I do not eat my food
with as much pleafure as you can do, though perhaps with lefs coft and variety? Is your fleep
founder than mine? Have not I as much fatisfaction
in focial life? It is true, to join much with the gay
fluttering tribe, who fpend their days in laugh and
fing-fong, is equally contrary to my duty and inclination. But I have friends and acquaintance as
well as you. Among the many who favour me
with their efteem and friendfhip, there are fome
who are perfons of fenfe, learning, wit, and (what
perhaps may weigh as much with you) of fortune
and diftinction. And if you fhould fay, " Ay, but
they are all enthufiafts like yourfelf," you would
fay nothing to the purpofe, fince, upon your max-
im,

im, that " happineſs is according to opinion," it
cannot be an objection, but the contrary, to have
my acquaintance to my own taſte. Thus much for
the brighter ſide of your ſituation ;—or let me add
one thing more. I know you have thoughts of
marriage : do you think, if you ſhould enter into
this relation, your principles are calculated to make
you more happy in it than I am ? You are well
acquainted with our family life. Do you propoſe
to know more of the peace and heart-felt joy of
domeſtic union, than I have known and continue
to know to this hour. I wiſh you may equal us ;
and if you do, we ſhall ſtill be as before, but upon
even ground. I need not turn Deiſt, to enjoy the
beſt and the moſt that this life can afford.

But I need not tell you, that the preſent life is
not made up of pleaſurable incidents only. Pain,
ſickneſs, loſſes, diſappointments, injuries, and affronts
will more or leſs, at one time or other, be our lot.
And can you bear theſe trials better than I ? You
will not pretend to it. Let me appeal to yourſelf :
How often do you toſs and diſquiet yourſelf, like a
wild bull in a net, when things croſs your expectations ? As your thoughts are more engroſſed by
what you ſee, you muſt be more keenly ſenſible of
what you feel. You cannot view theſe trials as appointed by a wiſe and heavenly Father, in ſubſer-
vience to your good ; you cannot taſte the ſweetneſs
of his promiſes, nor feel the ſecret ſupports of his
ſtrength in an hour of affliction : you cannot ſo
caſt your burden and care upon him, as to find a ſenſible relief to your ſpirit thereby, nor can you ſee
his hand engaged and employed in effecting your deliverance. Of theſe things you know no more than
of the art of flying ; but I ſeriouſly aſſure you,
and I believe my teſtimony will go farther with you
than my judgement, that they are realities, and that
I have found them to be ſo. When my worldly
concerns

concerns have been moft thorny and difcouraging,
I have once and again felt the moft of that peace
which the world can neither give nor take away.
However, I may ftate the cafe ftill lower. You do
pretty well among your friends; but how do you
like being alone? Would you not give fomething
for that happy fecret, which could enable you to
pafs a rainy day pleafantly, without the affiftance
of bufinefs, company, or amufement? Would it
not mortify you greatly to travel for a week in an
unfrequented road, where you fhall meet with no
lively incidents to recruit and raife your fpirits?
Alas! what a poor fcheme of pleafure is your's, that
will not fupport an interval of reflection!

What you have heard is true; I have a few friends
who meet at my houfe once a-fortnight, and we
fpend an hour or two in worfhipping the God who
made us. And can this move your indignation, or
your compaffion? Does it fhew a much nobler fpirit, a more refined way of thinking, to live altogether without God in the world? If I kept a
card-affembly at thofe times, it would not difpleafe
you. How can you, as a perfon of fenfe, avoid
being fhocked at your own unhappy prejudice?
But I remember how it was once with myfelf, and
forbear to wonder. May he who has opened my
eyes, open your's. He only can do it. I do not
expect to convince you by any thing I can fay as of
myfelf; but if he be pleafed to make ufe of me as
his inftrument, then you will be convinced. How
fhould I then rejoice! I fhould rejoice to be ufeful
to any one; but efpecially to you, whom I dearly
love. May God fhew you your true felf, and your
true ftate; then you will attentively liften to what
you now difdain to hear of,—his goodnefs in pro-
viding redemption and pardon for the chief of finners, through him who died upon the crofs for

fins not his own. Keep this letter by you at my
requeſt; and when you write, tell me that you receive it in good part, and that you ſtill believe me
to be

Your ſincere and affectionate friend.

FOUR

FOUR

LETTERS

TO

The Rev. Dr ——.

LETTER I.

Dear Sir,   *April* 17. 1776.

BY this time I hope you are both returned in peace, and happy together in your stated favoured tract; rejoicing in the name of Jesus yourselves, and rejoicing to see the favour of it spreading like a precious perfume among the people. Every day I hope you find prejudices wearing off, and more disposed to hear the words of life. The Lord has given you a fine first-fruits, which I trust will prove the earnest of a plentiful harvest. In the mean time he will enable you to sow the seed in patience, leaving the event in his hands. Though it does not spring up visibly at once, it will not be lost. I think he would not have sent you if he had not a people there to call; but they can only come forth to view as he is pleased to bring them. Satan will try to hinder and disturb you, but he is in a chain which he cannot break, nor go a step farther than he is permitted. And if you have been instrumental to the conversion of but a few, in those few you have an ample reward already for all the difficulties you have or can meet with. It is more honourable and important to be an instrument of saving one soul, than to rescue a whole kingdom from temporal ruin. Let us therefore, while we earnestly desire to be more useful, not forget to be thankful for what the Lord has been pleased already to do for us; and let us expect, knowing whose servants we are, and what a gospel we preach, to see some new miracles wrought from
day

day to day : for indeed every real converfion may
be accounted miraculous, being no lefs than an
immediate exertion of that power which made the
heavens, and commanded the light to fhine out of
darknefs. Your little telefcope is fafe. I wifh I
had more of that clear air and funfhine you fpeak
of, that with you I might have more diftinct views
of the land of promife. I cannot fay my profpect
is greatly clouded by doubts of my reaching it at
laft; but then there is fuch a languor and dead-
nefs hangs upon my mind, that it is almoft amazing
to me how I can entertain any hopes at all. It
feems, if doubting could ever be reafonable, there
is no one who has greater reafon for doubting than
myfelf. But I know not how to doubt, when I
confider the faithfulnefs, grace, and compaffion of
him who has promifed. If it could be proved that
Chrift had not died, or that he did not fpeak the
words which are afcribed to him in the gofpel, or
that he is not able to make them good, or that his
word cannot fafely be taken; in any of thefe cafes
I fhould doubt to purpofe, and lie down in defpair.
        I am, &c.

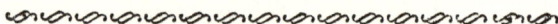

L E T T E R   II.

My dear Sir,   *July* 15. 1777.

I Begin with congratulations firft to you and Mrs
——, on your fafe journey and good paffage
over the formidable Humber. Mrs —— has another river to crofs (may it be many years before
fhe approaches the bank) over which there is no
bridge. Perhaps at feafons fhe may think of it with
                                        that

that reluctance which she felt before she saw the
Humber; but as her fears were then agreeably difappointed, and she found the experiment, when
called to make it, neither terrifying nor dangerous,
so I trust she will find it in the other case. Did
not she think, The Lord knows where I shall be,
and he will meet me there with a storm, because
I am such a sinner? Then how the billows will
foam and rage at me, and what a long passage I
shall have, and perhaps I shall sink in the middle,
and never set my foot in Hull. It is true, I am
not so much afraid of the journey I go by land,
though I know that every step of the way the horses
or the chaise may fall, and I be killed; but how
do I know but he may preserve me on the road on
purpose to drown me in the river? But behold,
when she came to it all was calm; or what was
better, a gentle, fair breeze, to waft her pleasantly
over before she was aware. Thus we are apt per-
versely to reason : he guides and guards me through
life; he gives me new mercies, and new proofs of
his power and care every day; and therefore when
I come to die he will forsake me, and let me be
the sport of winds and waves. Indeed the Lord
does not deserve such hard thoughts at our hands
as we are prone to form of him. But notwith-
standing we make such returns, he is and will be
gracious, and shame us out of our unkind, ungrateful, unbelieving fears at last. If, after my
repeated kind reception at your house, I should
always be teasing Mrs —— with suspicions of her
good-will, and should tell every body I saw, that
I verily believed the next time I went to see her she
would shut the door in my face and refuse me ad-
mittance, would she not be grieved, offended, and
affronted? Would she not think, What reason
can he assign for this treatment? He knows I did
every thing in my power to assure him of a welcome,

come, and told him fo over and over again. Does
he count me a deceiver ? Yes, he does : I fee his
friendfhip is not worth preferving ; fo farewell.
I will feek friends among fuch as believe my words
and actions. Well, my dear Madam, I am clear I
always believed you ; I make no doubt but you will
treat me kindly next time, as you did the laft.
But pray is not the Lord as worthy of being trufted
as yourfelf ; and are not his invitations and promifes as hearty and as honeft as yours ? Let us
therefore beware of giving way to fuch thoughts of
him, as we could hardly forgive in our deareft
friends, if they fhould harbour the like of us.

I have heard nothing of Mr P—— yet, but that
he is in town, very bufy about that precious piece
of furniture called a wife. May the Lord direct
and blefs his choice. In Captain Cook's voyage to
the South Sea, fome fifh were caught which looked
as well as others, but thofe who eat of them were
poifoned : alas ! for the poor man who catches a
poifonous wife ! There are fuch to be met with in
the matrimonial feas, that look paffing well to the
eye, but a connection with them proves baneful to
domeftic peace, and hurtful to the life of grace. I
know two or three people, perhaps a few more,
who have great reafon to be thankful to him who
fent the fifh, with the money in its mouth, to Peter's hook. He fecretly inftructed and guided us
where to angle ; and if we have caught prizes, we
owe it not to our own fkill, much lefs to our deferts, but to his goodnefs.

I am, &c.

LET-

L E T T E R   III.

My Dear Sir,   *Sept.* 4. 1777.

——— Poor little boy ! it is mercy indeed that
he recovered from fuch a formidable hurt. The
Lord wounded, and the Lord healed. I afcribe,
with you, what the world calls accident to him,
and believe, that without his permiffion, for wife
and good ends, a child can no more pull a bowl of
boiling water on itfelf than it could pull the moon
out of its orbit. And why does he permit fuch
things ? One reafon or two is fufficient for us :
it is to remind us of the uncertainty of life and all
creature-comforts; to make us afraid of cleaving
too clofe to pretty toys, which are fo precarious,
that often while we look at them they vanifh, and
to lead us to a more entire dependence upon himfelf ; that we might never judge ourfelves or our
concerns fafe from outward appearances only, but
that the Lord is our keeper, and were not his eye
upon us, a thoufand dangers and painful changes,
which we can neither forefee nor prevent, are lurk-
ing about us every ftep, ready to break in upon us
every hour. Men are but children of a larger
growth. How many are labouring and planning
in the purfuit of things, the event of which, if they
obtain them, will be but like pulling fcalding water
upon their own heads. They *muft* have the bowl
by all means, but they are not aware what is in it
till they feel it.

I am, &c.

LETTER IV.

Sir,   *July* 7. 1777.

I Have had a letter from your minifter fince his
arrival at ——. I hope he will be reftored to
you again before long, and that he and many of
your place will rejoice long in each other. Thofe
are favoured places which are bleffed with a found
and faithful gofpel-miniftry, if the people know
and confider the value of their privileges, and are
really defirous of profiting by them: but the kingdom of God is not in word but in power. I hope
thofe who profefs the gofpel with you will wreftle
in prayer for grace to walk worthy of it. A minifter's hands are ftrengthened, when he can point
to his people as fo many living proofs, that the
doctrines he preaches are doctrines according to
godlinefs; when they walk in mutual love; when
each one, in their feveral places, manifefts an humble, fpiritual, upright conduct; when they are
Chriftians, not only at church but in the family,
the fhop, and the field; when they fill up their relations in life, as hufbands or wives, mafters or
fervants, parents or children, according to the rule
of the word; when they are evidently a people feparated from the world while converfant in it, and
are careful to let their light fhine before men, not
only by talking, but by acting as the difciples of
Chrift: when they go on fteadily, not by fits and
ftarts, prizing the means of grace without refting
in them: when it is thus, we can fay, Now we live,
if you ftand faft in the Lord. Then we come forth
with pleafure, and our fervice is our delight, and
we are encouraged to hope for an increafing bleffing. But if the people in whom we have rejoiced
                                                        fink

fink into formality or a worldly fpirit; if they have diffentions and jealoufies among themfelves; if they act improperly, and give the enemies occafion to fay, There, There, fo would we have it; then our hearts are wounded and our zeal damped, and we know not how to fpeak with liberty.   It is my heart's de-fire and prayer for you, that whether I fee you, or elfe be abfent from you, I may know that you ftand faft in one fpirit and one mind, ftriving together for the faith of the gofpel.

I am, &c.

The End of the SECOND VOLUME.

www.ingramcontent.com/pod-product-compliance
Lightning Source LLC
Chambersburg PA
CBHW022115080426
42734CB00006B/139